Routledge Revivals

THE CAMBRIDGE EVACUATION SURVEY

THE CAMBRIDGE EVACUATION SURVEY

A Wartime Study in Social Welfare and Education

Edited by

SUSAN ISAACS

With the Co-opration of

SIBYL CLEMENT BROWN & ROBERT H. THOULESS

Routledge
Taylor & Francis Group

First published in 1941 by Methuen & Co. Ltd.

This edition first published in 2018 by Routledge
2 Park Square, Milton Park, Abingdon, Oxon, OX14 4RN
and by Routledge
52 Vanderbilt Avenue, New York, NY 10017, USA

Routledge is an imprint of the Taylor & Francis Group, an informa business

Publisher's Note
The publisher has gone to great lengths to ensure the quality of this reprint but points out that some imperfections in the original copies may be apparent.

Disclaimer
The publisher has made every effort to trace copyright holders and welcomes correspondence from those they have been unable to contact.

A Library of Congress record exists under ISBN:

ISBN 13: 978-0-367-14377-0 (hbk)
ISBN 13: 978-0-367-14379-4 (pbk)
ISBN 13: 978-0-429-03171-7 (ebk)

CONTRIBUTIONS TO MODERN EDUCATION

General Editor; **Susan Isaacs, M.A., D.Sc.**

THE CAMBRIDGE EVACUATION SURVEY

CONTRIBUTIONS TO MODERN EDUCATION

General Editor; Susan Isaacs, M.A., D.Sc., Head of Dept. of Child Development, Institute of Education

THE NEW ERA IN THE JUNIOR SCHOOL

BY E. B. WARR. 4*s*. net

THE CHILDREN'S PLAY CENTRE

BY D. E. M. GARDNER. 4*s*. net

PLAY IN THE INFANTS' SCHOOL

BY E. R. BOYCE. 6*s*. net

THE HUMAN PROBLEM IN SCHOOLS

BY MARION MILNER. 9*s*. 6*d*. net

WHAT DO BOYS AND GIRLS READ?

BY A. J. JENKINSON. 7*s*. 6*d*. net

THE CAMBRIDGE EVACUATION SURVEY

EDITED BY SUSAN ISAACS. 8*s*. 6*d*. net

THE CAMBRIDGE EVACUATION SURVEY

A Wartime Study in Social Welfare and Education

edited by

SUSAN ISAACS

with the co-operation of

SIBYL CLEMENT BROWN & ROBERT H. THOULESS

---

written by

GEORGINA BATHURST
SIBYL CLEMENT BROWN
JOHN BOWLBY
G. A. BULLEN
NANCY FAIRBAIRN
SUSAN ISAACS
N. S. MERCER
MADELINE ROOFF
R. H. THOULESS

METHUEN & CO. LTD. LONDON
36 Essex Street, Strand, W.C.2

First published in 1941

PRINTED IN GREAT BRITAIN

PREFACE

IN JANUARY 1941, when this volume goes to press, some of the situations with which it deals seem already to belong to a remote past. A gulf of terrible experience and the most urgent need and effort divide us from the first quiet months of the war, when there was no more than a threat of danger and destruction. Even the summer months, after our friends and allies were laid low and yet the terror had not come to our own doors, now seem to be no more than a dim memory, so crowded, so intense, and so dramatic have our days and nights been since the full attack began.

Since then, the need for evacuation has been enforced by events and it has been carried out on a larger scale than at the beginning of the war. Many of its attendant circumstances have changed. Yet the essential problems remain the same. It still seems a wise thing to look with sober detachment into its first successes and its first failures. There is still ample scope to apply the lessons which can be learned from such an inquiry.

The work of the Survey was completed in July 1940, but the preparation of this report has had to be fitted by its authors and editors into the spare moments of busy practical lives.

The editors, on behalf of the Research Committee, wish to acknowledge the encouragement, help, and advice received from many sources. In particular, grateful acknowledgment is made to the following:

For permission to carry out the Survey, and for much detailed advice and help, to the Education Authorities of the Boroughs of Cambridge and Tottenham and the London County Council, and especially Mr. T. F. Foreman, as Education Officer in Cambridge, Dr. C. F. Strong, as Director of Education for Tottenham, Dr. E. M. Rich, and, on his retirement, Mr. E. G. Savage, as Education Officer to the London County Council.

Professor F. C. Bartlett and other distinguished men and

women, who consented to form a Consultative Committee and to give their criticisms and suggestions, as well as, in many cases, to share the financial burden.

For generous co-operation in the work of the Survey, the Women's Voluntary Services engaged in organizing and supervising billeting in Cambridge; and, above all, Mrs. Hester Adrian, Chairman of the Reception Committee, and the Senior Voluntary Workers and Friendly Visitors.

Miss S. M. Fry, for her wise guidance and ungrudging labours in the first part of the work.

The Mental Health Emergency Committee, for very generous financial help in loaning the services of three psychiatric social workers. Two of these, Miss N. M. Lindzell and Mrs. K. Edkins, made a study of the families of children returning to their homes, and one, Miss K. Davies, carried out the work of surveying the children in Cambridge from the Borough of Islington.

The Head and Assistant Teachers from Tottenham and Islington schools in Cambridge, as well as those from Cambridge schools. Without their devoted co-operation and their skill, the Survey could not have been carried out.

Mr. Aymeric Straker and Mr. John Whitfield, who with Dr. Thouless made the statistical studies, Mrs. Bathurst, who carried out the intelligence testing, Miss Fairbairn, who gave unstinted labour in too many directions for detailed acknowledgment, and Dr. John Bowlby, who made many valuable suggestions for the clinical study of the material.

The Child Guidance Training Centre, who loaned material and members of the staff to assist in the field work and in the special studies of individual cases.

The London School of Economics, who kindly lent office accommodation for the headquarters of the Survey.

The students of the London School of Economics and of Bedford College, who helped in some of the field work.

Lastly, Miss Th. Alcock, founder and Hon. Secretary of the Child Discussion Group (in London), at a meeting of which, in October 1939, it was first suggested that this Survey should be made.

Owing to the present abnormal cost of printing and our wish to keep the price of the book within the reach of as many readers as possible, we have not reproduced, in their original shape, the four forms of inquiry used in the study of the child's relationships in the foster home and the school, of the children who went home and of the point of view of the teachers; but all the questions used in these forms are given in Appendix IV.

January, 1941

S. I.
S. C. B.
R. H. T.

CONTENTS

CHAPTER I

INTRODUCTION

IN SEPTEMBER 1939, the family life of large numbers of parents and children in England and Scotland was voluntarily broken up. 750,000 school children, 542,000 mothers with young children, 12,000 expectant mothers, and 77,000 other persons left their homes and agreed to go wherever they were sent, in small country towns and rural areas.[1]

This great upheaval was made necessary by the threat of large-scale bombing. It was needed partly in order to save the lives of helpless civilians, partly in order to prevent panic and the consequent hampering of military operations in national defence, and to lessen the problems of the distribution of food and essential services in a major crisis.

The mechanics of evacuation had been discussed and planned by Government and local authorities during the previous twelve months. It was carried out in the first three days of the war more or less according to plan, although the mothers and children who proved willing to be dispersed when the time came were a good deal fewer than had promised to go. There were many breakdowns in the working of plans for transport, and unexpected stresses and strains in the hastily carried out billeting. Yet on the whole, evacuation seems to have been achieved with a fair measure of success, and the officials and private persons responsible breathed a sigh of relief to know that such large numbers of people had been removed in time from the threatening danger.

Yet no sooner was the great migration accomplished than its reversal began. Mothers and children began to trickle back to the industrial centres from every district. The trickle became a spate in the case of mothers with young children, until by January 1940 86–88 per cent were at home again.

[1] Figures quoted from Padley, Richard, and Cole, Margaret, *Evacuation Survey*, A Report to the Fabian Society, Routledge, 1940, p. 42.

The return of the unaccompanied school children was slower (43 per cent by January 1940), and it lost momentum as the months went on.[1]

These returns to the danger zones gave by no means the only sign of failure in the plans for dispersal. From every quarter came rumours and reports of distress and disillusion. The town was ill at ease in the country. The country was shocked at the manners and morals of the town.

Yet from every quarter, also, there came stories of new health, newly discovered pleasures among those dispersed, of generous care and devotion among foster families, of disinterested service from voluntary social workers. Clearly many unexpected things were happening. Officials and authorities were faced with acute personal problems which were quite outside their traditional knowledge or routine skill. Evacuation was proving a powerful social ferment. The lives of numbers of people, those who had been moved from their own homes alike with those who had received strangers in theirs, were being changed and their spirits stirred in unfamiliar ways.

We were all eager to know how much good, how much ill was being achieved. What mistakes in the execution of the scheme were at the root of its partial breakdown? How could they be remedied and avoided in future schemes? How could the drift back to the areas of danger be halted? And in the long run, what was this jar to family life doing to the children and parents who were parted, or to those whose privacy was intruded upon? What were the true effects of this impact of town upon country and country upon town? What would be the ultimate outcome of these changes in personal and social life? What was happening to education?

Some of us knew that from our general experience we could give partial answers to some of these questions. But partial answers are never as good as truth and not always better than ignorance. And much that was happening in this great social experiment was unknown, much that was known was not understood, much was being lost before it could even be

[1] Ibid., p. 43.

recorded. Events were changing rapidly before our eyes, and an opportunity to learn priceless lessons for future social service was melting away.

The Cambridge Evacuation Survey arose from a discussion, in October 1939, among child psychologists and social workers, many of whom had taken part in the actual evacuation, or were engaged in some form of practical work among children. Our sense of the urgency and importance of the problem was great, our resources in labour and finance meagre. The Survey had perforce to be limited in scope. Yet we felt that a detailed study of what was happening in one area might bring out causal sequences which would become blurred and lost in a larger and more comprehensive study.

In the Borough of Cambridge we had at hand not merely a compact field of study, but also many personal contacts which ensured the essential co-operation of officials and voluntary workers. Moreover, we had similar contacts with people in the London areas from which the children had come to Cambridge, as well as some first-hand knowledge of those districts.

The Survey was not only limited in scope, but also had to be limited in method, owing to various circumstances discussed in Chapter II. We have tried in the accounts which follow to make clear the deficiencies and even the makeshift character of some of the methods which circumstances forced upon us.

Our conclusions are therefore in large part tentative. Some of them apply only to the children in the areas studied. Others from their very nature have a more general bearing. They are at least more likely to be true and just, not merely than opinions based upon hearsay evidence, but also than broad impressions not formed upon a close study of detail.

The detailed facts and the various conclusions arising from them are set out in the chapters which follow. In this chapter we wish only to summarize the broad conclusions emerging from our study as a whole, and to discuss some of their general implications.

It seems certain that even the high measure of success

attained in areas where the reception of children was well carried out might have been greater and more enduring, might have been gained at less cost to the families concerned, to officials and to the public generally. And where and when it failed, its failure might have been much less. All this might have been, if the Government and the authorities co-operating with the Government, as well as the general public, had seen that evacuation, from its very nature, was necessarily far more than an emergency military measure. It was a process which could not occur without creating far-reaching social and educational problems. If we had planned for these problems with a tithe of the labour and intelligence which we put into questions of transport, if human nature had been taken into equal account with geography and railway time tables, there would in all likelihood not have been so serious a drift back to the danger areas. The evacuation of September 1939 would then have provided a better example for the enforced transfer of people from the bombed areas in the summer and autumn of 1940. Moreover, the dispersed children would have gained far more from their new experiences, for learning and living.

These general conclusions go beyond the Cambridge data, but are fully supported by them.

In Cambridge, the public response to this emergency had been generous and devoted. The planning and preparation for the work had on the whole been carefully done. (One great advantage was that the Chief Billeting Officer was the Education Officer for the Borough.)[1] A considerable body of practical women had been found who could devote part of their time regularly to aiding and supervising the billeting arrangements. And the bulk of the households who had been willing to receive children had proved themselves sensible and friendly, indeed in many cases astonishingly helpful, to the strangers.

The facts and figures which are presented in later chapters show that the large majority of the school children from two

[1] Compare the state of things described in *Evacuation Survey*, Ch. XXIV, 'A Small Market Town'.

boroughs in the London district, Tottenham and Islington, who were still in Cambridge on December 1st, 1939, and March 1st, 1940, respectively,[1] were satisfactorily settled and contented in their foster homes.

Yet the most casual inquiry, after the first month of evacuation, showed that everybody concerned with billeting —officials, voluntary workers, parents, and teachers—was heavily overworked and overburdened with the acute personal problems of parents and foster parents and children. And there were exceptions, some of them outstanding exceptions, to the general satisfactoriness of the billeting. A small proportion of the Tottenham and Islington children at the given dates had an unsatisfactory relationship with their foster parents, and many had gone home. The detailed analysis of our data, together with the special studies of individual children, showed that some at least of these failures and distresses could have been avoided if more had been known beforehand, by those engaged in billeting, of the characteristics of the particular child and of the foster home in question, and if more trained skill had been available for the work.

This was further borne out by the experience of the staff of the Child Guidance Training Centre, in dealing with the more difficult children and the serious failures.

The majority of children temporarily sent away from their homes can be happily placed in some household or other. The majority of households can be relied upon to care for a child properly and make him happy. But some children have characteristics which call for special care in choosing a foster home. They will thrive in one but not in another. And some foster homes will do well with certain types of children, but not with all.

The intelligence of the child does not appear to have much importance for success in billeting, as one would expect. But his personality is a weighty factor. Even among normal children certain temperaments and types of character are easy to fit in anywhere; others are less ready to adapt to

[1] About one quarter of the Tottenham children and about one half of the Islington children had returned to their homes by those dates.

strange people and apt to give rise to friction. Certain sorts of neurotic difficulty in a child make very special demands upon a foster home. Anxious, aggressive, or delinquent children are not easy to place satisfactorily, but far from impossible if their needs are understood and an appropriate home is chosen. Even children with quite serious psychological difficulties can be so happily placed in the right foster home as to be accounted satisfactory in their relationships there.

On the whole, depressed or anxious children seem to prosper most in quiet, rather conventional homes, where they are by themselves and free to follow their own devices. Whereas the more aggressive boys and girls do better in homes with a more lively atmosphere, where there are others of much the same age and the children can be kept actively interested and employed.

The age of the child also affects the ease with which he can be happily placed in a foster home. The difficulties of billeting showed a sharp rise, with the children we studied, at or after thirteen years of age. Possible reasons for this fact are discussed in later pages, but it is not very surprising that the years when boys and girls commonly tend to be most difficult at home should also be a time of special trouble in the foster home. Particular care in selecting the home is called for, and special help and advice should be available for the foster parents.

The immense value, for children of these years, of proper opportunities for social pleasures, for games and sports, for clubs and hobbies and practical interests, was brought out in our study of children's recreation. After the choice of the foster home, nothing is more important than to provide for such activities and enjoyments.

It was found, also, that most children were happier if their brothers and sisters were living in the same foster home. And, contrary to what many people assumed, the visits of the children's own parents tend not to be unfavourable to their settling down in the new surroundings.

Of the importance of the family tie, we gained ample

evidence. The children themselves, in the essays which they wrote for us, whilst letting us enjoy the special flavour of their individual values, yet showed us how dominant in their feelings is the love of home, of parents, of brothers and sisters, how intensely even the happily placed child may feel the loss of his own family. They showed us, too, how responsive they are to goodwill and friendliness in the foster home and the neighbourhood, how appreciative of what is done for them, even though they do not always know how to express this appreciation directly.

The value, for the purpose of successful billeting, of experience in social work and understanding of the psychological needs of individual children was further borne out by the calls made upon the staff of the Child Guidance Training Centre. It was found that if the complaints of children or foster mothers were investigated as soon as they were made, much serious friction and distress could be avoided. If a billet had to be changed, this was better done before tempers were frayed and goodwill exhausted. But skilled visitors, with training and experience in personal problems, were often needed to get at the heart of a complaint, to give the advice needed in any crisis, and to recognize the foster mother who would be likely to deal happily with a specially difficult child. The choice of a new foster home for an unsettled and difficult child may, and often does, call for the special knowledge of the social worker trained to deal with psychological problems.

It was furthermore found immensely helpful to establish and maintain a hostel which could receive any child whose affairs had reached a crisis, and could give special guidance to the more restless and unhappy ones for a period.

Our study of the families of children who went home emphasized still more deeply the crucial importance of family ties and of the feelings of parents and children towards and about each other. It was far from easy to discern and disentangle the many and complex motives which led parents to take their children home again. Many different reasons were discovered. But the dominant motives seemed to fall into three groups: (*a*) Those relating to family feeling—the anxiety and loneliness of the parents, the homesickness or worry of the children. (*b*) Complaints about the foster homes or foster parents. In some cases at least these seemed to be justifications for bringing the children home rather than the real grounds for this action, which actually sprang from the parents' own longing to have the children in the home. (*c*) The third reason was the financial burden of keeping part of the family away from home, a burden which in many cases the billeting allowance by no means fully eased.

The feeling of family unity and the intense resistance to its being broken up was apparent, too, in the reasons which many parents gave for not wishing to send their children away again, even should the need become more imperative.

Much more might have been done than was done, however, to allay the anxieties of parents about their children, in the first few weeks and months. If the tensions arising between parents and foster parents could have been dealt with when they arose, and the parents given more direct help in keeping alive their own natural ties with the children, there would have been fewer withdrawals.

Our inquiry into the experience and considered views of evacuated teachers brought many confirmations of the conclusions we had arrived at from our study of the children's relationships in the foster home. The difficulties which arose in the life and work of the teachers, and the handicaps to the educational progress of the children, came from faults not in the routine organization, but in personal relationships. 'It may well be that too long was spent in perfecting the mechanics of evacuation, while the personal problems of the "evacuee" were too quickly dismissed from mind. A happy settled community in the reception area would surely have been ample recompense for some slight loss of precision during the journey out.'[1] And a closer contact between the educational authorities in the visiting and receiving areas, beforehand, would have obviated many of the difficulties and the waste which occurred.

The teachers reported that the health of the children had

[1] See p. 176.

certainly improved. So had their relations with their teachers —had become more intimate, more trustful and confident. There had been a slowing down of academic learning, but against this could be set great gains: in liveliness of general outlook, in new and satisfying pursuits and fields of knowledge, and in a greater self-reliance.

Among themselves, too, the teachers saw more intimate, more co-operative and enjoyable relationships appearing in response to the new situation. Many new and varied responsibilities had come to them. Their financial position had in most cases worsened. But for the teachers as for the children, the chief loss and chief source of difficulty was the break in family life, the parting with loved ones and the securities home. And the chief complaint of the teachers was that their knowledge and skill had not been made use of more fully in planning the details of evacuation for their own pupils. The knowledge which every teacher has of his own children had been left largely waste and neglected, in the first distribution, and even in later redistributions of children to their foster families, as well as in the planning of their education in its new setting.

This, then, is our broadest and most general conclusion, namely, that the first great scheme for evacuation might have been far less of a failure, far more of a success, if it had been planned with more understanding of human nature, of the way in which ordinary parents and ordinary children feel and are likely to behave.

In especial, the strength of the family tie,[1] on the one hand, and the need for skilled understanding of the individual child, on the other, seem to have lain too far outside the ken of those responsible for the scheme.

In the Practical Recommendations which were drawn up

[1] Since the bombing of London's East End, we have seen how this need to keep the family together and to cling to familiar home surroundings may override even the worst dangers. Among the simple and the poor, where there is no wealth, no pride of status or of possessions, love for the members of one's own family and joy in their bodily presence alone make life worth living. So deeply rooted is this need that it has defied even the law of self-preservation, as well as urgent public appeals and the wishes of authority.

and circulated among authorities and interested private persons in March 1940, and which are printed in Appendix II, the Research Committee of the Survey strongly urged the value of appointing trained social workers to help generally in billeting, and to give special advice and guidance with difficult children. Many people who have commented privately upon these recommendations and agreed generally with their wisdom have hesitated to consider them practicable, because of the probable cost of such services. Yet this cost would be measurable and limited, even if greater than authorities are accustomed to, whilst the waste, the tragic and irremediable waste of money, of effort and goodwill, or the time of officials and the future of children which has already been incurred by the failure of the actual scheme is not to be measured. 'It is extravagant *not* to provide a personal service to which individuals can turn for understanding and help'[1]—especially when the success of a vital public operation depends upon such understanding and help. There has already been, and still exists, an enormous double waste—of private and public goodwill, on the one hand, and of the expert knowledge of child psychologists and trained social workers, on the other.

If such help is made available, people will and do make use of it. The skilled social worker does not have to go out and look for people who need her. The existence of some one with special knowledge of parents' and children's concerns has only to be made known to be sought and used.

It seems an extraordinary thing that we should have allowed so much neglect of human feeling and personal issues in a scheme which proudly emphasized its voluntary nature; that is to say, a scheme which relied upon people's wishes and understanding, upon their confidence and content, for its maintenance. Had evacuation been compulsory we should not have been open to this reproach, since the authorities would have drawn upon the sanctions of the law. But when the whole plan rested upon the ability of the ordinary man and woman to co-operate in a public undertaking of such

[1] p. 155.

gravity and urgency, it is hard to believe that we could be so foolish, so self-contradictory.

Again, if evacuation had been forced upon us by war in September 1938, we might have been excused for thinking only of immediate military necessity and questions of transport. But when we had a whole year in which to plan, it is bitter to think that we in our proud democracy showed so little prevision, so little knowledge of the parents and children upon whom we were to act so disturbingly, and in whose hands the success or failure of the scheme rested.

This sharp lesson in the ineffectiveness and waste of a partial approach to a great human issue, one which from its very nature touches every side of human life, applies by no means only to the temporary crisis of dispersing urban populations during a war. It has an equally direct and urgent bearing upon the whole field of education and of social reconstruction during and after the war.

This is not the place to enter into such larger questions. We feel justified, however, in stressing our conclusion that a true understanding of the feelings and aims of ordinary human beings is an essential condition of success, whether we are concerned with the replanning and rebuilding of our great cities, the renewal of life in the countryside, the humanizing of our town schools, the training and teaching of youth, the education of adult citizens, the revision of economic structure.

Every one of these purposes not only requires a co-operative effort from the departments and sectional authorities now so often working isolatedly; it demands also the full knowledge and understanding of human nature as a whole.

CHAPTER II

HOW THE SURVEY WAS CARRIED OUT

THE WAY in which any investigation is carried out has to be determined by various considerations. First, there is the purpose of the study. If its aim be mainly a practical one, then we need to arrive at conclusions quickly, although we still wish them to be as reliable as can be in a short time. If our purpose be chiefly to add to our store of lasting knowledge, then absolute reliability is more important than speed and immediate applicability.

Secondly, the method is naturally forged from the kind of problem presented. Human relations cannot be arranged to suit the convenience of the person who is interested in finding out what they are like. Human beings will not stand still for the students' time exposures; they are always on the move, so that we must often be content with snapshots. This is particularly true of a study of which change is the very essence, as in this case.

Finally, there are limits set for social studies by all sorts of other facts. For example, whilst it is very generally found by research workers that most people like talking about their experiences when inquiries are made with honesty and consideration, it is also true that at periods of special strain, any extra demand upon time and thought may be felt as an impertinence. Each step in method must therefore be weighed against the particular demands that it will make upon the people concerned.

In this study we were primarily interested in the welfare of children sent away from their own homes in wartime. The Survey had its origin in a discussion which took place in the Child Discussion Group. But we were also concerned with the effect of this migration of children upon family life; the home deprived of its own children, and the home offering hospitality. Bound up closely with the whole scheme was the school. The school appeared in a rather new rôle. The boundaries of education were suddenly vastly widened when the child was entrusted by his parent to the teacher who thus became for the moment the only link with all that had gone before in the child's life.

In the Survey, we had both a short range and a long range purpose, and we tried to reach a compromise between them. In time of war, immediate practical results must needs assume a special urgency. Here was an important part of national policy carried out in a time of grave crisis. Success or failure, in the early autumn of 1939, might even have proved crucial in the prosecution of the war. If it were necessary to sustain this family separation, how could it be done with the least damage and the most benefit to those who were involved—children, parents, teachers, and private citizens? In October 1939 this immediate question was being answered partly by the breakdown of the scheme itself, and partly by ill-founded statements in the Press and elsewhere. Clearly the truth could only be discovered by a sober collection of facts.

It was this short range purpose which led us to publish preliminary reports and practical recommendations before our Survey was completed. We did not offer them as final conclusions, but we were satisfied that they approximated more closely to the truth than the kind of generalizations which were then being widely accepted as fact, and were apparently based almost wholly upon complaints.

If it were found, for example, that a proportion of children did settle down happily, then it seemed worth while discovering how this came about, for in new schemes more careful methods might increase the number of children and foster parents who became good friends.

We were also interested in adding to our knowledge about children, and about family life. We had in mind some of the social services in peace time, and their possible improvement. In Great Britain at peace some 40,000 children at least are boarded every year in private families. About ten years' ordinary experience in the placing of children had been condensed into one week of evacuation. Surely something could be learned from this. Many countries are far in advance of Great Britain in this kind of knowledge and skill.[1]

The situation was of course a very different one from that of boarding out dependent or difficult children in peace time. The parents who parted from their children, far from having failed them, were acting from a sense of duty, often at great sacrifice. The foster parents felt at first that they were offering shelter from immediate danger and there was a true element of rescue in the motives of many. But the bare fact of separation of child and parents remained the same. The study might throw light upon the effect of sudden parting on children of different ages and temperaments, upon their powers of adaptation to new people and new surroundings. The work of Child Guidance Clinics had shown clearly that the emotional difficulties of children such as anxiety, temper, upsets in feeding, sleeping and elimination, were generally bound up with the child's relationship with his parents. But Child Guidance Clinics admittedly saw selected members of the population. It would be interesting to discover what happened when the basis of selection was a different one. The study might also be a means of finding individuals who had a capacity for mothering, undiscovered perhaps to themselves or to other people. If they existed, then perhaps not only could the care of the 40,000 children generally looked after in private homes be improved, but a better sort of upbringing might be devised for the much larger number of children brought up in institutions.

The practical problems of parents and foster parents were obviously of the utmost importance both in themselves, and in the effect they must inevitably have upon relationships. If, for instance, the parents were having great difficulties in supplying clothes which at home they would have cut down and patched, this might lead to the child's return; or, if he stayed, to a sense of injury on the part of the foster parents, and humiliation on the part of the child. For example, efforts

[1] League of Nations Child Welfare Commission. Placing of Children in Families. 1938.

made by one Central School to get girls to bring their underclothes to school for laundering, and so to relieve the foster parents, failed, apparently because of the girls' embarrassment. It is always misleading to separate material facts from human attitudes.

These were some of the questions which the Research Committee considered at its first meetings. This volume is evidence of their compromise between immediate practical issues and discoveries which might have permanent value. We have had to be content (partly for reasons of time), with second-hand evidence, when, in other circumstances, we should certainly have insisted upon special research interviews. We have not had enough resources to enable us to round off the study by getting records of individual children before they left home, or of their homes while they were in Cambridge. We have studied the children from different London boroughs at different times, so that it is difficult to assess the extent to which our findings are affected by events in time, and to what extent by real differences of fact. In spite of all these handicaps we have, however, thought it worth while to record our study in some detail.

The method will be described in terms of history rather than of logic. Each step had in fact to be thought out afresh, and it would give a false impression to suggest that the final scheme was planned as a whole. Both subjects and investigators had a way of disappearing, the one group to their homes, the other generally further afield. Conditions were constantly changing, and with each change came new practical problems which momentarily distracted us from the main theme of our inquiry. It is therefore probably both more accurate and more interesting to give an account of the method as it was actually evolved by the Research Committee.

We decided in the first place to confine our study to children of school age whose mothers were not in Cambridge. It became evident within the first few weeks of evacuation that the scheme for mothers and young children was breaking down, and, even if it had been possible to carry out a study of those who remained, the problem was such an entirely different one that we could not have done justice to both. We decided also that we should have to look upon the problem of evacuation mainly from the standpoint of a Reception Area. It would have added greatly to the interest and value of our research if we had been able to discover why the families who lived in the same London boroughs had not sent their children away, but this was not practicable. In different parts of the country the proportion of school children evacuated varied as widely as from 8 per cent to 76 per cent, and for the country as a whole it was 47 per cent.[1] It is important to bear this in mind, since there is a tendency to pass easily from generalizations about evacuated children to generalizations about the school population as a whole, and this is not justifiable unless we are able to measure the main influences at work in the decision reached by parents.

In September about three thousand school children were evacuated to Cambridge. These children came mainly from the Metropolitan Area of London. It was decided that, since the study must be limited, there would be considerable advantages in confining ourselves to the children from one or two boroughs. This had obvious gains from the administrative point of view. Before any first hand study could be undertaken it was necessary to get permission not only from the local Education Officer and Billeting Officer (who, in the case of Cambridge was, most fortunately, one and the same person), but also from the Education Committees of the evacuating authorities. In spite of their burden of work and responsibility in the autumn of 1939, we were able to get co-operation from all those officials and authorities whom we approached.

There were certain other advantages in selecting the school children from one or two boroughs. It was more possible to get general information about the neighbourhoods from which the children came. In Tottenham a survey of school

[1] Padley, R., and Cole, M., *Evacuation Survey*, A Report to the Fabian Society, Routledge, 1940, Chapter III, pp. 46 and 47.

children had been carried out two years previously.[1] It was hoped that it might be possible to form some general impression of the difference in incidence of children's difficulties at home and with strangers, and that in some cases individual records might be pieced together. We knew that in the case of children who had attended special clinics this could be done, but of course these were likely to be exceptional children, and it would have been particularly interesting to know what happened to the child who had not already been singled out for any special treatment. This Tottenham survey was useful as a general background of knowledge about the children from the Borough, but we were not able to use the individual records as we had hoped—partly because only a very small sample of children had been studied in 1938, and few of these happened to be children who had been sent to Cambridge, and partly because it was difficult to make sure that definitions of difficulties, such as 'delinquent' or 'aggressive', would be used in the same sense.

The boroughs we chose, then, were Tottenham and Islington. It so happened that a large Central School had been moved from Tottenham, and that some members of the teaching staff were particularly interested in the scheme; indeed, if it had not been for the enthusiastic help of the teachers it is doubtful whether the study could ever have been carried out at all, and every chapter in this book is evidence of their interest. Tottenham is mentioned first because the part of the survey carried out between November and February 1939–40 was completed and reported upon separately. It consisted of individual records of 373 children, about one quarter of whom had returned home by December 1st 1939.

It is worth while noting that the proportion of children returning from Cambridge was, at this date, probably rather lower than the average proportion for the country as a whole. By January 8th this proportion varied from 35 per cent to

[1] Rawlings, Grace, *A Psychological Survey of Elementary Schools in the Borough of Tottenham*, published by the Borough of Tottenham Education Committee, 1939, p. 79.

69 per cent, and the total proportion was 43 per cent.[1] The parents of most of the Tottenham children who had returned to their homes before December 1st, 1939, were interviewed during the first two months of 1940.[2]

The Committee was aware that in some ways the Tottenham children could not be taken as a representative sample of evacuated children as a whole. To start with, there were few homes in this district which could be said to be of extreme poverty. Many of these children came from the homes of artisans or skilled labourers in fairly comfortable circumstances. They lived in a neighbourhood where there was plenty of space, not only for formal recreation but even for wandering about by a river side. The contrast in surroundings for a child moving down the line from Tottenham to Cambridge cannot have been anything like so striking as for the child who was moved from, say, Bethnal Green to Somerset, or from Stepney to Cornwall; indeed one teacher maintained that there was more 'open space' in the borough of Tottenham than there was in the borough of Cambridge! Then the age distribution of the children was not a 'true' one; it did not correspond either with the age distribution of school children of Tottenham, or with that of all the evacuated children from the Borough. There was an undue proportion of children of eight years old or more. Only one quarter of the Tottenham children in Cambridge were less than eight years old, whereas the proportion in the Tottenham schools is one third. This meant that the number of young children was not large enough to justify fine statistical measurements in the lower age groups. Finally, it seems probable from the tests of general intelligence which were carried out on a proportion of the children[3] that those of over eleven were of higher intelligence than the average child of that area attending the elementary school.

All these facts affected our conclusions, but they did not of course invalidate them, so long as we did not attempt to

[1] Padley, Richard, and Cole, Margaret, ibid., p. 50.
[2] See Chapter VIII, p. 125.
[3] See Chapter VI, p. 91.

generalize without keeping them clearly in mind. In point of fact some of our conclusions have corresponded so closely with other studies where these limiting conditions have not been present, that it is possible that we have over-estimated their importance.[1] We thought it worth while, however, to extend our study to another group of children, and we chose 352 children from the borough of Islington. This time the sample had its proper quota of young children. It was unfortunate that we were not able to carry out these two studies simultaneously, because conditions had changed in many ways by the spring of 1940. To start with, a larger proportion of the children had returned (roughly half, as against one quarter), and it was probable that new factors influenced their return. The Christmas holidays, the establishment of parents' payments, raised billeting allowances, and new phases of the war had intervened. We were fortunate, however, in being able again to visit a proportion of the homes of returned children. In the selection of these homes we were careful to take a random sample of children corresponding in sex and age proportions with those who at that time were still in Cambridge. Again, the Islington children came from a poorer neighbourhood; it was partly for this reason that they were chosen, for we were anxious to see whether the standard of the home did affect significantly the child's adjustment to new surroundings. We realized, of course, that this was a very complicated question, and that no conclusions could really be reached unless some way could be discovered of measuring the relationship between the standards of the child's home and the foster parent's household. Even then it seemed probable that subtle questions of manners and customs, not by any means simply related to income or occupation, were likely to be involved. It would be impossible to measure such attitudes as were expressed by the child who remarked: 'The country is a funny place. They never tell you you can't have no more to eat, and under the bed is wasted.'[2]

[1] Cf., for instance, the estimate of general success and failure, Chapter IV, p. 53, and that contained in the Liverpool University study, *Our Wartime Guests—Opportunity or Menace*, p. 10.

[2] Cosens, M., Evacuation, A Social Revolution, *Social Work*, Jan. 1940, p. 9.

The Research Committee was constantly confronted with the dilemma of the social investigator: how to find out what the general tendencies were without destroying the portraits of individuals. The dilemma was made particularly vivid to us because on the Research Committee we had individuals whose work had been almost wholly of the 'case-study' variety, and others whose discipline was mainly statistical. This combination was in itself of great interest, and suggested the need for further experiments in joint social research. The problem is, of course, presented as soon as any outline for a study of individual cases is designed. The 'free' interview, in which certain topics are introduced, and the conversation is allowed to take its course, is perhaps more likely to give a true picture of attitudes and, if conducted by a skilled and disinterested investigator, is less likely to suggest certain stereotyped answers. The interview in which standardized questions are put and space on the form is left for additional comment is infinitely easier to compare and to classify.

Suppose, for example, that we are interested in the subject of the parents' supply of clothes to their children in foster homes. The question might have been left unasked, to see whether it was 'uppermost' in the mind of the foster mother, and brought spontaneously into a general discussion of evacuation. But if in these circumstances clothes had not been mentioned at all, there would be no way of telling whether in this particular instance they had in fact been important. They might have been outweighed by other troubles, such as wet beds or bad table manners, or compensated for by quietness and obedience. In such a free conversation features of the situation which are giving no trouble or no outstanding pleasure tend not to be mentioned, although they may be just as important. A foster parent would be likely to remark on specially good clothes sent by parents, or on the fact that nothing had been sent at all, but the 'ordinary' would tend to pass without comment. Yet almost any form of question suggests a certain kind of response, and this was certainly true of the question on this subject that was finally framed: 'Have there been any difficulties about the child's clothes?'

It is obvious that the method finally used must depend upon the skill of the investigators and also upon the uniformity of this skill. Summaries of 'free' conversations can only safely be used if similar standards of judgment are employed by all those undertaking interviews, for in this type of study there must always be selection and interpretation.

The way in which our data were obtained was actually largely determined for us by local conditions and by our own resources. It was felt, by those responsible for billeting, that the foster mothers who had already been liable to callers on many different errands should not be visited specially for purposes of this inquiry. We had therefore to be content with such information about the child and the foster home as was already in the minds of those who had supervised the children for the first two months of evacuation, or could be obtained by them in a further visit, after discussion with the Survey investigator. The cards of inquiry were completed in the offices, and none of them were taken to the homes. Owing to the large number of different visitors involved in the study, and the fact that they were volunteers with varying degrees of efficiency and skill, it was evident that the information itself would be of uneven value.[1] In view of this fact the committee felt it necessary to make the answering of the questions as simple as possible, and many of them were of the 'tick' variety, such as 'What is the foster mother's attitude towards having the child'? *Answer* (Please tick) 'Likes. Tolerates. Is Dissatisfied.'[2] Even so it was felt that the outline, as it was finally used, was too complicated, particularly in relation to special difficulties of the child about which the Friendly Visitor would only have accurate information if she had kept in very close touch with each foster mother. In the Tottenham study various methods were used in the actual completion of the cards: some of the Senior Voluntary Workers preferred to fill in their own for

[1] For a description of the work of reception in Cambridge, see Chapter III.
[2] For reproduction of forms, see Appendix IV, p. 222.

the whole district, and others left them to the Friendly Visitors. In some cases the Survey investigators made the entries on the dictation of the voluntary workers. In the Islington part of the study we tried to improve the standardization by arranging for our investigator to complete all the entries in an interview with those who had been supervising the children, and in this way she was able to make some estimate of the knowledge which the visitor had of this particular case, and to discount those in which it seemed unreliable.

We should hardly have felt justified in drawing conclusions from these cards if we had not been able to supplement our information from other sources. The interest of the school teachers has already been mentioned. In both the Islington and the Tottenham part of the inquiry we were fortunate in being able to get cards completed on each child by his teacher. It so happened that from the school point of view the Tottenham information was of greater value for our inquiry. At the time this was undertaken most of the teachers who came away from London were still with the same children, though some of them disappeared before the study was completed. In the Central School where the senior children were working, the entries were made by a group of teachers under the guidance of a member of the Research Committee. Most of these teachers had been in touch both with the child's parents in London and with his foster home in Cambridge, so that we were able to cross-check the entries of the visitors and the teachers. By the time the Islington study was undertaken, many of the teachers had left to look after those children who by that time had drifted back to London, and some of those who were left in Cambridge had only known the child for a comparatively short time, and had not had so much to do with the foster home, although there were some notable exceptions. On the whole, therefore, in spite of our greater care in standardizing the entries of the foster home cards, we regard the Tottenham information as more reliable than that obtained about the Islington children in Cambridge.

There was a third source of information which we found very valuable, and which was given by the children themselves in an essay written in an ordinary school class on 'What I like in Cambridge', and 'What I miss in Cambridge'. These essays are summarized in Chapter V. In some cases, the teachers talked with the small children, and sent in notes of what they said about their stay in Cambridge. The interpretation of the essays themselves was of course no simple matter. Some of them proved to be far more stereotyped than others, although we had carefully asked that no suggestions should be made to the children. It could of course by no means be assumed that the older children would speak of those things which touched their feelings most deeply; indeed for many children the reverse would be more likely. We felt, however, that when we set these three kinds of information side by side—the Friendly Visitor's report, the teacher's card, and the child's essay, we could in most cases gain a clear picture of how the child was getting along, together with certain definite facts about their circumstances at home and in Cambridge.

The next stage in our inquiry was decided in January 1940. At this time reviews were being made by the Ministry of Health of the number of children who had returned home, and it was not difficult to foresee that there would probably be a second evacuation scheme. The Research Committee felt that it was urgent, for practical reasons, to discover something about the successful and the unsuccessful billets. So far the comments or studies that had been made elsewhere seemed to be one-sided, dealing with things only from the point of view of the foster parents, of the teachers or of the parents. In our case material, we had data from at least three points of view about each child. It is true that the parents' point of view was lacking. Possibly, if we could plan our study again, we should have used the professional assistance which we were offered in London[1] to complete our knowledge of the child

[1] Through the generosity of the Mental Health Emergency Committee, we were loaned the services of two psychiatric social workers to undertake our London visits, and of one to undertake the Islington inquiry in Cambridge.

still in Cambridge rather than use it, as we did, for visits to the families of the children who had returned home. But there was good reason for our choice of these visits at the time. The obvious reply to any general statements about the children in Cambridge would be: 'but the others have gone home'. If, for instance, we were to find that a large proportion of children in Cambridge were visited by their parents without ill effect, or were causing trouble in the Juvenile Court, then the rejoinder might be that all those children who had been upset by their parent's visits had returned; or that the 'good' children had belonged to the more united families. Therefore, in order to make sure that our data in Cambridge were significant, we felt that we must make some study of the children who had returned to the two boroughs.

It seemed that the answer to the question as to whether the present billeting was a success could only be determined by a composite judgment based upon all the material available on each child. The satisfactoriness of the billet could not be determined alone either by the behaviour of the child, or by the attitude of the foster parent, but must be the product of both. Admittedly we had more material on the child, and we did not have a close enough measure of the degree of sacrifice or hardship which the foster mother had undergone in making a home for the child. It was decided to use the device of the five-point rating scale, in which the relationship between child and foster family was assessed from 'very satisfactory' to 'very unsatisfactory', with three intermediary classes. The interpretation of these different categories will be further explained in Chapter IV.

After a preliminary trial of this method carried out by all the members of the Research Committee, it was decided to leave the rating to two individuals, one of whom, in the case of the Tottenham group, knew a large proportion of the children, and could often supplement the available information. The method seemed justified in that, although the assessments were made independently, there were only two or three cases in which there was a difference of more than one point in the judgments. In the Islington study, such differences were referred to a third member of the committee for final decision.

Having completed this rating, it was possible to single out various facts upon which we had precise information and to see whether there was any significant correlation with the whole picture of relationship as it had been judged.

The Research Committee had hoped from the outset that it would be possible to see some of the children and the foster parents themselves. The visits which had been carried out to the parents in London had shown that they welcomed an opportunity for discussion. 'Those who felt injured were glad of any opportunity to voice their grievances, and those who were grateful liked to be able to express their feelings', ran the report of the social workers to the committee. No visits were refused by the parents, although in one borough the Education Committee ruled out certain families from the list of about one hundred children that was submitted.

In the assessment made in Cambridge it was found that there were certain significant differences between the circumstances in which children settled down well, and not so well, in homes other than their own. These facts might be of value in administering the scheme for large numbers of children, but would not necessarily be of assistance in dealing with the individual child. It is this disconcerting truth which has often made social workers rely completely for their progress upon unclassified studies of individuals, rather than upon analyses of large number of cases. If, for instance it is found that most children settle down better in their billets when they are placed with their brothers and sisters, it does not mean that all evacuated children will do better if they stay with members of their own family; what it does mean is that if a general plan must be made, there will, in the long run, and under similar circumstances, be fewer failures by keeping *all* the children together than by separating *all* of them. If generalizations on this subject had been made from cases which received special attention from visitors and clinics in Cambridge, it seems likely that separation of all brothers and sisters would have been the verdict, for family wrangles have a way of making themselves felt more forcibly than happy families.

Just as case work must supplement wholesale social planning in order to meet the infinite variety of human needs, so in studies of social relationships, there must be both a separating out of certain features for purposes of measurement, and also a study of the individual cases in which all the influences may be seen merging with, supplementing, or counteracting one another to produce a constantly changing pattern of behaviour.

The Research Committee welcomed the opportunity, then, of making this 'case study' approach to all the children in the two boroughs who were rated, in relation to their billets, 'very unsatisfactory' or 'rather unsatisfactory', and to a group matched in sex and age who had been rated 'very satisfactory'. The children were seen by an educational psychologist in the school, and while a test of general intelligence was the focus of the interview, there was plenty of opportunity for a talk with the child about his life in Cambridge and for forming some idea as to his personality and how well he had settled down. The number of children interviewed was forty from Tottenham and forty from Islington. This part of the study is described in Chapter VI.

We should like to have completed the picture by a special visit to the foster homes of these two groups of children, but again the exigencies of wartime made it impossible for these visits to be undertaken, and we had to be content with the information that had already been gained about these families by the Friendly Visitor.

There were three other ways in which we were able to add to the Survey. It was evident in every stage of our inquiry that the teachers had carried the main burden of work in connection with evacuation. Although they were not officially responsible for the welfare of the children (this responsibility rested finally with the Education Officer of the Reception Area and the Billeting Officer), yet the parents had been told that the children would go with their own teachers, and when, as in Cambridge, this promise had been carried out, the teachers *felt* responsible. Children and parents naturally turned to them rather than to strangers when they were in difficulty. When the Research Committee came to consider practical recommendations at the time the second evacuation scheme was being devised, in April 1940, one of their main problems was how to lighten the burden of the teachers, leaving them free for their proper responsibilities, while at the same time making the best use of their unique knowledge of the child.

We were therefore particularly glad when a representative of the London teachers on our Research Committee offered to make an inquiry which would be of a rather different kind from the records already described. It was decided to send out a questionnaire to the London teachers, asking them for their views about some of the subjects which had formed part of our study of individual children, and some which belonged more closely to educational progress and teaching conditions. The inquiry included also their attitude towards their own evacuation, and how it had affected their professional work. Unfortunately, this inquiry was sent out at a critical stage of national affairs, when second evacuation schemes were already under way, and out of consideration for the teachers only a small proportion of the questionnaires were sent to those who were still in Cambridge in May 1940. The result of the teachers' inquiry is described in Chapter X.

The chapter on Recreation is another study carried out by one member of the committee. This originated in the reading of the children's essays, which were full of references to their enjoyment of the special clubs and play groups which had been arranged by local citizens and students. In the spring of 1940, the Board of Education called a conference of all those who were concerned with the recreation of the evacuated children in Cambridge, and it was evident from the lively discussion that there were many interesting experiments taking place, and many differences of view about what was needed. This encouraged the continuation of the small survey of recreation that had already been started.

Practical plans for the employment of more skilled

organizers of recreation were at this time being considered by the Board and by local authorities, and it was thought that, apart from the interest of knowing more about the social life of the children belonging to our study, it would be of value to make some record of what had taken place in one borough in which hospitality had been arranged for a large number of school children.

Finally, this book includes a chapter on Child Guidance and Evacuation. This subject, too, takes us beyond the scope of our original inquiry, since only a proportion of the children referred to the Clinic came from the boroughs of Tottenham and Islington. It was thought, however, that a record of the kind of cases for which special advice was asked from the staff of a Child Guidance Clinic would be of value from several points of view.

In ordinary circumstances, children are referred to such clinics because other methods of handling either the usual or the unusual difficulties of childhood have failed. It became evident during the first few weeks of evacuation that this threshold of breakdown must be reached sooner under conditions of evacuation. Not only were certain kinds of difficulties likely to be increased by the children's separation from their parents, but foster parents could not be expected to bear without help the strain of difficult or nervous children in addition to the extra responsibilities which billeting had involved for them. Then again, the social services of the neighbourhood, augmented as they were by the work of the Women's Voluntary Services, could not expand indefinitely to meet the needs of children, foster parents and teachers when relationships became strained to breaking point. The Child Guidance staff were therefore asked to help in all kinds of small emergencies, as well as in more serious cases of disturbance.

It so happened that evacuation had itself led to an increased number of Child Guidance workers in Cambridge. For many years, Addenbrooke's Hospital had provided this service for the borough and the neighbouring counties. At the outbreak of war, social work students, training for the mental health services, were moved with the London School of Economics to Cambridge. Through the courtesy of the staff of Addenbrooke's Hospital, a plan was worked out whereby the staff of the Child Guidance Department of the Hospital and of a Training Centre worked in close co-operation, and this led to an increase in the psychiatric social service available. A record of the work undertaken with evacuated children by the Training Centre is described in Chapter VII.

This, then, covers in general terms the content and method of the Survey. The Research Committee has been painfully aware of its limitations. The difficulties have sometimes been so great that we were only led to persist in our efforts by our concern for the welfare of children, and our desire to reap from the first year of the war some record of experience which might add in a small way to wisdom for the future.

CHAPTER III

PLAN FOR EVACUATION: THE ORGANIZATION IN CAMBRIDGE

AFTER THE Munich crisis of September 1938, A.R.P. propaganda started in Cambridge as elsewhere, and the anxiety of preparing for war conditions began to stir the Local Authority. Teachers helped to assemble and distribute gas-masks, and in this way were able to gauge public feeling. The London Women's Voluntary Services asked the Chairman of the Cambridge Women Citizens' Association to suggest a local representative of the Women's Voluntary Services to assist the Local Authority if required to deal with problems of evacuation. The local A.R.P. Authority was then approached by the London W.V.S. offering them the appointed representative. This was accepted and the Reception Assistant, as she was called, was co-opted on the Evacuation Sub-Committee of the Borough A.R.P. Committee. The appointment of Chief Billeting Officer, originally the Clerk to the Borough Council, was then, after a special A.R.P. meeting, transferred to the Education Officer. It was he who undertook in February 1939 (through the teachers and with the help of the W.V.S.) to carry out the survey of available accommodation. The staff of the Education Department of the Council became almost continuously occupied with the administrative details of the plan.

In November 1938 the Reception Assistant, after consultation with the officers of those Local Authorities concerned, had drawn up a 'draft scheme for the reception of refugees'. This dealt briefly with the following suggestions:

1. *The reception of mothers and children at the station.* The arrangements were to be in the hands of a Reception Officer to be appointed by the Clerk to the County Council. They included suggestions for the distribution of the children to various centres, arrangements for their reception there,

provision of temporary accommodation for late arrivals, distribution of rations, and provision of sanitary and first-aid arrangements at the station.

2. *The allocation of mothers and children to the County and to the Borough.* This was also in the hands of the Reception Officer.

3. *Transport from the station.*

4. *The selection and equipment of assembly halls* for the final distribution of mothers and children, in the first place as temporary accommodation, and possibly for use at a later stage for communal feeding. The staffing and equipment of these halls, other than schools, with canteens, first-aid and sanitary arrangements should, it was suggested, be undertaken by various women's organizations. Medical inspections on arrival, immediate hospital accommodation for some, and the special needs of pregnant women were all mentioned, and the co-operation of the various health services visualized.

5. *Billeting Organization.* This was to be divided according to the existing political wards with a local officer in charge, a representative from the staff of each school and assistant billeting officers. Their duties were to include the making of the register of accommodation and later of the billeting forms; the after care by periodic visiting to hear complaints, discuss difficulties, and arrange transfers; and the helping of district and school nurses, whose duties would be greatly increased.

Finally, the Billeting Organization would have to take steps to provide camps, huts, and unoccupied houses should the numbers of children and their mothers outstrip available accommodation.

The memorandum enlarged on the services which women's organizations might provide. Transport, distribution of rations, clerical work, collection of bedding and crockery, helping to look after children in private and empty houses, recreational facilities, washing and mending of clothes, settlement of disputes between householders and visitors, were also mentioned. The memorandum also emphasized the wisdom of compiling particulars of available accommodation *before* a state of emergency existed. Complications with army billeting, private arrangements with householders' own relatives and friends, and interference with householders' outside work, paid or voluntary, were all considered. Altogether it was a far-seeing memorandum. Although not officially stated, an increase in emotional problems, including bed-wetting, was also contemplated, and the whole complex question of the inevitable friction arising out of two women who were strangers to one another sharing a house as hostess and guest was given serious thought.

In June 1939 a meeting of teachers was held, one of many being called from time to time to keep abreast of and to interpret the Ministry of Health's memoranda. The teachers asked that a complete card index should be sent with the school parties, that the earlier survey of billets should be revised, that a police constable should be at each dispersal centre, and that a list of voluntary workers should be available. In at least one of the wards, a careful analysis was made of the billets and a joint meeting was held with the staff of a large private secondary school for girls and an excellent scheme for co-operation in billeting worked out. A senior voluntary worker had already been allotted to each billeting officer.

A major worry which was not solved until too late was that many householders promised billets if beds and bedding could be provided. These the Ministry of Health only provided in bulk on November 9th, but in the meantime the local authorities were authorized to buy up blankets from local stores, and school infant department beds were unofficially loaned to householders.

On August 23rd, 1939, a further memorandum was drawn up by the Centre Leader of the W.V.S. and the Reception Assistant. Thirteen Ward Billeting Officers, all head teachers, had been appointed by the Education Officer. A Senior Voluntary Worker had been appointed for each ward by the W.V.S. Reception Assistant. These Senior Voluntary Workers were to work in close touch with the Ward Billeting Officers to assist in after-care 'to promote the general welfare of evacuees and to help the householder in what must inevitably be a difficult situation'. They were selected because of their organizing ability or experience in social work. They were to be responsible for the visiting done by the group of Friendly Visitors. These varied in numbers in each ward from twelve to thirty-six, and were expected to submit regular reports to their Senior Voluntary Workers.

This recognition of the necessity for regular house-to-house visiting had been difficult to establish, but in practice it has proved, even with its failures, to be a bulwark in the scheme. If more trained visitors had been available many of the difficulties which occurred need never have arisen.

Education and Recreation. The memorandum discussed briefly the necessity for a double shift system in schools, since there were only 8,000 school places and about 16,000 school children were allocated to Cambridge. Recreation under discipline was to be the plan for the second session in the day and volunteers with experience in teaching or handling children were registered. Vacant halls were listed.

For evening and week-end recreation eighty volunteers were enlisted, mostly inexperienced and untrained, but ex-guides and scouts were also included. Advice from an experienced organizer of play-centres was available. Lectures were also arranged, both for householders and for Friendly Visitors.

Three lectures were given by experts at various schools in the summer term 1939 for those who offered to receive children. They dealt with health, nutrition, and the possible reaction of a child to a strange environment. A further memorandum outlined the way in which such visiting could contribute to the stability of reception and made valuable suggestions for approaching so delicate a task.

Numbers. The survey of accommodation yielded a total of 26,000 billets for 12,000 unaccompanied school children and 13,000 'others' (mothers, helpers, and children under school age), with 1,000 to spare. The provisional allocation to Cambridge of 16,000 evacuees was made up of 8,000 unaccompanied school children and 8,000 'others'.

These 16,000 evacuees were to be accommodated in approximately 8,000 households.

The scheme in action: Reception. On Sunday, August 26th,

the Reception Officer for the County, the Chief Billeting Officer of the Borough, and the station marshal appointed by the W.V.S. drew up a plan for the reception of the parties at the station. The numbers expected were 8,000 a day for three days.

On Friday, September 1st, a key man for each train load was placed on the arrival platform. Trains began to unload at 11.30 a.m. The control-room tried to give some information as to the number and composition of each party, but this proved to be quite inaccurate. The key-man sent a slip giving the name of the school party and the numbers of girls and boys to two men in the bus yard who directed transport to dispersal centres for both County and Borough. The only differentiation was that all secondary school children were to remain in the Borough. Parties suitable to the school accommodation available in each ward were sent out, e.g. Junior School children were sent to an area with enough places in a Junior School.

At the ward dispersal centres, the organization and the tasks varied a little. Medical inspections in some revealed no ailments, no verminous children. At one a few sore throats were found and gargles provided. At another centre receiving some 500 children, one or two minor operations were performed, one child was found to have scarlet fever and sent to hospital; several were incipient cases. The heads and tongues of the elementary school children in this area were found without exception to be clean and healthy, while among the children of a secondary school were many coated tongues. The only known bed-wetter announced, 'Mummy said I was to tell you I'm weak at night.' Much bed-wetting cleared at once. Many householders did not divulge, till it was cured, that they had had to deal with it. Mackintosh sheets were not available for the first three weeks.

Numbers of evacuees. The number of evacuees received at the beginning of September was estimated at about 6,700, about half of whom were unaccompanied school children and the remainder mothers, babies, teachers, and helpers. During the first month about 2,500 returned to London, and by the end of the second month at least a further 800 returned. During these two months by far the greater number returning were mothers and babies, the figures being about 2,700 adults and babies and 600 unaccompanied school children.

Of the total of 3,650 remaining on November 11th, when the first accurate count was possible,

3,128 were children (2,703 unaccompanied and 425 accompanied),
522 were adults (268 mothers, 197 teachers, 57 helpers).

As time went on, fewer and fewer went back to London. At the beginning of December about 100 a week returned. By February 1940 the number had dropped to about fifty a week, and although Easter slightly increased the number, in early June the number had fallen to about twenty. After the evacuation of Dunkirk, the numbers of those who returned rose in one week to over 160, almost entirely children. Householders began to feel that the responsibility of caring for other people's children was too great, and parents were more anxious without them. During succeeding weeks the numbers stabilized considerably; only thirty-two left during the week of July 7th to 14th. At the end of this week the numbers remaining in Cambridge were:

1,371 children (1,218 unaccompanied, 153 accompanied),
253 adults (69 mothers, 85 teachers, 25 helpers).

During the first two weeks in July about 100 additional evacuees, mainly adults, were transferred here from the coast.

Billeting. In spite of organization at the station, the children were very unevenly distributed in the wards—some having one-twelfth of their available billets used, others five-sixths, whilst in one outlying area the billets were completely used up and children had to be retransported to another. Compulsory powers were not used except in one or two cases, and in one street where these were used on the second night, all the children had to be rebilleted and the street refused to receive any others again for several months.

Although in some areas the billeting was fairly satisfactorily completed by the end of the first day, in others those responsible felt that they were working against time, that nightfall was imminent, and there was no time for careful sorting out. This element of speed was felt to have spoiled a great many billets, householders being bullied rather than persuaded, and this made some children temporarily more unhappy than they need have been. In one ward two people went round with every four children and one person undertook the doorstep discussion with the householder. In another it had been arranged by the Senior Voluntary Worker that the Friendly Visitor who introduced the children to their foster mothers should continue visiting these same homes. This made for great stability, many children remaining in the same billets for at least seven months.

On Saturday, September 2nd, no more unaccompanied school children arrived, the parties being composed of mothers and babies with some older children attached. Pregnant women were also in this group, and a special dispersal centre was in readiness and billeting was done near to a maternity ward. Although careful preparations for blind persons had been made, none arrived.

Relatively few householders' offers were available for mothers and babies, and this day's billeting was much less easy. The organization at the station, too, had been more difficult, confused as it was by the arrival of great numbers of eager volunteers who carried luggage hither and thither and led parties off with no clear directions. Owing to the kindly zeal of porters at exchange stations, the mothers' often ill-labelled luggage was piled into vans with the result that in a number of cases it took several weeks to recover it for the owners and much time was spent by officials on this tiresome task. The stationmaster remained throughout unruffled and a tower of strength, and to distracted staff and helpers he offered a seat and a cup of tea. Workers had to be ready for all sorts of emergencies. At the end of the second night, after a wearying day, a Billeting Officer had to find billets for sixteen lorry drivers.

There was a wide range of nationalities among those

arriving—Austrian, French, German, Greek, Hungarian, Irish, Italian, Yiddish-speaking Jewish, Polish, Rumanian, Russian, Siamese, Turkish. Billeting for many of these was a complicated matter. Five hundred mothers and babies had to be accommodated in five colleges and halls. Of these sixty, mainly Greeks, were placed for the night in a youth hostel and remained there in dwindling numbers for several months, whilst a German refugee scientist, speaking modern Greek, helped to sort out their problems.

In one area, where the residents consist partly of skilled artisans and partly of professional and business people, the London children, some of whom came from a large elementary school and some from a secondary school, were able to find appropriate homes after the correction of the first disastrous attempt by some over-zealous person to put children from very poor homes into houses with a staff of maids. In one case two small children from a poor London home did settle down very happily with a professional family with children of their own, and all was well until the first visit of the parents after five weeks. The two pairs of parents seemed to speak a different language. The London parents felt the Cambridge parents 'too uppish' and removed their youngsters. This was not the only instance of great sensitivity on the part of the children's parents. But nevertheless some happy temporary billeting occurred between parents of very different social groups. A solicitor took a mother and two children, had them waited on for five weeks, and gave the husband a holiday. After they were all rested, the W.V.S. then arranged for their transfer to a household where the father was in the same semi-skilled occupation as the evacuees' father. This worked admirably with good feeling throughout.

By September 5th most of the evacuees were in private billets and in empty houses, bare necessities being provided by neighbourly people from all over the town. One Billeting Officer said of the night of September 2nd: 'It was a pitiful sight in the school. We were packed with women at the fag end of their endurance, anxious, afraid of the unknown. But a cup of tea worked wonders. There was no hysteria, they were sensible. Their morale, even with babies crying in their arms and toddlers at their feet, was excellent.' On the other hand, other mothers were on that same night trying to return to London, demanding return fares under the impression that this was their due.

There was a rapid return for the next fortnight of unhappy, troubled women and children. Some were extremely difficult and unreasonable and some were verminous and dirty, and thus resented by Cambridge women, whose standards were often considerably higher, even with rather primitive sanitation in their houses. But often there were real grievances. No one would want to take, naturally enough, a woman with five children; but in this strange and terrifying new world, the mother could not allow any of them to be separated from her. She was quite quiet but firm about it. Another woman found herself alone in an isolated cottage with an old shepherd. Some London mothers were terrified at night of the great trees round the youth hostel. A Greek head-waiter's wife was given a bed inferior to that of an under-waiter's wife. Greeks and Turks found it difficult to live under the same roof.

One Senior Voluntary Worker who built up an active community life for the mothers in her ward said that the main reason for return after the first week of panic was sheer economic necessity. She quoted a typical case where the father was a milk roundsman earning £2 13*s*. with commission, amounting to a weekly rotal of £3 3*s*. Of this 17*s*. 6*d*. went in London rent, 2*s*. 6*d*. in coal. His income was reduced rapidly to £2 7*s*. 6*d*. total because of the decrease in his clients. He kept 4*s*. for meals and paid several shillings in insurances. The remainder he sent to his wife to feed and clothe herself and three children and to clothe two other children who were billeted elsewhere.

In other cases it was the loneliness of the husbands and the fear of 'the woman round the corner' which sent mothers with young children back to London. Occasionally women lived with great fortitude in very bare houses lacking all the household goods which are so dear and necessary to the hearts of many of us, finding the absence of the street market for food and second-hand clothes a serious deprivation. Or, still more precariously, they found themselves lodged in another woman's house sharing her much-prized equipment.

Naturally the local authority wanted the householders disturbed as little as possible, for their dislocation was already great; there was a short time when it was enough in some areas for a householder to complain that a child had been rude to her at table to have the child rebilleted without due investigation of all sides of the question. On the other hand, one mother used the lavatory pan to wash her child's clothes in because that was an easy way of getting rid of the water, and some lay abed in the morning while the householders did the work. Billeting Officers had constantly to play on the goodwill of the householders whose generosity was often quite astonishing. The impression is that these irresponsible mothers were isolated cases, due to a chronically low economic level and to poor mental development, aggravated by depression in the face of the overwhelmingly new situations that had to be faced.

The rapid fall in the numbers of mothers with young children remaining in Cambridge (and in the reception areas generally) seems to show that their evacuation was on the whole an unworkable proposition, and that not nearly enough imaginative thinking went into the Government's planning of the scheme.

Plans for After Care. By September 3rd the Evacuation Department of the Guildhall and the Ward Billeting Officers were being inundated with complaints from all sides, and from then on these places have continued to function as clearing centres for difficulties. There was no precedent for any single thing. Mistakes were inevitable, but many were easily rectified once and for all, whilst others, owing to the frailty of human nature, go on being made.

For instance, the Reception Assistant thinks that, instead of remaining at her headquarters for the first fortnight dealing with detailed complaints, she would have been wiser to see all the head teachers in order to come to some working arrangement with them as to the demarcation of function.

As it was, every one was doing some rebilleting; local head teachers, London head teachers, voluntary workers, school helpers, and mothers and children themselves, whilst householders would exchange children amicably without notifying any in authority. Tracing people was a time-consuming job and full of minor irritations to all concerned. The Reception Assistant began to see the head teachers individually about the middle of September, but it took the best part of two weeks before all twenty-six had been seen, and many misunderstandings which might have been cleared up easily in the beginning were difficult to remove after the lapse of three or four weeks.

After the first two weeks the consensus of opinion was that the local headmasters could not continue the work of billeting and run their own schools, complicated as they were by the influx of visiting children. At this point, therefore, the Senior Voluntary Workers already attached to the Billeting Officers took over the rebilleting. It seems to have been somewhere assumed that, once billeted, people would 'stay put', and that nothing more than a good card index was necessary. But in fact human life when uprooted is even more complex than it is normally. Problems that would have been taken in one stride at home became greatly magnified and needed all the patience and skill of a large number of people working long hours, turning their homes into offices, being indeed at the beck and call of every one. As one helper said, 'We saw so much anger and distress in the early days.'

Every system has its disadvantages. Too great standardization is devitalizing and too great freedom in organization may waste time and create difficulties. The latter certainly increased the tasks of a London head teacher who had children scattered in at least five wards, and found no standard procedure in matters of billeting among the various Senior Voluntary Workers who took over billeting duties. Moreover, visitors poured into the schools all day and every day, generally on quite important tasks, but they were none the less distracting to those who were trying to find their way in a quite new educational plan.

A further difficulty was that it was not clear to whom the school helpers arriving with the school parties were responsible, although in the Ministry of Health memorandum it appeared that they were to work under the jurisdiction of the Local Authority. Many of these helpers have been excellent people, stepping into the breach in countless ways, escorting children to hospital, washing, mending, visiting; but they have often found themselves in a quandary as to whom they served.

Perhaps it was insufficiently recognized that every one was keyed up with the imminence of bombing and its effects, and that this movement of people of different ways of life would create strains which inevitably led to a lowering of normal patience, resourcefulness, co-operativeness.

One outstanding difficulty peculiar to a University town was met with in the first month. It had been assumed that, as the number of undergraduates coming up for the session would be immensely curtailed, University lodgings could be included in available accommodation. It actually turned out that students from other colleges evacuated to Cambridge brought up the numbers of students to more than the normal total. After about three weeks, therefore, all the University lodgings had to be cleared of mothers and children. This amounted to some five or six hundred adults and children and the change produced a generally disturbing effect of incompetence and confusion. A good many parents on their second visit found their children in poorer billets and the changeover accounted for a fairly large number of those who returned to London in the early days.

Billeting is necessarily one of the most complex tasks—so many people and so many considerations are involved; even for skilled social workers many mistakes are possible. It is little wonder therefore that billeting used up so much time and energy and was at times such a nightmare to those responsible for it. Of course it had its bright spots. Many middle-aged childless couples were made really radiant by the care of their young guests and the co-operation of householders anxious to take their share in a great national task and to help the local people who were organizing was a constant encouragement.

In the first instance no complete card index of the children who actually arrived in Cambridge was available and this took many weeks to build up. Some schools produced indexes but this was not general; there was a very real possibility at first of losing track of a child.

Some four hundred children and adults privately evacuated or on holiday in Cambridge at the outbreak of war had to be included in the work of the Education Department, and this entailed much investigation and correspondence.

Some Senior Voluntary Workers had little or no clerical help at first and they and teachers spent long nights overtaking correspondence, keeping in touch with parents, making weekly returns and keeping case records.

A great deal of overlapping of visiting was at first almost inevitable. Some wards, however, reduced this rapidly and arranged that only one visitor should be responsible for each household, no matter on what score. An attempt was made in October 1939 to centralize billeting, and for this purpose the L.C.C. were asked for five assistant organizers of Care Committee work, professionally trained social workers accustomed to act as liaison between school, home, and the various health services. On paper the plan seemed to be an excellent one. In practice, however, the social workers found that they always had to refer to the Senior Voluntary Workers for first-hand knowledge of the billets, and although they did greatly relieve the excessive strain on Senior Voluntary Workers, this subordination, together with the decrease in the numbers remaining, led the L.C.C. to withdraw all but one of their staff. This one social worker remained to help in special emergencies and to act as a liaison between the Education and Public Health Departments.

One general problem, perhaps inevitable with authorities responsible for special groups of people to deal with special things, has been the difficulty of considering the child as a whole, as a person needing billets and clothes and education and recreation, perhaps medical and psychological care, one who is a member of a family which makes demands upon him, and to which he is still profoundly attached. Perhaps if the work had *started* from the actual child (or other evacuated person), it would have been simpler, more complete, and better integrated. But the child or the mother was not there when plans were being improvized; there were only 'such and such numbers' of children or of mothers, of 'evacuees'. Hence it has sometimes appeared as if the organization ranked higher in value and importance than the people it was designed to serve.

The Education Department was throughout grossly overworked, helped though it was by a voluntary group of three or four whole-time women and several part-time, whose past experience ranged through University lecturing, Froebel training and the running of their own households. They dealt mainly in the early days with illness, blankets, assessments and with children who could not be satisfactorily placed. In October a salaried inquiry officer was appointed for several months.

Emergency hostel. The crying necessity for a clearing hostel to deal with emergencies of householders and to take really difficult children was one which the Education Department had stressed from the beginning. Yet months elapsed before the Ministry of Health sanctioned the appointment—in February 1940—of two superintendents to take over the youth hostel which was suitable for such a function. In the meantime a few young children were placed in an entirely unsuitable institution for the aged and infirm; yet they flourished there under the kindly eye of the matron. Others were moved about from household to household for want of better arrangements. The hostel has become one of the many bright spots in the whole plan. It has provided for some twenty-five children at a time—most of them quite seriously unstable and in need of the most patient and understanding handling and a really secure background. The degree of freedom allowed to the children has sometimes been criticized, but those who have worked closest with it have seen the evidence of a real basic control which yet allows to children, already bearing the marks of unstable heredity or unwise upbringing or both, an opportunity to discover for themselves their own capacities and limitations. It is one of the happiest houses to visit and provides the prototype of what many psychologists and social workers have long wanted—an informal small home for children of both sexes who need special handling and treatment over a prolonged period.

After the hostel was opened on February 19th, 1940, there were (to June 1940) 55 admissions and 36 departures.

Of the admissions 39 were admitted on account of difficult behaviour.
16 were admitted on account of emergency in billet.

Of the departures 24 were billeted.
10 were removed by parents.
2 were unsuitable and returned to their Education Authority.

Of the billeted 8 returned to their old billet
16 were placed in new billets

Of those who returned to their old billet seven were emergency cases and one was difficult, and of those who were placed in new billets thirteen were difficult and three were emergency cases. Of the twenty-four who left the hostel for billets only two returned, one for unsatisfactory behaviour and the other temporarily, owing to an emergency in the billet.

Social Welfare. The Senior Voluntary Workers each worked out her own scheme for the welfare of the evacuees under supervision, and especially for mothers and their young children. In one ward, for instance, with a total of 480, every one had been visited by Sunday, September 3rd, and an invitation to tea on September 4th was given to some eighty mothers and babies. Vicars and Ministers were present and gave out the times of their services and meetings. Information about Infant Welfare Centres and Health Visitors was given. In this and in other wards, the Church Hall was open every afternoon including Saturdays and Sundays for mothers and babies from 2.30 to 5 p.m. for recreation and tea, entertainments, special talks on every kind of subject, and for an opportunity for those in charge to get to know people personally. Every Saturday children came in relays of sixty to seventy for tea and games.

In other wards, students from Training Colleges took charge of the toddlers in a separate room, while mothers were free to talk, to knit and to machine the garments they were making for their children. 'Keep Fit' classes, in which both London and Cambridge mothers joined, were very popular in the winter. But it was noticed that some mothers were quite depressed and the dwindling numbers in the early days of the new year added to the feeling of apathy. Many mothers drifted back to London about February 1940 because things appeared to be so normal there. In June 1940 clubs were meeting about once a week, but those in charge were ready to start a full programme should the coming winter make a demand for them. Some mothers felt they would not return to London, and hoped to establish their homes here after the war. Mothers wanted to talk seriously at the clubs, and to get another person's point of view on all the problems confronting them, and Senior Voluntary Workers felt that perhaps this intimate exchange of ideas and feelings had been the most valuable part of their work.

Church. Children were taken regularly to Church by their teachers until the late spring—some went as a matter of course with their foster parents. Many attended Sunday Schools.[1]

Communal feeding. The Women's Voluntary Services were prepared to undertake this but so few requests for it were at first made—as few as five out of eighty mothers in one ward—that no communal feeding for adults was arranged for some time. With the help of the Education Authority and W.V.S., a large Central School was able to make an arrangement with a local store for the provision of the midday dinner for most of its scholars in the store's staffroom at 4*d.* a head. The W.V.S. from the beginning supplied a voluntary staff to work with the store's cook, and this has worked excellently and has saved foster mothers much labour. The same store

[1] For the children's comments, see Chapter V.

provided the food for a tea party for school leavers while another gave a large room and provided music for dancing, and a conjurer. The generosity of local shopkeepers in all sorts of ways has added greatly to the happiness of evacuees.

Recreation and entertainments. These are dealt with specifically in the chapter on Recreation.

Health. At the outbreak of war Cambridge, like other towns, lost several of its assistant medical staff. The influx of women and children put a heavy burden on those remaining, and whilst the original medical inspection was here carefully done, no routine medical inspections were started till February 1940. Minor ailments were treated either at the existing school clinics or under the Ministry of Health scheme by a private doctor. A scheme for the treatment of eye troubles has been in operation since March, but few, if any, children have been able to have tonsils and adenoids dealt with, partly because of quarantine in the hospital ward for a prolonged epidemic of German measles. The assistant organizer of children's care sent by the L.C.C. has worked out a scheme for the follow-up of all children who have been found in need of treatment.

For many months there was no organization for the treatment of scabies which was a rather unknown disease hitherto in Cambridge: consequently some foster parents dealt with it without any guidance and without realizing its infectious nature.

The cleansing of heads was another problem. Cambridge parents deal with any verminous heads amongst their own children, so that no public cleansing stations existed. Under the direction of the Ministry of Health, the Red Cross took this in hand as well as the treatment of scabies, but it was some time before it could be dealt with effectively.

The lack of a home for the temporary care of cases of illness was a real difficulty, but early in 1940 a sick bay was arranged about twenty miles away.[1]

Dental treatment was at first difficult to obtain, but a plan

[1] See reference to the number of children who returned home for reasons of health, Chapter VIII, p. 136–9.

has been in progress for dealing with preventive work since Christmas 1939.

In spite of these administrative and practical problems the health of the children seems to have improved steadily, and there was comparatively little illness, although foster mothers had to nurse children during the spring through a number of minor infectious illnesses. But on the whole they took this in their stride admirably.

Bed wetting. This subject, which has been such a burning problem, deserves a paragraph to itself. There has been an amazing ignorance on the point throughout the whole community. For some it would appear that it was an entirely unknown phenomenon in the past, and that the evacuation produced a Niagara all over English and Scottish country beds. As a matter of fact bed wetting is a fairly common symptom not only of inadequate training but of temporary emotional disturbances. It is known for instance that it occurs frequently in institutions for children, in training ships and in boarding schools. It may be aggravated by the lack of affection. A child who has had a little difficulty in establishing normal bladder control rather easily breaks down in moments of slight or greater stress, such as separation from his mother, the birth of another child, anxiety over school, or new situations. One mishap seems quickly to breed a lack of confidence about it, especially if it is frowned upon and made a matter of shame by the grown-ups. Is it therefore to be wondered at that during evacuation there was a sudden and rather widespread appearance of this childish symptom, amongst children of a nervous temperament? The unfamiliar house, the outside lavatory which was common in many of the poorer homes in Cambridge where children were billeted, the excessive cold of the winter, all added to the difficulties.

There is, of course, a nucleus of chronic bed wetters, but it has been the experience of most of those who have been dealing with it that the trouble generally tends to clear up fairly quickly with sympathetic, practical handling. Most foster parents say that in fact it did clear up after the first few weeks, but, of course, when it is unwisely treated it can be very persistent. The practical difficulty was that it was not sufficiently foreseen, that no provision was made for it, that careful householders had their good mattresses spoiled without warning, and had a deal of washing to do for which the Government gave no compensation and for which no one had time to be particularly grateful. This has mostly been rectified, but not before wild stories were spread and justifiable indignation expressed and the small victim of the trouble made to feel rather an outcast.

Clothes. It is hardly necessary to mention how difficult it is for the poorer London parents to provide money for clothes. The weekly budget is often not sufficient to include such expenditure. Most families belong to clothing clubs and for the rest shoe repairs are done at home by fathers, and the market stall or church jumble sale provides clothes for a few pence that can be 'made down' for the children. The demand for 2*s*. 6*d*. for shoe repairs, for changes of everything, for special clothes for Sunday, for night clothes, is therefore beyond the capacity of many to provide. In spite of the generosity of local people who have organized work parties near and far, of teachers who have gathered from their friends, of churches and local societies who have given from their stores and of the good heartedness of foster parents themselves, clothing has been a perpetual but not altogether insurmountable problem.

The Women's Voluntary Services organized a depot for the collection and distribution of clothes, but for some reason this has not been as effective as it might. The difficulty seemed to be that clothing could not be issued from the depot until inquiries had been made in London as to the parents' ability to provide it. The need was generally so urgent that Senior Voluntary Workers and others could not wait for this and made desperate efforts, as they had done for bedding, old sheets, etc., to provide the necessary clothes and shoes from other sources. Many better off parents have been punctilious about supplying clothes, and there has been a touching generosity on the part of foster parents. Cambridge mothers set a high standard in the matter of 'best' clothes, and quite a few minor crises have arisen over this deeply-laid convention.

Visits of parents. Visits paid by sensible, wise parents were always helpful to every one concerned but all parents were not wise and sensible and many were unusually disturbed and lonely, and none had ever been in a position of accepting graciously private hospitality for their children paid for by the Government. Theirs was a peculiarly delicate position. Some managed it with fine sensibility and showed by their warmth and in countless small ways the gratitude they felt for the security that their children were experiencing. Visits were short and had often to be divided between two different foster households. Discrepancies in social status made for awkwardness, and the affection which children began to show for their foster parents was sometimes hard for their own parents to bear.

On the other hand, some children were made temporarily homesick after their parents' visit, and foster mothers had much to do to get the children settled again. There was also the difficulty of getting inexpensive meals in a country town on Sunday, the usual visiting day. Some parents thoughtlessly invaded the privacy of foster homes and took hospitality for granted, with not a word of recognition. Some who ought to have known better came frequently and yet did not send necessary clothes when they were asked. If in each ward a centre on quite a small scale had been opened at once for the provision of meals for these visits, the knowledge of this facility would have spread rapidly and saved many a difficulty. Canteens were later open for parents on the few cheap fare days but were little used and consequently it was assumed that they were not needed.

4

CHAPTER IV

CHILDREN AND FOSTER PARENTS

ONE OF the purposes of the Survey was to obtain quantitative information about the consequences of evacuation, especially those affecting the children themselves. In particular, we wished to find out how far a satisfactory relationship had been established between the evacuated children and their foster parents, and to discover the causes of such unsatisfactory adaptations as there were. To begin with, the inquiry was restricted to the children evacuated from the Tottenham area, of whom about 300 were still in Cambridge at the time of this part of the inquiry (that is, on December 1st, 1939).

These Tottenham children cannot, however, be regarded as a completely representative sample of the children evacuated from London; few, if any, of these children would have come from homes of extreme poverty. It was, therefore, felt to be necessary to make a further investigation of children from a poorer district and in the spring and early summer of 1940 this was done with a somewhat larger number of children who had been evacuated from Islington. Unfortunately the difference in time of the two parts of the inquiry make a direct comparison between the two groups very unreliable. Partly because the expected aerial bombardments of London had not taken place and partly for other reasons, there had been a continual leakage back to their London homes of the evacuated children. This process had been going on for some months longer in the case of the Islington children, and the somewhat contradictory results of the Tottenham and Islington inquiries may have been partly due to the fact that this process of returning home had affected particularly those children whose adjustment to their foster homes had been unsatisfactory. The Islington group may, therefore be supposed to have differed from the Tottenham group in the fact that there had been a process of elimination in the Islington group which had removed from the Survey a considerably greater proportion of the children whose adjustment to their foster homes was not a happy one. It is true that, at the time of the Islington part of the inquiry, approximately the same proportion of children unhappily adapted to their foster homes was found as amongst the Tottenham children. This is not, however, inconsistent with the possibility that a larger proportion of these children had returned home, since it seems extremely likely that there were more of these less well-adapted children amongst the Islington children at the beginning. Children from the less poor areas may be expected, on the whole, to be more acceptable to the average foster mother.

It is also necessary to bear in mind that the assessments of the foster home relationships for the Tottenham and Islington groups may not have been exactly equivalent. Only one of the two people making the ratings was the same for both groups. This also might be part of the reason for the fact that the more prolonged drift home of the unsatisfactorily billeted children was not reflected in a smaller proportion of such children in Cambridge for the second part of our inquiry. There were also small differences in the two parts of the inquiry which make of doubtful validity any direct comparison between the two sets of figures. The information contained in the cards was no doubt much more reliable for the Islington group, and this information was largely relied on for making assessments in this group. The relative unreliability of the card information for the Tottenham group was, however, compensated for by the personal knowledge which one of the assessors had of a large number of the children, and this personal knowledge was often one of the deciding factors in the assessment. It is difficult to say which gave, in the end, the more accurate assessment of the real happiness or unhappiness of the relationship between foster child and foster parent, but it is clear that they must not be considered as the same assessment and that we must not assume that each would give exactly the same proportion of happily and unhappily adapted children even if both were applied to equivalent groups of children.

The assessment of how satisfactory or unsatisfactory was the relationship between each child and his foster parents was made by considering information derived from four sources. These were: (1) entries made in an inquiry card based on the knowledge obtained by 'friendly visitors' who had made a number of official visits of inquiry to the child's foster home; (2) entries in a similar (but not identical) card of inquiry filled in by the child's teachers; (3) two essays done by each child (except those of the lowest age groups) on 'Things I like in Cambridge' and 'Things I miss in Cambridge'; and (4) (for the Tottenham group only) information received from two teachers who were on the committee who had personal knowledge of most of the children. The questions asked on the cards referred to above are given in Appendix IV. The essays are separately discussed in Chapter V.

The method of assessment was by the use of a five-point scale in which the mark +2 was given to a child whose relationship seemed to be as happy as could be expected, −2 meant that the child appeared to be outstandingly unhappy in the foster home, while +1 and −1 meant respectively that the child was on the whole, though not outstandingly happily and unhappily adjusted. The mark 0 was given when there appeared to be no indication that the child was either happily or unhappily adjusted to his or her new circumstances.

The figures for both girls and boys are shown in Table I in Appendix III (p. 207) for both the Tottenham and the Islington groups of children. Although this arrangement in five classes is convenient for statistical purposes as containing more information than a simpler classification, it is somewhat cumbersome for a more general discussion. I propose, therefore, in this chapter, to simplify the discussion by considering only two classes: those marked as −1 or −2 who are all in some degree known to be unsatisfactorily adjusted to their foster homes, and the remainder (0, +1 and +2) who are on the whole satisfactorily adjusted or, at any rate, have shown no evidence of unsatisfactory adjustment.

We may first consider the total number of children who seem to be more or less unhappily adjusted to their foster homes. This number is 25 out of 304 Tottenham children and 29 out of 352 amongst the Islington children. That, in all, only 8·2 per cent of the children appear to have developed an unsatisfactory relationship with their foster parents is a striking indication of the success of the evacuation of these children, and is a tribute to the devotion and self-sacrifice of the foster mothers. There are, of course, other questions in connection with the success of the evacuation policy on which this Survey obtained no information. We do not, for example, know how the burden of extra work imposed in many cases by the presence of evacuated children may have affected the foster mothers themselves. Many such factors would also have to be considered in order that a satisfactory judgment might be made of the success of the evacuation policy as a whole.

It would be unprofitable to inquire whether there is any significant difference between the satisfactoriness of relationship between the Tottenham and the Islington children. Obviously there is none between the proportion of children falling into the (−1, −2) class, but a greater proportion of the Islington children have been classed as very satisfactory (+2) and a smaller proportion as very unsatisfactory (−2). This difference might, however, be due either to the difference in the time at which the two parts of the Survey were made or to the difference in the method of assessment which has already been discussed. No conclusion could be drawn as to a real difference between the Tottenham and the Islington children.

Another question which may be asked with respect to these figures is as to whether they show any difference between the ease of adaptation of the boys and the girls to the billeting situation.

Both Tottenham and Islington groups show a slightly greater number of boys in the maladjusted group. In both groups taken together, 9·6 per cent of the boys and 7·1 per cent of the girls were classed as either −1 or −2. As shown in the Appendix, however, this slight preponderance of boys is no greater than might arise by chance if both boys and girls were equally likely to be unsatisfactorily adjusted to their foster homes, and provides no evidence of a tendency for greater difficulty or adjustment amongst the boys.[1]

When, however, we turn to the relationship of the age of the children to the satisfactoriness or unsatisfactoriness of their relationship to their foster homes, more positive results begin to emerge, at any rate amongst the Tottenham children. The detailed figures are shown in Table IIa (p. 208). The most striking feature of this table is the sharp rise in the percentage of unhappily adjusted children at and after the age of thirteen. Below the age of thirteen, only 2·7 per cent were classed as −1 or −2. At the age of thirteen, however, this percentage rises sharply to 13 per cent, while at fourteen and fifteen this rise is maintained at 24 per cent and 23 per cent respectively. This rise is unquestionably significant and we may safely conclude that billeting difficulties are greatest at the period of adolescence amongst these children.

We might also be tempted to conclude from this table that billeting difficulties were particularly slight below the age of 7. No children below this age were classed as −1 or −2. The total number below 7 was, however, small (only 24) and the information about them was relatively meagre. They did not write the essays which were found very useful in the assessment of the older children, and the teachers on the research committee did not know very much personally about the youngest children. It is, therefore, very likely that the assessments are not particularly reliable for these children and there may have been more cases of unhappy adjustment to billeting conditions than our figures show. If, however, the figures for these youngest children are omitted, there remains a percentage of only 3·3 per cent of more or less unhappily billeted children below thirteen years of age, which is a sufficiently striking contrast to the 18·5 per cent

[1] There was, however, a difference in the proportion of boys and girls referred to the Child Guidance Training Centre (p. 118).

above that age. The conclusion that the onset of adolescence increases billeting difficulties remains clear.

While the figures of the Survey point to this fact, they provide, of course, no explanation of the fact. There may be many reasons for increased difficulty of satisfactory billeting after adolescence. The restlessness and instability of the adolescent often cause a certain amount of strain with the parents even in the child's own home, and this strain is not likely to be felt less in a foster home. Also it seems likely that a younger child will more readily give affection to a foster parent than will an adolescent. A contributory factor in causing a less easy billeting situation for the older children may sometimes be the greater expense of feeding them.

Since we have this clear indication amongst the Tottenham children that the onset of adolescence is a factor of primary importance in determining difficulty of adjustment to the foster home, it is disappointing to find that no such indication is given by the later figures obtained for children evacuated from Islington. The percentages of children unhappily adjusted to their foster homes shown in Table IIb vary somewhat irregularly for the different age groups with no definite change at the age of thirteen. The number of children of thirteen or over more or less unhappily adjusted to their foster homes was 5 out of 43 (11·6 per cent), while below thirteen the number was 24 out of 309 (7·8 per cent). This is only a difference such as might occur by chance alone, and indicates no real tendency in these children for the billeting difficulties to increase with adolescence. The figures are in strong contrast with those of the Tottenham group where the proportions were 18·5 per cent and 2·7 per cent respectively.

The discrepancy between these two sets of figures is puzzling. We have already discussed the relative reliability of the assessments of satisfactoriness of foster home adjustment for the two groups. On the whole the fuller information for the Tottenham children from other sources than the inquiry cards probably made the assessments of these children somewhat more reliable. It must also be remembered that unreliability of the assessments is more likely to obscure a genuine relationship of billeting difficulty with age than it is to create a spurious appearance of such a relationship. For both of these reasons, if it were necessary to make a choice between the indications of these two sets of figures, we should choose to accept the positive conclusion of the Tottenham group rather than the negative one of the Islington group.

There may, however, be no reason for making this choice. Both sets of figures may be correct and there may be a real difference between the two groups due to the later date of the Islington inquiry. The discrepancy would be explained if there were any factor at work during this interval which tended to reduce the number of older children who were unhappily adjusted. It does not seem to be an unlikely hypothesis that amongst the large number of children going back in the interval between the two parts of the inquiry, those most likely to return were the older children who were unhappy in their billets. Younger children also unhappily billeted would be less likely to be able to influence their parents to bring them back, and older children happily billeted would have less reason for return. If this is the true explanation, the effect indicated by the Tottenham figures is a real one, which has been masked amongst the Islington children by the process of selective return of the older less happily billeted children.

This explanation is rendered more plausible by the observation that amongst the returned children the proportion of the older children (over twelve) to the younger children whose principal reason for return was given as some unsatisfactoriness of the foster home was much larger amongst the Islington returned children than amongst the Tottenham ones. This is to be expected if dissatisfaction with the foster home became increasingly operative amongst older children with the lapse of time. Similarly a larger proportion of the older Islington returned children gave homesickness or desire to work as a reason for return. The numbers of returned children were too small for any of these indications to be separately significant but they give some confirmation to an explanation originally suggested by quite different facts.

Having settled, so far as we can, the problem of how success in billeting is related to the age of the child, we may next consider the question of how it is related to the age of the foster mother. For this purpose, the foster mothers were divided into three age groups, those below forty, those between forty and sixty, and those above sixty. The results are shown in Tables IIIa and IIIb respectively.

There is again a difference between the indications of the figures obtained from the Tottenham and Islington children. In neither case is there any important difference between the foster mothers below forty and those between forty and sixty. Amongst the Tottenham children, however, there are no children unsatisfactorily adjusted to their foster homes amongst those with foster mothers of over sixty. The total number of such foster mothers is small and, it is found, when statistically treated, that the deviation from expectation is no greater than might occur by chance. This, however, is not true of the considerable excess of unhappily adjusted Islington children with foster mothers of over sixty. Here there are 26 per cent unhappily adjusted children (all graded as -1) against a general percentage of 8·5. By every method of treatment, it is clear that this excess is significant and indicates that, in this group, the over-sixty foster mothers were less successful than the others.

This is a result which might well be expected. It remains to be considered why this relative greater difficulty was not found amongst the Tottenham children. There does not appear to have been any difference in social status between the homes to which the two groups of children were sent. If there had been, it might have provided the explanation for the difference between the success of the older foster mothers in the two groups since to an elderly woman of the working classes with no domestic help, the presence of billeted children would be a severe burden, whereas in a more prosperous home with perhaps two servants and the possibility that the billeted children might be living with the servants and not with the family, the advanced age of the foster mother would make no extra difficulty in caring for the children. It might even in some cases mean that the foster mother was more ready to give the affection which must play a large part in making the billeting relationship a satisfactory one.

Since this explanation is, however, ruled out, it seems reasonable to surmise that here again we have a difference which is due to the difference in time of the two parts of the inquiry. The majority of the children in both groups were billeted in working-class homes. In such homes, an elderly foster mother, often of uncertain health in the winter months, must have found the presence of billeted children an additional burden whose weight tended to grow more severe as time went on. A burden willingly borne at the beginning might be found more irksome as time went on and perhaps illness may have added to the already considerable strain of caring for billeted children. Under such conditions of strain on the foster mother, unhappy relationships with the foster children might be expected to develop. If this is the explanation, we must regard billeting with foster mothers of over sixty years of age as always unsatisfactory, although its unsatisfactoriness may only be apparent after some months.

Another question of some interest to which the figures of the Survey seem to give a definite answer is the question of the relationship between change of billet and satisfactory adjustment of the child to his foster home. Some children have remained all the time in the same billet; others have changed their billets more or less frequently. These changes have sometimes taken place through causes which depend in no way on the child himself (he may, for example, have been originally placed in undergraduate lodgings from which he had to move when the autumn term began). In other cases, however, there may be some factor in the child himself which makes him unable to form a satisfactory relationship with any foster parent, and this may be a cause of the changing of billets. If this were so, we should expect to find that those children who had changed their billets were, on the whole, assessed low in the scale for satisfactoriness of relationship between foster mother and child.

This appears to be the case. It will be seen in Table IV (p. 211), showing the combined figures for the Tottenham and Islington children, that amongst those children who have had one or more changes of billet, 12 per cent were classed as more or less unhappily adjusted to their foster homes, whereas there were only 5 per cent of such unhappily adjusted children amongst those who had had no change in billet.

The indications of these figures are not altogether unambiguous since they are consistent with two possible explanations: (*a*) certain children may have difficulties of character or temperament which make them unable to settle down happily in a foster home and which lead both to an unhappy relationship with foster parents and also to change of billet, or, (*b*) children who might have settled down happily in one foster home may find it difficult to transfer their affection to a new foster parent and the change of billet may, therefore, be a cause of the development of an unhappy relation between foster child and foster parent. It seems not unlikely that both directions of causation may have acted to some extent: that inability on the part of the child to adapt himself to any foster parent may have caused change of billet, and that changes of billet produced by conditions external to the child may have caused the development of unhappy relations with the foster parent. If the first of these explanations were the sole one, it would appear that more than half of the total number of children who changed billets did so because of some degree of 'difficulty' in the child himself, and that such difficult children comprised between 3 per cent and 4 per cent of the total evacuated population. Since explanation (*b*) may also be the cause of some of the excess of unhappily adjusted children amongst those who have changed billets, these suggested figures for children who will be troublesome in all foster homes are probably an over-estimate. They may, at any rate, be regarded as a maximum figure, and we may safely conclude that not more than 4 per cent of the evacuated children (and probably less) show such difficulties of character or temperament as to lead to change of billet.

The visits of parents have sometimes been supposed to have an unsettling effect on children in foster homes and to disturb their relationships with their foster parents. Whether this is so in particular cases depends, no doubt, on the suitability of the behaviour and conversation of the visiting parents and on the kind of bond that exists between the parent and child. Our figures, shown in Table V (p. 212), do not support the view that, on the average, parental visits are unsettling. The highest percentage of unhappily adjusted children is found amongst those whose parents have paid them no visits, and the lowest percentage amongst those whose parents visit them frequently (more than once a month).

There may, of course, be other explanations of these figures than the obvious one that frequent visits from parents are favourable to the formation of a happy relationship between children and foster parents. It is probable, for example, that when parents visit their children frequently, those children who are unhappy in their foster homes are more likely to be taken home. It seems reasonable to suppose that this is a ground for at least part of the better adjustment of children whose parents visited them often, although this, too, might well be considered a reason for encouraging parental visits. It is better that the child should return home than that he should remain in isolated unhappiness in a foster home with which he has not succeeded in making a satisfactory adjustment. The figures of Table V seem, at any rate, to contradict the view that frequent visits of the parents are unfavourable to the satisfactory settling of the child in his foster home.

Another factor which may determine the happiness or unhappiness of the child in his foster home is the presence or absence of other children. In Table VI (p. 213) are shown the ratings for satisfactoriness of adjustment of children with and without other children in their billets. There are three kinds of other children who may be present in the billet: the evacuated child's own brothers or sisters, other children (also evacuated), or Cambridge children (normally the children of the foster mother). The presence or absence of other children of any of these three groups gives eight possible combinations which are shown in the eight rows of this table.

A cursory examination of the table shows that the homes with the second largest number of difficult adjustments (10 per cent) are those with no other children, while the homes with other children of all three classes shows nearly the lowest incidence of difficulty (4 per cent). The presence of other children appears, therefore, to be favourable to a happy adjustment.

Closer examination of the table leads to a more specific conclusion. The first four rows of figures of children with their own brothers or sisters in the billet show, on the whole, a lower percentage of difficult adjustments than the next four rows in which brothers and sisters were not present in the billet. It is not so clear that the presence of fellow evacuees or of Cambridge children has the same favourable result. The figures are displayed in the form necessary for a solution of this question in Table VII, where the whole group of children are subdivided separately into those with and without the companship of brothers or sisters, of other evacuated children, and of Cambridge children respectively. The smaller incidence of difficulty amongst the children accompanied by their own brothers and sisters is obvious (5 per cent as against 10 per cent when no brothers or sisters are present). Statistical calculation shows that this difference is significant. The differences in the other two parts of the table, showing the effect of the presence of evacuated children and of Cambridge children respectively, are small and insignificant.

The presence of the child's own brothers or sisters in the foster home is, therefore, clearly favourable to ease of adjustment to the new home, while, so far as our figures show, the presence of other evacuated children or of Cambridge children has no such effect. This suggests that it is not the presence of other children but the continuance of part of the child's own family life that is important. The breaking-up of family life and the consequent removal of one of the main foundations of the sense of security is, no doubt, one of the factors causing difficulty in the child's adaptation to unfamiliar surroundings. Separation from the parents is generally an unavoidable accompaniment of billeting, but if so much of the continuity of family life as is implied in the billeting together of brothers and sisters can be preserved, our figures show that this will cause an easier adaptation.

A last question which was considered was whether a difference between the social and economic status of the foster home and of the child's own home was a considerable cause of difficulty of adjustment. It was clear from the Tottenham children's essays that a certain amount of difficulty was in some cases caused by such a difference. The social superiority of the foster home was occasionally commented on, sometimes favourably and sometimes unfavourably. Resentment of a foster home of lower social status than the child's own home was also sometimes expressed. It would seem, so far as possible, desirable to make any such differences as small as possible, since they may be causes of difficulty even if such difficulties are successfully overcome. Our figures do not, however, give any support to the idea that differences in economic and social status between the child's own home and his foster home are a measurable factor in determining the likelihood of an unsatisfactory adjustment to the foster home.

We had no data on which to base a comparison between the status of the foster home and of the real home of the Tottenham children. For the Islington children such data were obtained, but reference to Table VIII shows that the percentage of unhappily billeted children was virtually the same whether the foster home was superior, equal, or inferior in social and economic status to the child's own home. It seems likely that the quality of individual affection and care is of greater importance for the child than the more easily defined differences of material circumstance and characteristic manners and customs.

CHAPTER V

WHAT THE CHILDREN SAY

WHEN THE Survey was being planned the desirability of obtaining direct evidence from the children was recognized, and it was decided that one method of doing so was to ask every child to write two 'essays', the first on 'What I like in Cambridge', and the second on 'What I miss in Cambridge'. The word 'miss' was preferred to 'dislike', as the investigators were under a pledge to do nothing which could possibly have an adverse effect on the actual billeting situation, and it was felt that to ask children to express themselves freely on their dislikes might, when the fact was retailed at fourth or fifth hand, have disturbing results. The word 'miss' is ambiguous, and it was occasionally difficult to discover whether the child meant 'regret' or 'notice the absence of'. A boy aged twelve wrote: 'What I miss most in Cambridge is the thick fogs and fish and chips', apparently utilizing both meanings simultaneously; another aged fourteen: 'I miss getting hidings from my dad when I get into trouble', and a girl aged thirteen: 'I miss my brother always teasing me'; and there are a fair number of similar instances.

The essays were written by two groups of children, one from Tottenham and the other from Islington. For various reasons the Tottenham ones only have been utilized in this chapter. The Tottenham children were in four parties. All those over eleven were at the Central School, Cambridge. Most of these were pupils of a Central School in Tottenham. There were attached to this party a considerable number of children from other London Central and Secondary Schools, but their essays are not included in any of the statistical work of the Survey, and where a quotation from an essay has been used it has been marked with an asterisk. The younger children were mainly the pupils of a Junior and Infant School in Tottenham, but there was also a number of Tottenham children who came to Cambridge with their elder brothers and sisters in the Central School, and these were sttending two Cambridge schools. All these children's essays were included in the Survey.

The purpose for which the essays were written was not literary excellence but frankness of opinion. In the Central School the following method was adopted. The Hall would hold half the children. The children were therefore divided into seniors (thirteen and over) and juniors (under thirteen). The seniors were taken one morning into the Hall. No previous warning was given. There they were told what they were wanted to do, and what its purpose was: to try to help them and other evacuated children by giving them more of what they liked, and trying to supply what they missed. They were asked not to speak to another child, nor to see what any one else was writing, but to put down as briefly and clearly as they could what they liked and what they missed. They were not to try to please the teachers or any one else; on the other hand they were not to try to be clever or funny. They were given one or two illustrations, but told they were not to use these unless they expressed their own feelings. They were then given half an hour to do both sections, and were warned after a quarter of an hour that the time was half gone. As soon as the seniors had finished the juniors came into the Hall, and the process was repeated.

The children were sitting fairly close together, and the time was deliberately cut down to ensure as far as could be that no one having finished would copy extracts from his neighbours, with or without discussion. But it is important to remember that the children wrote at some five minutes' notice, and very hurriedly in most cases, so that the omission of anything does not mean that the child did not like or miss it. There is also no doubt that the illustrations used by the speaker had some effect on the essays. He had said that if fish and chips were what they most missed, they were to say so. In a large number of cases they did. Similarly, parks and fens were referred to as 'wide open spaces', although this may have been first-hand from the cinema and not second-hand. Although the children were urged to give only their own views and opinions, the effect of previous propaganda on behalf of parents, foster parents, and the home school cannot be supposed to have been without effect. But on the whole the essays were both spontaneous and individual. The subjects obviously appealed to most of the children. Some, however, showed little interest. The difference in length between the longest and shortest essays was noticeable in each age group.

With the younger children the usual method was for the class teacher to give the essays, after a talk on the same lines as to the seniors, to one class, but all the classes in a school wrote during the same morning or afternoon. With very small children the teachers made a note of what the children said when talking freely to them.

Younger children are less conscious of the exact nature of their likes and dislikes than older ones: also they find the labour of using pen and ink, or pencil, so great that their energy is absorbed in the task of writing, to the detriment of both their ability and their desire to express themselves. They needed more help than older children, and even then their essays were more standardized.

The essays were divided for statistical work into boys' and girls', and these into age groups. They were then examined for topics. It will be obvious from what has been said about the method in which the essays were written that conclusions from statistical analysis could be drawn only with great caution, and there were other factors which strengthened this view. The number of boys and girls was approximately equal, but the age groups were of very different sizes.[1] The children came from a very limited and homogeneous district in Tottenham, but they were billeted all over Cambridge, and in many billets of very differing social grades.

A comparison was drawn between the frequency of comments about various subjects, made, respectively, by the boys

[1] For an exact account of the age distribution, see pp. 208–9.

and the girls. In the following lists, stated in order of frequency, there are included only those subjects mentioned in the essays more than half a dozen times. In the case of the boys the subjects have been numbered consecutively, and, for purposes of comparison, the same numbers have been given to the girls' list. Those subjects peculiar to one or other of the lists have been marked with the letter 'S'.

'WHAT I LIKE IN CAMBRIDGE'

	BOYS	*Number of Times Mentioned*		*GIRLS*	*Number of Times Mentioned*
	1. Rivers and Fens	(59)		5. Commons	(64)
	2. Colleges	(50)		4. Foster Parents	(54)
	3. School	(48)		2. Colleges	(53)
	4. Foster Parents	(37)		6. Play Centres & Clubs	(43)
	5. Commons	(35)		3. School	(41)
	6. Play Centres & Clubs	(33)		1. Rivers and Fens	(33)
	7. Food	(27)	S.	Country Walks	(31)
S.	8. Games	(26)		11. Cambridge People and Children	(27)
	9. Cinemas	(26)		10. Billets	(26)
	10. Billets	(23)		7. Food	(25)
	11. Cambridge People and Children	(21)		13. Shops	(21)
S.	12. Farm Animals	(18)		9. Cinemas	(12)
	13. Shops	(16)	S.	Church	(10)
S.	14. Airport	(15)			
S.	15. Pets	(9)			

The similarity of these lists is perhaps more marked than their differences. It is possible that suggestion was at work in the more conventional references to commons and to rivers and fens, which together figure more often than any other single subject. The same influence may perhaps also be recognized in the references to colleges, though a few of the remarks bear the quality of quite spontaneous feeling. Many children chose to write about their foster parents and their billets, and in the girls' essays, the people in their new homes have found their way into the essays more often and at greater length than for the boys. This must partly be accounted for by the fact that there was a large proportion of adolescent girls than of boys of similar age. Country walks seem to have taken the place of games for the girls (possibly more because of circumstance than of choice). Church is entirely absent in the boys' list, as the airport is from that of the girls'.

'WHAT I MISS IN CAMBRIDGE'

	BOYS	*Number of Times Mentioned*
	1. Parents & Relatives	(65)
	2. Friends not Evacuated	(35)
	3. Home Activities	(28)
	4. Home School	(28)
S.	5. Ice Hockey	(25)
S.	6. Speedway	(22)
	7. Home (apart from parents and activities)	(21)
	8. Pets	(21)
	9. Parks	(18)
	10. Cinemas	(17)
S.	11. Indoor Swimming Baths	(17)
	12. Toys	(16)
	13. Fish and Chips	(12)
	14. Clubs, Scouts, etc.	(10)
S.	15. Bus Services	(8)
S.	16. Professional Football	(8)
S.	17. Teachers	(7)

	GIRLS	*Number of Times Mentioned*
	1. Parents & Relatives	(81)
	2. Friends not Evacuated	(43)
	8. Pets	(34)
	4. Home School	(33)
	3. Home Activities	(25)
	7. Home (apart from parents and activities)	(24)
	12. Toys	(22)
	9. Parks	(22)
S.	Shops	(14)
	10. Cinemas	(11)
	14. Clubs, Guides, etc.	(10)
	13. Food	(9)

The lists are again so closely similar that the few differences between the boys and the girls are obvious. It is quite clear that it is their own families and friends whom most of the children miss, and there seems little conventionality about their expression of this need. Again, it is the girls who seem more often able to express this, though it can hardly be assumed that the separation means more to them than it does to the boys. It is interesting to notice that of the six subjects peculiar to the boys, three are 'spectator' sports.

The essays tend to fall into two groups, those written by children who are fairly content, and those written by the homesick. The second group is very much smaller. Then there is a third group of essays which defy classification.

TYPICAL ESSAYS

I. *Boy, aged 14. Apparently contented.* This boy was billeted with his younger brother, and received frequent visits from his parents. To his teachers and to the psychologist who gave him an intelligence test, he gave the impression of being particularly well suited to his foster home. He was found to have a good average intelligence, though his reasoning was slow and laborious, and his memory poor.

The psychologist concluded that, though he seemed on the surface a quiet, accommodating person, there was considerable underlying worry, which came out in a rather uneven performance. He said that his real desire was to join the Air Force and train as a pilot. His parents were opposed to this, and he was complying with their wishes in taking up electrical engineering.

The essay was written in December 1939. In July 1940 this boy was still in his same billet.

'WHAT I LIKE MOST IN CAMBRIDGE'

First of all I like the people's spirit of Cambridge always willing to help you e.g. The people in my billet are very good, they give me the same type of food as I have at home, and best of all they have the same ideas of home life, so I am very happy. I like the town for there is not much difference than the one we had at home except it is made up of shops in different streets where as my town in one long 'High Road' full of shops.

I like to look at the Colleges which are beautiful. The free swimming pool is very handy in the summer to have a swim especially as we have no mother to get threepence off, to go, if the baths were not free. The river's for fishing in the summer not very far to walk or ride to where ever you like in Cambridge. There are also plenty of places to ride on a cycle to, not very far away.

The school is a good one with a marvellous gymanasiom.

I have a friend named Jack Robinson who comes in my billet nearly every night to play draughts and dominoes. There are plenty of open spaces to play football and other games.

'THINGS I MISS MOST'

I only miss Mum and Dad and my sister and relations most and few friends that have stayed behind. Also just my house.

I am so happy I miss nothing else what so ever. Except the school rules of not running in the playground.

II. *Girl, aged 14. Apparently contented.* This girl, the daughter of an artisan, was living in a foster home of about the same social standard. She had a room to herself, and was well supplied with clothes from home. Her parents visited her occasionally, and she once went home on a visit herself. She was a friendly, sociable child, on good terms with her foster parents and with other children. The foster parents were fond of her, though the foster mother found the extra washing something of a strain. The fact that they grew their own vegetables made it possible to manage on money which she would otherwise have regarded as inadequate.

In July 1940 this girl was still in the same billet.

'THINGS I LIKE MOST IN CAMBRIDGE'

For nearly eleven weeks I have lived in a completely different place to me and I have found Cambridge a very interesting place. I like the beautiful Colleges especially King's College Chapel which I consider very beautiful. I like meeting people who come to my new home to tea, and I enjoy the food I have which is like the food I have in my real home. Fortunately I have a bedroom to myself which I prefer to sleeping with any body else. At home I usually have pocket money allowed me each week, but now I am away from my home I have a much larger amount sent me and I buy my own clothes which I like choosing very much, as it is a privilege which I have never been allowed at home. I have several letters a week and this cheers me up immensely. Most of all things I like in Cambridge is the 'homely' feeling in my new home and I very much like the ways my foster parents treat me—for several girls I know live with the maids but fortunately I am allowed to live with the family which is much nicer. I also enjoy going cycling Sunday afternoon with friends my foster mother lending me her cycle. I also liked my foster grandmother sending me a gas-mask carrier before she had even seen me and when my foster parents went to see her in Ipswich they offered to take me there for dinner as they thought I should enjoy the change which I thought was very nice of them. Amusement is provided by the students of several colleges when we go dancing with them and they are all very nice and kind towards me. Newnham students also invite us to play games in their rooms which is very nice for I meet so many new and interesting people in this way.

'THINGS I MISS IN CAMBRIDGE'

Most of all the things I miss in Cambridge are my favourite friends who are all in London. Naturally I miss my parents and sister, and I also miss going to different places of amusement with my special friends in London. I very much miss winter swimming here as there are no public baths. In my new school I very much dislike the open cloisters which are very cold and draughty. On Sunday mornings at home I usually have an extra hour in bed and I miss this very much in Cambridge. I also miss suppers which I used to have in London. I usually have a dinner for supper in London but here I don't have such a heavy one.

III. *Boy, aged 13. Tendency to Homesickness.* This boy changed his billet three times, and went home at the beginning of January 1940. There is little doubt that he had been thoroughly spoilt at home, and that his discontent was largely brought about by his mother's letters and visits.

'WHAT I LIKE IN CAMBRIDGE'

There are not a lot of things I don't like but here are the things I like: First I like my foster Parents and their boy, the undergraduates because they entertain us and arrange games and other things for us. I like the town because we don't have to go far and we are in the country. I like the school here because it has a better gym than what we have got in London. The town has not got any factories in it and it is not very dirty, as London.

'WHAT I MISS IN CAMBRIDGE'

The things I miss most in Cambridge is my Father and Mother and family. I miss my dog and cat and I miss going to the Pictures on a Friday Saturday and Monday. I miss going errans here and I miss the People who live near me my friends. I miss going to see Ice Hockey Played at Harringay Areama. I miss Playing on my skates with a hockey stick. I miss my sister saying 'Come for a Ride on your bike'. I also miss playing football in Playground at school. I miss going swimming at Tottenham Baths.

IV. *Girl, aged 13. Homesick.* It is interesting to notice that although this child writes as though she were constantly missing her *home*, her mother and four younger children were in Cambridge, though not in the same billet. She is the second child in a family of seven. The foster mother complained that her own mother refused to take any responsibility for her, and said that she herself grudged working for a girl whom she described as 'sulky, selfish and ungrateful'. This girl had already had two changes of billet. Comments on the records of the younger children confirm the fact that the mother was off-hand with the foster parents and neglectful of the children. Three other members of the family were described, respectively, as excitable and fidgety: (Boy, aged 12); cheeky and excitable; (Boy, aged 10), disobedient, and lies; (Boy, aged 8), though they were all in different foster homes.

The writer of this essay is, according to intelligence tests, a girl of average ability whose reasoning is, however, slow and uncertain. She is poorly developed for her age, and has a squint. With the psychologist her manner was subdued, and she seemed very anxious to say and to do the right thing. She was below the level of intelligence of most of the Central School children, and said that she was more fond of doing things than of book-work. There were no particular problems in school, but she was described as 'undeveloped'.

This girl was still in the same billet in July 1940, and was then described as 'very happy'.

'WHAT I LIKE IN CAMBRIDGE'

There isn't much that I really like in Cambridge. I like going to the playcentre at Newnham College and the amusements that are prepared for us. I like the gymnasuim in the Central School in Cambridge. I like the meadows and parks in the Summer but it is too cold in the winter to go there. I like the colleges and their grounds. I like the church service in Cambridge better than the one I go to in Tottenham.

'THINGS I MISS MOST IN CAMBRIDGE'

I miss my home in Tottenham and I would rather be there than where I am. I cannot find much to do down here. I miss my sister and my friends. I haven't any of my friends living in Newnham where I live and I never know where to go on Saturday and Sunday as I have no one to go with. At home I can stop in on Saturday if it is cold, but I have to take my brother out because the lady in this house goes to work and sometimes it is too cold to go any-where. I miss my cup of tea which I always have at home after dinner. I miss my mother's cooking because the lady does not cook very well.

V. *Boy, aged 8.* This little boy is an only child, the son of a carpenter. His foster parents seemed rather indifferent about him, and he was described by the friendly visitor as 'not too bright'. He had once been visited by an aunt in Cambridge, but apparently not by his parents. The foster parents complained of his lying—an accusation which, in view of the unusual essay, should have received further investigation. His parents were attentive to him, writing at least once a week. He was said to be 'lethargic' in school, but his teachers noticed nothing unusual in his behaviour or interests.

He stayed in the same foster home till June 1940, when he was taken home because a bomb dropped near the billet.

'WHAT I LIKE IN CAMBRIDGE'

I like my dog I like my cat I like my Granny dog to it is dead my Granny did not cry I made the grave *the other dog run and run he nock the grave down.*

'WHAT I MISS IN CAMBRIDGE'

I miss my tortoise in lanDon he is Robert taylor he bit me once he bit me. And I tod (told) him he wac (was) a note (naughty) boy and I fod (fed) him a los (lots) of tam (times).

VI. *Boy, aged 6.* (Notes taken after a talk with the child.) This child is the youngest in a family of three children, all of whom were evacuated to Cambridge. His thirteen-year-old sister was in his foster home with him, and his brother was staying in the same road.

He seemed happy and friendly at school and in his foster home, and all the children had apparently settled down away from home.

He and his sister stayed in the same billet during the six months they were in Cambridge.

He likes to go and watch the ducks on the river. He doesn't like to see the bulls going into the slaughter-house, which is next-door to where he is living and he can hear the gun going off plainly when they are slaughtering cattle. He may return to Tottenham soon, but he likes Cambridge better.

VII. *Boy, aged 14.* This intelligent boy is an only child who was placed by himself in a foster home rather more well-to-do than his own. He was frequently visited by his parents and wrote to them every few days. At school he was usually solitary, except for a curiously dependent relationship with one other boy. His teacher commented that he seemed to 'lack separate individuality', and he was described as 'lethargic'. He was described by the psychologist as 'A boy of superior intelligence, with an unusually keen and lucid reasoning capacity when dealing with abstract problems, and an exceedingly good command of words. When, however, it was a question of applying his ability to the solution of practical problems he failed completely'. He gave the impression of 'a seriously unstable character who will have considerable difficulty in adjusting himself to practical life when he leaves the shelter of school, if indeed he succeeds at all. He is conscious of both his ability and his disability, but seems to doubt his capacity to settle down to what seems to him the drudgery of tackling hard facts. He would like to be a journalist, but cannot endure the prospect of going through the donkey work to attain his end. He is quite happy, as he is now billeted alone, very much to his satisfaction; he has made little use of the various club activities which were available. He prefers staying at home in the evenings playing about with a microscope or fixing up his stamp collection or reading'.[1]

'THINGS I LIKE BEST IN CAMBRIDGE'

One of the most pleasant things that I find here is the kindness with which I was received. To receive town children who they have never seen was most difficult, yet within a week we were as happy as if we were at home. When the first strangeness had worn off we seemed to be part and parcel of Cambridge. The historic buildings was another source of enjoyment to me, in my early days.

'THINGS I MISS IN CAMBRIDGE'

The things about which I now intend to write hardly fit here, but I must say them. If these things give pain to anyone I ask their forgiveness. The

[1] For a full description of this boy in another context, see Chapter VI, p. 103.

over-enthusiasm of the Undergraduates, and their promises which were not kept. I am expected to attend Socials and Dances, to learn to dance. But I do not wish to dance, while not doubting that this is a 'social asset', I do not wish to be possessed of it. If I do not attend these functions I am regarded as 'one aside'. Then the present 'hate propaganda' which has invaded a once sane country. This propaganda is shouted at us from all quarters. The Press roars its encouragement, and the preachers from the pulpit glorify these things. And we are expected to attend church and sing war-like psalms.

Naturally I miss most of all the 'home atmosphere' and my relations and friends. But little else.

VIII. *Girl, aged 15.* This girl is the only child from a rather poor London home. She had had no visit from her parents, though they wrote to one another every week. Her foster mother was a fussy, complaining woman, whom even the Friendly Visitor avoided because of her constant grumbles. She had some reason for worry, since her husband had fallen out of work after she had agreed to take in the children. In school this girl's record was entirely satisfactory, though she was described as shy. The psychologist found that her intelligence was well above the average, and that she made excellent use of it, particularly in practical situations. She found her a mature, competent young person, friendly, sensible and co-operative. She made no complaints about her billet, but said that she would much prefer to be at home. She wanted to become a post office clerk, and was regarded as entirely suitable for this type of work.

She remained in the same billet for eight months. When it became certain that no Civil Service Examinations would be held, she returned home for employment.

'WHAT I LIKE IN CAMBRIDGE'

When I first came to Cambridge at the end of August I spent most of the time walking with my friends that's one thing that I like, the open space that is good for walks. Sitting by the river watching the punts, fishing for the small fish that are in it. The school here, Cambridge Central School, in some respects is better than D.C.S. in Tottenham. The gym. which is set out so good, with the changing room and showers. On the other hand the cloisters which are all round the centre of the school are very cold. On Monday evenings we are allowed to go to Newnham College where several students look after groups of us. We all enjoy these evenings and I think that the students are very friendly to us. For one evening a week I go dancing with some of my friends and have a lovely evening there. The shops here are rather good for shopping purposes and they are all built close together only it is rather a long way to walk every time I want to buy anything special. I like the concerts they have had in the Guildhall especially one by Joan Metcalfe. On Armistice Day I thought the students were good sports the way they dressed themselves up in different costumes and didn't mind when everyone were laughing at them. The people of Cambridge were very kind when I first came to Cambridge. Cambridge is a very nice place but I shall be pleased when we are all together once more in Tottenham and the war is over.

'THINGS I MISS IN CAMBRIDGE'

One of the things I miss in Cambridge is when coming home from school in the evening if I'm not going to any school activities (e.g. Newnham College etc.). I know that the evening will be spent as usual knitting and sometimes reading. When I'm home in Tottenham I often go out to tea to a friend or relation of mine and spend an evening with them. Over the week-ends when I feel as if I'd like to stay in by the fireside the lady I'm billeted with generally expects us to go for a walk, and as it is almost wintry it is not very nice. I miss my relations, parents and friends who are in Tottenham. And often wish our foster mother wasn't so particular although she does that for our good, as she says.

IX. *Boy, aged 13.* Within three months of evacuation this boy had been charged in the Juvenile Court for stealing from shops with one or two other boys. The Child Guidance Clinic to which he was referred found him to be of outstandingly good intelligence, with unusual ability in dealing with abstract problems, and excellent concentration. The school noted that his behaviour had become markedly worse after evacuation. From the story given to the Clinic by the father and by the boy himself, it appeared that he had become seriously depressed several years ago after the sudden death of his mother when he was alone with her. Subsequently, after an operation on his eyes, which had taken him away from school for a period, he had dropped from the top to the bottom of his class, and had never regained the educational place appropriate to his intelligence. He had been anxious about leaving his father. Some of the stolen articles were sent as presents to him. He appeared deeply disturbed at the Clinic. At school he was reported as sullen, hostile, and obstructive. The psychiatrist regarded this boy's separation from home as an extra strain he was unable to stand during a period of depression.

This boy was removed from his first billet because his foster parents knew he had been pilfering from the shops. When he wrote the essay he was awaiting trial in the Juvenile Court for further thefts. The Court bound him over for two years and sent him home.

'THE THINGS I LIKE IN CAMBRIDGE'

I do not like Cambridge except for the people and the swimming facilities and the undergraduates who are a decent lot of chaps in my estimation if not in anybody else's. The swimming facilities are very good but being in the river it is rather cold in winter.

'THE THINGS I MISS IN CAMBRIDGE'

Most of all I miss my parents and brothers. I also miss the facilities for carrying on my hobbies: Radio (Short Wave) Technical Drawing and Model Aeroplanes. I also miss Sunday marches with the Communist Party and will miss the May-day Celebrations in Hyde Park next year. I miss the fellowship and good spirit of my comrades in the Communist Party. I miss the power to be allowed to choose whether I wish to go to church or not. I miss the safety of London in leaving your bike about without having a post-mortem on it by Cambridge boys who fool about with your brakes and my dynamo has been mucked about with lots of times already. I miss a decent and regular bus-service. I miss films that have any resemblance of being new. I miss the power to live as I do at home instead of being dictated to by the masters as they did on the question of us going on the river.

It may have been noticed that four out of five of the unusual essays reproduced were written by boys, and that the girl's essay is the least remarkable of the five. The general impression left on all who read the essays was that the boys wrote more frankly, spontaneously and characteristically. As far as the older children are concerned, the difference between the sexes may be due wholly or in part to the fact that all the arrangements for writing the essays were in the hands of two men, and the masculine nature of the explanation of what was wanted may have proved more stimulating and suggestive to the boys than the girls. With the younger children, however, the arrangements were in the great majority of cases in the hands of women.

Brief quotations will now be given. They do not offer a representative picture of the essays. Some of the principal topics called forth no striking expressions. Also the 'misses' tend to be more vigorously worded than the 'likes'. The arrangement under headings makes no claim to be systematic. Some of the extracts should be under more than one heading. Where the spelling is original it is the child's. A few spelling errors which seemed mere slips have been removed. Inserted words or comments are in brackets. Omissions are indicated by dots.

GENERAL REMARKS ON CAMBRIDGE

B. 14 years. I have liked the town also which is in my opinion a better town than Tottenham.

B. 14 years. The best thing about the town is that it is easy to get to other places as it is a big bus centre. (This idea appears in embryo in Essay No. III.)

B. 13 years. Cambridge is a dull dismal and awful place with hardly any entertainment.

B. 13 years. I like playing football here (better) than I do in London the ground is softer.

B. 13 years. The thing I like most in Cambridge is the fruit.

B. 12 years. I don't miss anything in Cambridge. I am perfectly happy.

B. 12 years. I do not want to go home for Christmas because I like Cambridge.

B. 7 years. I like it here because I have more toys.

B. 8 years. I miss the barage beloons as well.

B. 11 years. I miss nothing in Cambridge as I am enjoying myself to much to miss anything.

G. 12 years. All the surroundings are new and I feel very strange, though I am happy here and feel safer I am rather homesick. (The only reference to war risks in any essay.)

G. 9 years. I like Cambridge betther than London because it is much nicer and much clner (cleaner).

G. 12 years. I really miss everything in general.

G. 12 years. I like staying down here in a way because I have more pocket-money.

G. 13 years. I don't have no more time to miss anything else because I am always going somewhere were I am happy.

G. 13 years. Altogether I like Cambridge but I would like it better if it were home.

G. 13 years. I have a lovely time in my billet and never have time to think about my sorrows.

G. 13 years. In every way I miss everything in general.

APPRECIATION OF BEAUTY

(Many of the children, including the majority of the younger children mention the colleges with approval, but there are few statements that give an impression of genuine feeling. The absence of factories and smoke is generally approved from the hygienic point of view. A few boys and girls regret their lost music lessons.)

B. 14 years. I like to stand outside King's College Chapel on a Sunday morning and listen to the organ.

B. 15 years. Cambridge is a beautiful town with its colleges.

B. 14 years. . . . so many colleges and they are all beautiful.

B. 12 years. The thing that I like best in Cambridge are the lovely views.

B. 12 years. I like hearing my hostess play the piano.

G. 12 years. The parks are very nice here with the river running by and the trees and long stretches of grass.

G. 15 years. The colleges and bridges are marvellous for seeing, but you soon get tired of walking round them.

PUBLIC BATHS

B. 14 years. I miss not having a bath in the house and I don't like attending the public baths as I get rather embrassed.

B. 14 years. I also miss the enclosed swimming baths that we have in London. I do *not* like the dirty slimy rivers in which the people in Cambridge have to swim.

B. 14 years. Although there are free baths in Cambridge they have soft muddy irregular bottoms which can on no account be placed in comparison with the firm shelving bottoms of baths in London.

COUNTRY

B. 12 years. The best thing I like is a walk wright out in the wilds where all the rabbits and other wild creatures are. Last Saturday I went along the riverside for a mile and then I almost lost myself I walked on for about twenty minutes and found myself in the wilds of Chesterton. It was quite alright for I knew my way back then.

G. 11 years. And I like to go for some walks at Cambridge because you can go for some very nice walks and you ownly have to go a little walk and then you are in the fields and country.

CAMBRIDGE CHILDREN AND PEOPLE

B. 14 years. I like the two (Cambridge) boys in the house both and jolly good chaps and let me go with them when they go out. Also they share all their things with me.

B. 13 years. The people they seen to me more gernous.

B. 13 years. The first thing that struck me when a arrived in Cambridge was all the time and trouble the people of Cambridge must have spent in preparing for us.

B. 12 years. I also find the people of Cambridge are very friendly every time I see anyone in the road where I am billeted they always stop and talk.

B. 9 years. The next is that Cambridge children are will to show you anything, and always play with you.

G. 14 years. Cambridge is also interesting because the people seem so different from the Londoners and some of them are most funny and dress very queerly.

G. 15 years. I like *some* of the girls in the school.

G. 12 years. I have all our meals with the maids and not with the lady of the house. The maids are very nice.

G. 13 years. I don't like the way the people stare and think it rude if you do the same. I don't like the way the children go out of their (way) to pick quarrels with us.

G. 14 years. Cambridge people in most cases are snobs.

CYCLISTS AND TRAFFIC

B. 14 years. I miss the careful driving of the buses and cars in London, they are reckless and dangerous here. I have had accidents already in Cambridge which I didn't have in London.

B. 14 years. I miss the wide highways and the carefull drivers of London. The streets here are too narrow, the town streets are to crowded by parked cars.

B. 13 years. I miss the buses and the heavy lorries which go passed my house at home. (A common remark in the essays.)

B. 9 years. I dislike the people who show off on bikes and skates.

B. 10 years. The things I do not like in Cambridge is that the traffic is crowded in the road and people are easily knocked over.

B. 14 years. The bus service in Cambridge is greatly inferior to the London Transport Service. The streets in places are very narrow and crowded with traffic and pedestrians which makes it very dangerous. Also the danger is increased by the fact that the drivers of buses being used to it take unnecessary risks.

B. 14 years. I miss the thunder of the tube in the underground railway.

B. 13 years. There are *no* tramlines here, to the danger of cyclists on wet days.

CHURCH

B. 14 years. Another place I like going to is the Children's Service at St. Mark's Church at Newnham. I like the addresses given by Mr. Tullett and Vicar Robbs, who are both very nice people.

B. 7 years. I also like the choir . . . I like the vicar. I like him because he is kind to me.

G. 14 years. I like the Children's Church which is held at St. Mark's Church on Sunday morning.

G. 9 years. Another thing I miss is my Sunday school. I never used to miss unless I was ill or at my Auntie's.

G. 12 years. I do not like the Church service at St. Paul's Church as it is so different from my church at home.

G. 13 years. I like the vicar and the curate at the church which I attend better than the one at home.

FAMILY

B. 14 years. I like my brothers and sisters being at home and not messing up my belongings. . . . I miss getting hidings from my dad when I get into trouble.

G. 14 years. I miss having someone to look after my sister and do her mending.

G. 7 years. I miss dolls Pram and mummy and Daddy and granma and bathing her at night and putting her to bed and put cums down her throat and bits of fish and dressing her in the morning and put her plats in and cloming her hair and nursing her.

G. 11 years. I miss my two little brothers who make a lot of noise.

G. 12 years. My brother is down here with me so I am not lonely.

G. 13 years. Although it feels nice not to be teased I'm afraid I miss it.

G. 13 years. I like my sister being down here with me as she is a good sort.

G. 13 years. I miss my brother always teasing me.

G. 13 years. I miss my father most of all as there is no man in (the) billet where I am living.

FOOD

B. 15 years. Every Sunday at home we used to have a roast leg of lamb, and this is something which I miss now.

B. 15 years. I miss the food which I use to have because now as I live in a large house we have many fancy dishes.

B. 13 years. I like the meals which I am having in my billet the best of all apple dishes made with apples.

B. 12 years. I also miss a nice supper.

B. 7 years. I like the river but spesaly I like my Christmas pudding.

B. 8 years. Things I like in Cambridge
Cauliflower Sweets Country Walks Pets Apples.

G. 14 years. I also miss my proper English food because my people are continental, and so their taste is much different to ours.

G. 14 years. The dinners where we are staying are much more richer than we have at home.

G. 14 years. I miss my mother's cooking very much.

G. 14 years. We have very nice food such as venison, pheasant, hare and other luxury which we cannot afford at home.

G. 13 years. I like having my dinner dinnertime as at home I have it at night.

G. 13 years. I like the air in Cambridge because it makes you feel hungray.

G. 13 years. I don't care for the cups of tea after dinner but I don't like to refuse as I don't want to hurt their feelings.

B. 14 years. I miss the lovely cooking I get at home.

B. 14 years. . . . also the food I get here is not like I get at home.

G. 15 years. At home I also been used to a morning cup of tea, but here I am not able to have one.

G. 15 years. I also miss my fish and chip suppers and my peas-pudding and saveloy suppers.

FREEDOM

B. 15 years. The first thing I miss is the freedom, we are not allowed to do just as we would if we were at home.

B. 14 years. I also miss the freedom of my own house.

B. 14 years. I miss . . . the freedom of the house I used to get at home.

B. 14 years. I also miss going out at night after dark with my friends as in Cambridge we have to been in by black-out time.

B. 14 years. At Tottenham I used to go out at nights with my friends but here I have to stay indoors and sit about bored because we are not allowed out after black-out.

B. 13 years. I miss my home very much for I could do things there which I am unable to do in my billet.

B. 13 years. Then too the fact that you cannot 'mess' about in your billet is a disadvantage.

B. 13 years. I wish we did not have to carry our gas mask to and from school. (The only reference to gas masks.)

B. 9 years. I don't like staying indoors.

B. 10 years. I like my billet because sometimes I can do what I like.

G. 15 years. At home on Sundays I generally had an extra hour in bed which meant I did not have to get up until 9.30 a.m. but here I have to get up at 8 o'clock which makes a lot of difference.

G. 14 years. I miss being able to take an apple or some sweets when I want them and I miss being able to sing about the house.

G. 13 years. I like to think that I am able to keep one big secret from Mummy, Christmas Presents. It feels nicer not to have everyone fussing round you.

G. 13 years. I like the maid who is not very old and we have good times together when the cook is not there. . . . I miss sitting round a fire eating nuts and oranges and not minding how much mess is made as long as it is cleared up afterwards. . . . I do not like living in the kitchen of the house as the cook is very fussy. I do not like going to bed at half past seven.

G. 13 years. I miss not being able to do some painting at home.

G. 13 years. I miss the freedom I had when I was at home, and the liberty of the house, also the hot water bottle I had to warm my bed up. I fret more often than I thought I would, as nothing can be like one's own parents and home and everyday life. . . . I miss the freedom of talking and laughing in my billet, as there are no children.

G. 10 years. I do not like the stew my fosterparent makes. I do not like getting lost in the town. I do not like going to bed early and I don't like having to go out to play when I don't want to.

FOSTER PARENTS

B. 15 years. In Cambridge I a stranger am very struck by the way in which I have been received. My foster-parents have put themselves out for me, a person whom they have never seen before.

B. 14 years. I like the people I am billeted with, they are so kind and when I first went there they made me quite comfortable so that after a while I felt like one of the family.

B. 14 years. My foster parents are very good to me and there is plenty of food. My priviledges are exactly the same as at home.

B. 14 years. The people are kind to us and treat us like one of themselves. . . . I have met a lot of high friends of our foster-parents. Our foster-parent takes up to the pictures a lot.

B. 14 years. I like the game of cards which I play with my foster-parent and some friends.

B. 14 years. One outstanding thing I like in Cambridge is my foster-parents who I have been billeted on. I treat them like my parents and they treat me as if I was their son.

B. 13 years. The way our fostermothers treat us as if we were their own children and do the best they can for us.

B. 12 years. What I like best in Cambridge is my hostess.

B. 11 years. I miss . . . somebody happy in the house.

G. 15 years. The people who have billeted us in their houses have showered upon us such hospitality and kindness that we do not have any chance to feel homesickness. In the two billets that I have lived I have been very happy indeed.

G. 14 years. I am sometimes unhappy at my billet, as the maids quarrel a lot and make it awkward for us.

FRIENDS

B. 14 years. I miss in Cambridge my friends. At home we could go out at night and have fun, but here except on few night we have to stay in and amuse ourselves.

G. 15 years. Although I am with most of my friends here there is one I particularly miss who is still in London.

G. 15 years. I miss my friends because no one at all is near me. I miss somebody coming home with me, and coming to school with me. I have to walk two miles to school and two miles home again twice a day without talking to anyone.

G. 12 years. I like having my friend in as I do. I either go in with her or she comes in with me. . . . I like having my foster-parent's neices to sleep with me, and having my friend to sleep with me. I like having Dinners at Marks and Spencers as I can have them with my friends.

(These 'Dinners' were communal meals for such children at the School who found it difficult to get home in the lunch interval.)

(There are many references to pets and several to the baby next door.)

HOBBIES

B. 14 years. I miss not being able to carry on my hobby of science and chemistry as the house I am in is not big enough to do chemistry in.

B. 14 years. I miss my toolshed. At my billet there are only three tools, a screwdriver, spanner and hammer. I cannot clean my bike there is no place to do so.

B. 13 years. I miss Dad's shed were I use to go and make little things like scooters with ball bearing racers, we have no tools in my billet here.

B. 13 years. The lady in my house lets me do fretwork. The man in my house goes abroad and sends back letters with foreign stamps on.

G. 12 years. I like Sunday morning as I do most of the cooking.

(Several girls mention shopping, housework, and taking out the baby next door.)

HOUSES

B. 14 years. I live in a small four room house with no bath no hot water laid on only gas light where at home I lived in a nine room house bath hot water electric and all convenience should be in a house two of us have to sleep in a small single bed where at home I had a big one to myself there is only one lavatory to two houses where at home we had two in one house only a very small back yard instead of a big garden.

B. 14 years. The things I like in Cambridge is the large house and grounds which I live in. . . . I like the big garden in which we do gardening on holidays and Saturdays.

B. 14 years. The house which I am in is a large house and is a very comfortable one. The house is much better than our own and the food is excellent.

B. 14 years. I (miss) my home as the house I am in is smaller.

B. 13 years. I miss Dad's shed. . . . We have no tools in my billet here. I miss the electric light in my bedroom, we use candles here. I miss my sink at home, we have to go outside and wash under a tap here.

B. 13 years. I miss the shed down the bottom of the garden where I used to do a little woodwork or metalwork. I miss my patch of garden.

B. 13 years. I like bedtime because I have a very big bed to myself.

B. 8 years. I have a nice houses and my parents are very kind to me. I have a bedroom to myself.

G. 15 years. I also miss the bathroom that I have always been used to.

G. 15 years. I miss an eiderdown on my bed, and a warm bedroom, as I now sleep in an attic which is freezing. I miss my wardrobe and a chest of drawers to put my clothes in, as I now have a tin trunk.

OPEN SPACES

B. 14 years. (*et passim*) I like the wide open spaces.

B. 14 years. There are open spaces here but we cannot play games on them. Imagine playing cricket on the Fens. I miss all the recreation ground.

G. 14 years. I know they have lots of parks and open spaces but there is one park I miss and that is Downhills Park it is very big and has woods in it.

G. 14 years. I like the open spaces which we are allowed to play on (!).

G. 7 years. I miss the parks. (This child's only statement.)

G. 8 years. I have missed the nice parks.

G. 9 years. Another thing the parks are not divided into any parts like a racing track and American Garden.

G. 9 years. I miss Alexandra Park because I used to go there nearly every Satday.

G. 10 years. I have missed the swings and the seesaws, the traffic area.

G. 10 years. I miss a park called Downhills Park because there was a paddling pool and a traffic area in it and I used to go there every day. I miss a park called Woodlands Park because it is only a turning away from where I live in London and I used to take my dog for a run. I miss going to Grans on a Sunday and to go home through Finsbury Park.

G. 10 years. I do not like in Cambridge is the commons and the river because it has houses in the comon and the river is dangerous.

G. 10 years. There are many parks here but not many parks with swings, seesaws and rounderbouts.

G. 10 years. I miss playing on the swings and roundabouts, in Downhills Park.

G. 13 years. I miss all the parks and recreation grounds which was supplied for us.

(Many more children 'like' the Fens and Parks and Commons than 'miss' them, but as usual the complaints are more precise. It is perhaps right to note that Tottenham is particularly well supplied with public parks and open spaces, though it has little if any private open grounds.)

CINEMA

B. 13 years. I also miss the 3d rushes I used to go to in London.

B. 12 years. A thing I do not like is the difficulty getting into the pictures and not having the pictures on Sunday.

B. 13 years. I find the picture palaces have new films before they have them in London.

G. 8 years. I like to go to the pictures and see funny films.

B. 14 years. I miss the variety of pictures which one gets in a programme there being only one picture and the news for sixpence in the Cambridge cinemas.

B. 10 years. I do not like the pictures in Cambridge because they show all old films.

READING

G. 15 years. I miss the reading that I do at home as down here I do not get so many good books as I do at home.

G. 12 years. The library is a long way (a fairly common complaint).

G. 10 years. I miss my comics wich I have weekly.

G. 13 years. The library is very nice and very modern. Ther are books of every description which would suit everybody.

SCHOOLS AND TEACHERS

B. 13 years. Firstly there is the school building that we are now using it is a vast improvement on our old Central School. And there is the gymnasium, since we did not really have one in Tottenham I cannot compare them, but it is a delight to do P.T. in a properly equipped gymnasium. (The gymnasium is praised by very many.)

B. 14 years. In our school at Tottenham we were given privileges such as playing games in the playground we miss it very much for we are not allowed to run or jump. (A common complaint. The reason was the crowded condition of the playgrounds.)

B. 13 years. I miss homework which I think should be given in cases were it is convenient for the Lady in which you are billeted and I do not think the light is too bad to do homework and it would also occupy the time of the long evenings.

B. 13 years. I also miss homework and wish for more work to be done in school hours. Also not being able to do many science experiments in school is a great miss. . . . Another thing I miss are our two school clubs the 'Science Club' and the 'Magazine Club'. I also miss our art lessons. We now only have thirty minutes a week instead of the ninety minutes or more that we should have.

B. 13 years. I very much enjoy not having any homework in the evenings. I enjoy the woodwork lessons more than I used to at Downhills. I enjoy having the wireless layed on in practically every room of the school. . . . I miss not having a desk of our own.

B. 13 years. I do *not!* like the long way I have to go to school each day and I don't like the cold and bitter weather which I have to go to school in.

B. 12 years. I also like the school I am at but I hate coming from a nice warm room and going into a cold cloister.

B. 7 years. I like to go to school and I like sums.

B. 9 years. I miss Mr. Gordon and West Green caretaker I miss the hot water pipes.

B. 10 years. And I like going to school because I do not no what to do with myself when I am on a holiday from school.

G. 15 years. I miss our own classroom, having a room of our own. (Several older girls say the same.)

G. 15 years. I miss cooking lessons. I miss typing lessons very much.

G. 15 years. I especially miss the lessons which we have at our own School in Tottenham, the ones I miss most are the needlework lessons which we have in our own new Needlework Centre and housewifery when we have to clean out the modern flat.

G. 15 years. There are two teachers who I miss very much. I miss school itself because it was cosy during the winter but round the cloisters here of a cold December morning it not very pleasant. (A very common complaint.)

G. 14 years. The most pleasant thing I have experienced is that I am able to go about with my schoolfriends more and we have a lot more to do with school than we did in London.

G. 14 years. I do not like this school it is cold and draughty and it does not come up to our good old Downhills Central School. I miss our teacher Miss (. . .) very much. I miss my dancing on a Saturday night.

G. 9 years. I miss our electric light that we used to have in West Green School because here at Young Street School we have got gas.

G. 13 years. I miss the term exams which though hard were interesting.

G. 13 years. There is one thing I like very much and that is we haven't had much homework yet.

SHOPS

B. 14 years. I miss . . . shops near at hand were we can buy sweets and necessities. But in Cambridge we have to go a good few hundred yards to buy them. I also miss the near at hand cinemas which are a long way from our home in Cambridge.

B. 14 years. I miss the big shops in London, Selfridges and Gamages.

B. 10 years. I like (Cambridge) because there are plenty of Marks and Spencers, Woolworths and all the other shops.

G. 14 years. I think the shops down here are awful you can never get what you want.

G. 10 years. I went in a lift to the toy department and I liked it very much the shop was called Eaden and Lillies.

SOCIAL ACTIVITIES

B. 14 years. I like nearly everything, the Y.M.C.A. which is a jolly good club.

B. 14 years. The Scouts in Cambridge I dislike because they have not any idea of discipline and no knowledge of smartness, in London they have both of these and knowledge of companionship.

B. 13 years. I also miss the scouts which I used to attend in Tottenham and so far I have not seen a scout troop up to that standard.

B. 13 years. In some ways the Scouting has better facilities down here.

G. 14 years. The thing I miss most is the Girls Life Brigade which I used to go to at home.

G. 14 years. I miss having company as in the evening the three of us have to go and sit in our room by ourselves. I miss having the news in the papers which we never see and also we never hear the wireless which I miss very much.

G. 14 years. I like going to guides on Wednesday evening and our captain is lovely. I also like coming home in her big car. . . . I miss helping my mum do the shopping and cooking.

G. 15 years. Although I like the guides down here I miss our guides at home because they were much better girls.

G. 12 years. The dinner (Communal dinner at Marks and Spencers) for 4d. is very good and we get very good meals and I think that is a very good plan and very kind of Marks and Spencers to give us the loan of their canteen.

G. 12 years. I think going to Newnham of a Monday is very nice. Only I wish it was a bit longer.

(Appreciation of undergraduate activities very common.)

CHAPTER VI

INDIVIDUAL SUCCESSES AND FAILURES

WHEN AN assessment had been made of the relationship established between the evacuated children and their foster homes, it was thought that some more personal information of value and interest might be gained by interviews with some of the children individually. It was hoped that in this way we might discover the contribution of the child's own personality to his failure or success in his foster home relationships.

An examination of the records of children rated as unsatisfactory in their foster homes revealed that the causes of maladjustment between the child and the foster parent, though diverse, could be divided roughly into three classes: maladjustment due (*a*) to the child, (*b*) to the foster parents, (*c*) to both child and foster parents.

Of 46 cases rated as unsatisfactory this was definitely due to the child in 26 cases, and to the foster parents in 10 cases. These figures, however, do not mean that the 26 children could not be billeted successfully, nor that the 10 foster homes were unsuitable as such. The significance of the figures is that the billeting of these 26 children called for special care and they had not been lucky enough to meet immediately with foster parents who had the understanding and patience to deal with them successfully. In the same way, among the ten foster homes were some that would have made quite successful billets for easier children, but in which the foster mother had not the ability or the inclination to deal with special problems. In some cases the social standards of the foster home were somewhat rigid, and the foster parents found the London children's manners and speech intolerable; in other cases there was a tendency to exaggerate faults and fuss unduly over minor misdemeanours, and in yet others there was just a lack of patience on the part of the foster mother which led to the children's getting on her nerves until she felt that she could no longer put up with them. In a few cases of the older boys, complaints were made that the billeting money did not cover the children's feeding expenses, and the foster parents objected to being out of pocket on them. One boy, when asked why he had left his first billet, replied frankly: 'They said I ate too much.' Another remark made by a foster mother was, 'The billeting money is barely enough. P. has a very good appetite.' Of the 26 children who created difficulties in the home through their own personality, only two had to be sent permanently to a hostel for difficult children; and of the ten foster homes where the difficulty lay with the foster parents, there were only three cases where there was definite evidence that the foster home was unsuitable as such. In two of these the foster mothers were of the complaining type who could not help finding fault, though in both cases they had pleasant intelligent girls billeted with them; in the other case the children were overcrowded and uncomfortable and had evidently been taken in with the idea of making all that was possible out of them financially.

From these figures the incidence of children entirely unsuitable for billets is under 5 per cent, and the incidence of foster homes which are completely unsuitable as such is about 7 per cent, but the numbers dealt with are too small to allow of any reliable deductions. It seems, however, justifiable from our evidence to conclude that the great majority of children can be satisfactorily cared for in billets, if time and care can be given to the selection of foster homes, and that the great majority of foster homes can be utilized if only some knowledge is available about those women who have the patience and insight to cope with the more difficult children, and those who can only be entrusted with the simpler, more normal cases.

In order to gain more knowledge of the child's part in foster home relationships, it was agreed that the comparatively small group of children having an unsatisfactory relationship with their foster home should be personally interviewed and tested by an educational psychologist. It was also agreed to compare these children with a control group taken from the larger number of children whose relationship had been assessed as satisfactory. This control group was chosen to correspond in sex and age with the individuals in the original group.

The total number of children rated for success in billeting on the questionnaire cards was 656, and of these 54 had been rated as unsuccessful. Since several of these children had, however, returned to London shortly after the cards had been completed and assessed, there were in the end only 40 available for testing. With the corresponding control group this gave a total of 80 children who were tested as well as being personally interviewed.

The Tests used were the Revised Stanford-Binet Intelligence Scale, the Merrill-Palmer Scale of Mental Tests, Healy's Picture Completion, Numbers 1 and 2, and the Oakley Form Board. The Performance Tests were used chiefly as a means of observing the child's attitude to a practical situation. Such tests not only reveal to the trained observer the presence or lack of practical ability, but also yield a considerable insight into the child's characteristic traits such as his response to difficulties, powers of concentration, sense of reality, capacity for adaptation, and suggestibility. As a result of such observation it is possible to form a fairly reliable estimate of his temperament and type.

The time given to each child varied from an hour to an hour and a half, and he was encouraged to talk freely of his feelings about evacuation, of the difficulties or disabilities he experienced in his new setting, of anxieties about leaving his parents, as well as of more positive feelings of happiness and interest aroused by the sudden change in his life and surroundings. The older children were also questioned about the careers they would like to take up, and a few of the higher grade children asked the psychologist for definite advice on this matter, and were very interested in certain aspects of their ability which the tests revealed.

The reports on the tests were in every case submitted to the Head Master or the Head Mistress concerned, with a request for their comments and criticism. This request was complied with frankly, and in most cases considerable interest was shown in the reports. As often happens, there was in some cases a discrepancy between the measure of a child's ability as revealed by the test, and the measure of achievement attained in his school work. It was, however, very satisfactory to find that the teachers agreed substantially with the psychologist's report on the child's personality.

The psychologist would like to express her appreciation of the kindness and co-operation of both the local and the evacuated teachers. They did everything possible in difficult and congested conditions to give her facilities for carrying out the tests. From the educational point of view one of the most satisfactory results of the experiment was the interest it roused in the teachers themselves, and they acknowledged that the reports on the testing were of value to them. The words of one Head Mistress may be taken as representative of the general attitude of most of the teachers. She wrote: 'Perhaps there will come a day when every child will be tested by an expert as a help to her Class Mistress. It would be a real help.'

The children who were tested came from Infant, Junior, Senior and Central schools, but as half the number were Central School children whose intellectual standard is higher than that of the Senior School children, there is a tendency for the average Intelligence Quotients to be on the high side. Acting as a check on this tendency, however, is the fact that no Secondary School children, whose intellectual standard is higher still, were included. The Intelligence Quotients ranged from 81 to 141, with an average of 113·1. There was no significant difference between the Intelligence Quotients of the children who had a satisfactory relationship with the foster home, and those with an unsatisfactory relationship, the average Intelligence Quotients being 112·6 in the one case and 113·7 in the other. We may therefore presume that, within a normal range, intelligence is not an important factor in determining the children's happiness in their relationships in the foster home.

The numbers dealt with were too small to draw any general inferences about sex differences.

From the point of view of the Survey, there was nothing of any further significance to be drawn from the information obtained about the Intelligence Quotients of the children, but the evaluation of intelligence did not exhaust the possibilities of the Terman Test. The general attitude of each child to the test situation in its various aspects was carefully observed and the facts gleaned from such observation made an important contribution to the final assessment of personality.

Whilst the testing was going on, but independently of it, a psychiatrist made a careful scrutiny and analysis of the Tottenham school and foster home records, in order to gain some estimate of the type of character of each child, and of such difficulties of personality as were found. In addition to this, a certain number of children included in the Survey were referred to the Child Guidance Centre for various problems, and were seen by the same psychiatrist.

Assessments of the personality of the children were thus made in three different ways: some in a clinical examination; some through observations made during intelligence tests, and the rest indirectly on the information given in the foster home and school records. The last was naturally the least satisfactory method, since there were several cases in which the information was not enough to enable the scrutinizers to form a lively picture of the children. A special difficulty arose in the case of children who were marked on the school cards as backward, lazy, or lethargic, since backwardness and lack of interest may arise from a serious emotional difficulty or from an inherently dull intelligence. To give an intelligence test is the only reliable way of deciding this issue, indirect evidence alone being too speculative.

There was, however, some check on the assessments based on records only, in the measure of agreement found to exist between the psychiatrist's estimate from the records of the tested children and the psychologist's assessment from the personal interviews. In no case did it happen that a child was judged to have serious difficulties from scrutiny of the records who had not also been assessed as a problem on the Test interview. Out of the 40 Tottenham children who were tested, four who revealed serious difficulties of behaviour in the Test situation were not sufficiently defined in the school and home records to enable any judgment to be passed on them. It can, therefore, be assumed that the total number of children assessed in the original scrutiny as showing problems of personality is fairly reliable and if anything on the conservative side.

The normal personality is one which shows a certain balance of qualities and tendencies. Normal children, like normal adults, may differ a good deal from each other and show quite marked characteristics in one direction or another, but if any particular tendency or quality is exaggerated beyond a certain point, we all easily recognize such a person as being unbalanced. The ways in which lack of balance can be shown are very varied, but certain kinds of abnormal behaviour tend to go together, and it is therefore possible to classify abnormal types into definite groups. The classification used here was as follows: (A) Anxious children who may or may not be depressed as well; (B) Children who are 'shut in' and tend to withdraw themselves from relationships with other people; (C) Children who are jealous and quarrelsome; (D) Those who are over active and aggressive; (E) Those who show alternating moods of elation and depression; (F) Delinquent children.[1]

[1] This scheme was suggested and worked out by Dr. John Bowlby, who wrote the following account of the six types of difficult children.

Class A (those who are anxious and/or depressed), includes children whose fears and anxieties are in any way excessive. The usual symptoms are nervousness, diffidence, shyness, fear of failure which sometimes shows itself in frequent crying, depression and in an inability to respond to others, sometimes in a refusal to tackle anything difficult and in a constant need for reassurance and encouragement. This group also includes children of the 'perfectionist' type whose anxiety takes the form of a compelling need to excel in school and to be a pattern of goodness at home; such children frequently exhibit an obsessional desire for tidiness, method and routine. In the more severe cases they break down very readily in face of failure and are very prone to impute guilt to themselves for anything that goes wrong.

Class B (the 'shut-in', withdrawn children), tend to be solitary. They seem to have little need for human contact and find much satisfaction in their own world of daydreams. They are imaginative, often seem very

The children were classified according to these six ways of responding. They were also ranked according to the degree of disorder shown, in three grades. Grade I indicates a slight difficulty, in some cases not much more than a bare tendency, which with reasonable treatment and understanding in the ordinary course of events, in home and school, will right itself. Grade II indicates a fairly serious maladjustment which calls for clinical treatment, but one which may be

happy, but turn away from emotional demands of a personal nature. They have their heads in the clouds, and feel little contact with the things that belong to 'the light of common day'.

Class C (the jealous, quarrelsome children), are highly emotional, but their emotions are badly controlled. They seek human contact and affection and want to be the centre of attention. They desire power, and in face of a very slight frustration of these needs, they break down in fits of jealousy, temper-tantrums, and quarrelsomeness. In doing so they completely defeat their own ends by depriving themselves of the affection and admiration they wish to excite. They thus create for themselves a vicious circle in which their symptoms gradually become worse. Such children tend to be hysterical, uncontrolled and suggestible, and they are a source of difficulty and complaint in home and school, amongst both their fellows and the grown-ups. Clinical experience seems to show that more girls than boys belong to this category.

Class D (the over-active, aggressive type), is found more frequently among boys, and is in some sense a counterpart of the jealous, quarrelsome type among girls. The children in this class are openly aggressive, eager and ready to take the lead in the wilder and more active types of work and play. They are anxious to win at all costs, and they take a beating badly. They want power and attention, and set out to get it in a virile, even hostile manner. So intent are they on gaining ascendancy and subjecting others that they seem indifferent to affection, and it may be that these aggressive characters are frequently compensating for some such lack of love in themselves and from others.

Group E (those with alternating moods of elation and depression), is a general type of which the 'manic-depressive' illness is an extreme form. The members of this group are of a genial, friendly, type, easily raised to heights of optimism, easily thrown into depths of depression. When things go well they are boisterous and gay, and may be active and eager workers; when things go badly they are gloomy and dejected, cannot settle to anything, and exhibit alternating restlessness and lethargy. They are uncertain, unstable children, and difficult to assess in one or two interviews since the dominating mood of the moment is so strongly in the ascendant that its opposite tends to be altogether eclipsed. At the same time, this 'circular' type has more in common with the two previous groups, the jealous and the aggressive, than with the depressed and 'shut-in' groups. Even in his depressive phase the child of Class E may show glimpses of humour, and may keep in touch with the outside world of people and things in a way which the anxious, depressed, obsessional, 'shut-in' children fail expected to yield to skilled care and attention. Grade III indicates deeply-seated emotional disturbance which, unless treated at an early stage, will be likely to lead to serious breakdown later on.

It was hoped that the psychiatrist would find time to make a scrutiny and analysis of the Islington cards similar to the one he had made of the Tottenham cards, but unfortunately he was called away for war service before this was completed

to do. There is a tendency for the 'circular' character as observed in childhood to exhibit the aggressive, boisterous phase more frequently than the depressive, probably because of the resilience which is a natural feature of the earlier years of growth. In some cases, indeed, only prolonged and careful observation will reveal the depressed, anxious phase of the character. The difficulties of behaviour met with in children of this type are more likely to arise from their moods of boisterous elation than from their moods of depression. In relation to the problems of billeting, therefore, they approximate to groups C and D, and can be classed with them. Whilst for the purpose of treatment and clinical studies, the finer analysis is needed, from the point of view of a social survey they fall in with these other groups in being sharply separated from Group A, the anxious and depressed children.

Class F (the delinquent children), present a special type of affectionless, anti-social character whose delinquency is inherent in the lack of any feeling of social solidarity. This lack of social feeling may be only partial but is sometimes complete. Such children are isolated, solitary characters, whose affections seem to have been so completely frozen that it is impossible to make an emotional contact with them. They are delinquents because they do not feel any social ties. They are often children of much superficial charm and friendliness, but on closer acquaintance one soon begins to feel the utter lack of foundation in any contact that has been made; the apparent friendliness is found to be little more than a tool for achieving purely ego-centric ends.

It is obvious that the term 'delinquent' is used here in a very special sense, but it is just possible that in so narrowing its denotation we put a finger here on the basic type of persistent and chronic delinquent. The anxious depressed child may take to stealing as some kind of compensation for the thing he feels, rightly or wrongly, that he has been deprived of; the jealous child may steal to buy popularity among school friends or to exhibit herself in some unusual finery; the aggressive child may steal out of bravado, may form and lead a gang, or commit some breach of the peace out of sheer self-assertion. In all these cases the delinquency is a superficial symptom of some specific emotional disturbance, and if the emotional disturbance is cleared up and the abnormal temperamental features softened and harmonized, the delinquency is very likely to disappear. But in the case of the affectionless, anti-social character, the delinquency is the result of a deep-lying, fundamental lack of emotional life, perhaps due to certain special circumstances in the child's early years. The only possible cure lies in the very difficult task of reviving the human affection which has somehow failed to live.

and the scrutiny was continued by the educational psychologist, who was familiar with his methods of analysis and classification. The close correspondence between the psychiatrist's judgment on the school and foster home records and the psychologist's assessment during the testing makes it reasonable to presume that the completion of the scrutiny and classification was in line with the earlier work and produced comparable results.

The following table is based on the information given in the school and foster home records. It shows the number of children assessed as suffering from difficulties of personality, together with the type of disorder and the degree of such disorder.

ASSESSMENT OF DIFFICULTIES FOUND AMONG 656 LONDON SCHOOL CHILDREN
(Based on the school and foster home records)

Grade	*Personality Defect* I	*Personality Defect* II	*Personality Defect* III	*Sum of Grades* II & III
A. Anxious and/or Depressed	34	23	13	36
B. Shut-in, withdrawn	3	2	3	5
C. Quarrelsome, jealous D. Aggressive E. 'Circular': Alternating moods	} 24	11 14 } 30 5	3 3 } 6 –	36
F. Delinquent, affectionless, anti-social	–	5	5	10
Total No. with Difficulties	61	60	27	87

Omitting the children graded under Personality Defect I whose difficulties are such as are likely with reasonable treatment at home and in school to clear up of themselves, the figures show that in the total of 656 children 87, or 13 per per cent are in need of skilled therapeutic treatment, and of these 27, or 4 per cent of the total, are cases of considerable severity. When classes C, D, and E are grouped together, as already suggested, it will be observed that the great majority of the difficult children are absorbed in this group together with the anxious and/or depressed group, and that the numbers in each are the same, 36 in each group.

The following tables give the assessment of the children who were tested or interviewed without a test. The first table shows those children rated as unsatisfactory in foster home relationships and the second table those rated as satisfactory.

ASSESSMENT OF PERSONALITY OF 86[1] LONDON SCHOOL CHILDREN

I. RATED AS UNSATISFACTORY, 46

Grade	*Personality Defect* I	*Personality Defect* II	*Personality Defect* III	*Sum of Grades* II & III
A. Anxious and/or Depressed	7	8	5	13
C. Quarrelsome, jealous D. Aggressive E. 'Circular': Alternating moods	2 – –	4 6 1 } 11	1 1 – } 2	13
F. Delinquent, affectionless, anti-social	–	1	2	3
Total No. with Difficulties	10	20	9	

[1] Three of these children were not seen by the psychologist, but careful personal investigations were made by the psychiatrist. Eighty were given the intelligence test.

II. RATED AS SATISFACTORY, 40

Grade	*Personality Defect* I	*Personality Defect* II	*Personality Defect* III	*Sum of Grades* II & III
A. Anxious and/or depressed	5	5	–	5
B. Shut-in, withdrawn	2	1	1	2
C. Quarrelsome, jealous	–	–	–	0
D. Aggressive	2	–	–	
E. Circular	–	–	–	
F. Delinquent, affectionless, anti-social	–	–	–	–
Total No. with Difficulties	9	6	1	

Thus of the 46 children who were rated as unsatisfactory, only 7 were assessed as being perfectly normal, and another 10 gave evidence of only slight emotional difficulties not serious enough to cause concern about their future powers of adjustment. The remaining 29 were children suffering from emotional disturbances serious enough to call for treatment, 9 of them being definitely severe cases. As opposed to this, out of the 40 tested children rated as satisfactory, 24 were assessed as being perfectly normal, and another 9 gave evidence of emotional difficulties so slight as to be no cause for anxiety as to their later powers of adjustment. This left only 7 who were considered to be in a serious state of emotional disturbance, and only one of these was regarded as very severe.

These figures show that difficulties of personality in the child are a weighty factor in the success or failure of billeting.

Omitting those children graded as Personality Defect I, since their difficulties are not considered to be fundamentally serious, it will be observed that, just as in the case of the total number of children assessed as having psychological problems, the great majority of those rated as unsatisfactory in billets fall into the group covered by classes C, D, and E combined, and the group covered by Class A; in this case again the numbers in each are identical; 13 children in each group. Only three were regarded as showing definitely anti-social, affectionless, delinquent traits, and one was a seriously depressed child who had taken to delinquency as a compensation. It may thus be said, in broad terms, that those difficulties of personality which lessen the chance of success in billeting are of three main types: anxiety, aggressiveness and delinquency, the last being decidedly less common than the other two. In this investigation there was no case of a child belonging to the shut-in, withdrawn class giving rise to difficulties in the foster home. These children often make convenient lodgers, since they demand so little and assert themselves so little.

As examples of the types of children who are difficult to billet successfully, we present three cases, one from each of the above-mentioned classes.

There was among the children rated as wholly unsatisfactory in their relationships in the foster home a very clear-cut case of an anxious boy who could probably have been billeted quite happily if he had found a foster home which suited him. As it was, the mutual relation between him and his foster parents seemed to be very negative; there were no definite complaints about him, but just a general feeling of unsatisfactoriness and unfriendliness, as though the foster parents were looking for a more hearty response than the boy was capable of giving. On his side he was comfortable in his billet and liked it 'as well', he said, 'as he would like anywhere away from home', but he seemed quite detached about it, and showed as little personal feeling as one would in a hotel room. He was a boy of Central School age, of average intelligence, who worked with perseverance and meticulous care, and was most anxious to do well. In both scholastic and performance work he gave indications of a difficulty in readjustment; having once formed an idea of how a problem should be tackled he was inclined to try to force a result along those lines. Although he adapted himself fairly well to the Test situation it was essential to a successful procedure to let him go his own way and take his own time; it was even necessary to let him finish out a Test when the time limit was up, since to have interrupted him and started him on another test would almost certainly have resulted in blocking his further efforts. He had the rigid, anxious, obsessional characteristics which inevitably make adjustment to life difficult, and indeed in unfavourable circumstances must make it impossible. At the same time, in his own quiet way, he made quite a friendly contact with the psychologist, and the co-operation he showed in the test when free to move within his own personal limitations indicated that successful billeting was possible in his case. Such a child may get through life without serious breakdown if he is lucky enough to strike the favourable environment, but the chances are that in the rough and tumble of life he will sooner or later clash with his environment, and owing to the great rigidity of his character he will break because he cannot bend.

In the aggressive, over-active class there was a boy of Junior School age who finally had to be taken from his billet as his foster mother could put up with him no longer. Among the chief complaints was his constant bed-wetting. He was removed to a very happily run, free and easy hostel where his social adjustment improved considerably, and there was general improvement in the enuresis, although it did not altogether cease. In addition to the bed-wetting, the boy was described as being argumentative, hot-tempered, noisy and excitable; the school reported that he had been lying and truanting and that he had been caught pilfering. The Test showed him to be a boy of good intelligence, quick and active at things which interested him, co-operative, and keen on doing well in the Tests; he was particularly good at performance tests and showed quickness in grasping the point of a practical problem. Though nervous and ill-at-ease for a short time, he showed a capacity for friendliness and a sense of humour and fun. In the hostel this boy very quickly responded to the understanding treatment he received there. The Matron found him a delightful, open, friendly boy who got on well with the others, and who, owing to his good sense was soon regarded as 'one of the big ones'. He responded eagerly to the suggestion that he could do little extra jobs for which he would be paid, and out of the money thus acquired pay in to the school funds for what he had pilfered. The jobs were done willingly and he took regularly to the school Head the money he earned. During the whole period of his stay at the hostel he was found to be helpful, co-operative and popular. There were occasionally signs of depression, loneliness and unhappiness without any very definite cause, and he is almost certainly a typical example of the 'circular' character whom we have included in this general aggressive, over-active group.

Of the three children who were classified as delinquent, anti-social, affectionless characters, two eventually returned to London; the third has remained. The foster mother finds him an unwelcome visitor and is very anxious to get rid of him. He is described as dirty, disobedient, untruthful, dishonest, bad-tempered, lazy, and restless. No doubt some of this may be discounted as due to the disgruntled attitude of the foster mother. The school considers him to be a weak character who is easily led. He is a boy of rather less than average intelligence, works in a slow, laboured, uncomprehending way, and has difficulty in holding on to the central point of a problem. He gave the impression of being an anxious, self-centred child, jealous of other boys' attainments, both scholastic and social. He lingered about the room after the test was over, seemed anxious to make closer friends with the psychologist without being able to take any definite steps, and reluctant to give up the friendly contact, however superficial, which he had already gained. He was very uncommunicative and quite unenthusiastic about either his billet or his home; the only definite statement he made was that he would rather be where he was than return to London. He struck one as being an exceedingly unhappy child, who, through some fundamental emotional difficulty, was unable to make the friends he needed for happiness. As a consequence he was becoming more and more warped in his social relationships. It is improbable that evacuation had any effect on this condition which is too deep-seated for an external change to influence it either for good or for ill. He was a young boy of Junior School age, and it is possible that prolonged Clinic treatment might have an ameliorating effect; but unfortunately the case had not been considered serious enough to be referred to the Clinic.

While the figures indicate that difficulties of personality in the children were a definite factor in causing failure in foster home relationships, the fact that there were 7 children suffering from quite serious difficulties of personality who had adapted well to the foster home calls for further comment.

On an examination of the personality of these 7 children, it was found that all of them were either of an inhibited, anxious, or of a solitary, withdrawn type, this last being a type which did not appear at all among the minus ratings. It would appear, therefore, that children with definitely unstable characters of a certain type can live a seemingly satisfactory social life, by quiet withdrawn behaviour, up to, and even during, adolescence. The anxious child may appear to be of a passive nature, quiet and retiring, giving no trouble, or he may be actively helpful and dutiful, striving always to be a perfect child and thus gain comfort through praise and affection. The 'shut-in' withdrawn child seems to conform well with his environment simply because he skilfully fences himself off from it; the adjustment is superficial and in a sense negative, depending largely on the child's capacity to dispense with human relationships and to find satisfaction in a more or less remote phantasy life of his own. In both cases of this type noted here, the impression gained from talking to the children during the test was that they were in some ways happier than at home because no emotional response was expected of them, and they were free to indulge their inner phantasy life undisturbed by external demands.

One of these was a boy of superior intelligence, with an unusually keen and lucid reasoning capacity when dealing with abstract problems, and an exceedingly good command of words. When, however, it was a question of applying his ability to the solution of practical problems he failed completely. His work on the Performance Test was probably the most incompetent of that of any of the tested children, although he scored second highest in intelligence. He talked very freely about himself at the end of the test, and gave the impression of a seriously unstable character who will have considerable difficulty in adjusting himself to practical life when he leaves the shelter of school, if indeed he succeeds at all. He is conscious of both his ability and his disability, but seemed to doubt his capacity to settle down to what seems to him the drudgery of tackling hard facts. He would like to be a journalist, but cannot endure the prospect of going through the donkey work to attain his end. He is quite happy, as he is now billeted alone, very much to his satisfaction; he has made little use of the various club activities which were available. He prefers staying at home in the evenings playing about with a microscope, or fixing up his stamp collection, or reading. In his own home he spends a lot of his time over a coin collection, and he regretted that the coins were too numerous and heavy to have brought with him. This case was one in which the adjustment to the foster home was rated very high and yet he presents difficulties of personality which make him undoubtedly one of the most serious cases under observation. In cases of this kind the seriousness of the situation is enhanced by the fact that the deep-seated difficulty of personality may, through a facile adaptation, escape detection for so long that treatment must be difficult, prolonged, and, when at last it is considered necessary, possibly unsuccessful.

There is ample evidence, from the general success achieved in billeting after the first weeks of trial and error, that children of both the depressed and the aggressive groups can be satisfactorily billeted. It must, however, be noted that these two different types of difficult children settle down best in two different sorts of foster home. The nervous, anxious child is more happily placed in a quiet, conventional home where, if he is not actually alone, he at least has an opportunity to keep to himself and follow his own interests. The over-active aggressive child is happier in a tolerant, free and easy home, with companions of his own age, where he has not to fall back too much on his own resources. In her talks with the children, the psychologist noticed several quite anxious children who found considerable happiness in the quiet, undemanding kindliness of a home where they were the only children. One very anxious, sensitive, quiet child of thirteen had been most unhappy in her first billet where she was with a rather dense, insensitive foster mother whose attitude was that 'all London children were slum children', and that rough and ready, off-hand treatment was all they would expect: 'And I am *not* a slum child,' the little girl said very emphatically. In her second home she found the quiet protective kindness she was needing, and said with real affection, 'My lady treats me just like her own little girl.' On the other hand, some restless, active, out-going children, comfortably housed, and exceedingly well cared for as far as their physical needs were concerned, were wearied and made still more restless by the conventional propriety of the home and a lack of warm personal feeling. 'Oh! we are very comfortable,' they said, but complained of long, dreary, quiet evenings when they were left to find their own interests. The home had evidently only succeeded in creating an atmosphere of acute boredom which in itself was enough to encourage difficult behaviour.

It is interesting and important to note that whilst the normal children, those who showed no special difficulties, were not differentiated and classified in the same detail as were the abnormal group, it was yet clear that they also fell into two general types. Difficulties of personality are caused by the over-accentuation of certain feelings and attitudes which, in moderate and harmonious form, are found in ordinary children. We meet among normal children, too, the quiet, retiring type, and the more friendly, on-coming active type, each of whom may be quite stable, since his temperamental qualities are not ill-balanced or exaggerated.

A study of the reports of the tests, coupled with the very vivid impression which some of the children left, shows that more than half the normal children who had a good relationship with their foster parents, 17 out of 25, were of the friendly, cheerful, on-coming type who make easy social contacts, and are at home with their kind. They were sometimes described by their foster mothers as helpful in the house, and as having become 'quite one of the family'. The foster parents enjoyed their company and seemed to feel a genuine affection for them. There were three cases of the quiet, rather shy, self-contained type who, however, showed no indication of instability. They were all under eleven, and probably had not yet gained social confidence. The remaining five were rather negative characters, a little lacking in sensitivity to their environment. Their response was therefore inclined to be neutral; they did not appear to be unstable characters, but rather to be children who would fit in to most environments with a kind of stolid placidity without looking for or giving much emotional response.

The contrast between this group of normal children rated as satisfactory in the foster home and the group of abnormal children also rated as satisfactory is rather striking. It will be remembered that all the latter were of the quiet, inhibited, withdrawn type. The two groups serve to illustrate the broad classification of personality into the out-going, genial, extraverted type and the withdrawn, somewhat unsociable, introverted type. These facts seem to offer a clear if somewhat negative indication of the sort of child who is never likely to be a great success in an evacuation scheme. There is every prospect that the normal, friendly, genial child will in his own good time do credit to any billeting scheme; the quiet, withdrawn child, whether normal or abnormal, may still become a welcome guest; but the evidence suggests that the child who shows active, out-going, aggressive qualities to a marked degree will tend to remain a problem for foster mothers and billeting authorities.

A further general point of interest is that of the distribution in age groups of the children rated as unsatisfactory in foster home relationships, as quoted in Chapter IV (p. 54). The talks of the psychologist with individual children threw some further light upon this. The fact that amongst the Tottenham children the percentage rated as unsatisfactory in the higher age groups is much greater than amongst those of lower ages suggests that the older children found greater difficulty in making new social adjustments and possibly also that foster parents found it harder to make a happy and friendly contact with them. In the interviews the older children were on the whole more communicative and more ready to give voice to the difficulties which they had experienced. Among those children in their last school year, there was a feeling that if they had to make a change, it would have been more satisfactory to have gone straight into work instead of spending the year trying to adjust to temporary conditions and then making a further change and having to adapt once more. Moreover, the older children are more dependent on outside interests, and they missed the opportunities to which they were accustomed in London. The older boys in particular found the winter evenings long and dull. In a few cases the older boys and girls gave voice to anxiety about their family in London; a few of them thought that if there was danger and difficulty there, they would rather be with them,[1] but this expression of anxiety was by no means common. For the most part the younger children expressed real happiness in their surroundings, some of them quite definitely stating that they did not want to return to London, and wished that their mothers could come and live here. The great majority looked healthy, bright-eyed and happy, and in several cases the Head Master or Head Mistress remarked on a greater mental alertness and increased powers of concentration during their stay in Cambridge. Some of them developed an interest in natural history, and a few of the younger boys

[1] See Chapter VIII.

went so far as to express the desire to live in the country and become farmers.

A factor which undoubtedly helps the younger children to adapt more easily to the foster home is that their happiness is dependent upon simpler activities. So long as they have friends to play with and are accepted by the foster home as familiar inmates of the household, and are allowed to help and to take part in everyday family activities, they very quickly make themselves at home. Furthermore, Junior School children as a whole are less differentiated in their feelings and reactions than the older group, and a very strong impression was conveyed by these younger children that so long as their schools and classes remained more or less intact, the children felt that they were still moving in a familiar background, and this gave them a sense of security. One bright-eyed, rosy-cheeked Junior School boy gave definite expression to this general feeling when he said heartily, 'We are all very happy *together*'.

A few children had been drafted into new schools, either evacuated schools or local schools; this seemed to increase their difficulties even when they moved in small groups, for example, the eleven-year children transferring from a Junior to a Senior School. The trouble showed itself in a somewhat rigid demeanour, an uncommunicativeness, and a lack of spontaneity, as though they were ill-at-ease and afraid of committing themselves. It is possible that a similar attitude, although in a lesser degree, might be evident on any transfer to a new school even if it took place in their own home surroundings; but it seemed to bear out the general impression that the school unit is an important factor in giving the children steadiness and security in their new conditions.

There were two children who had been drafted into a new school without any of their old companions, a boy of five years, and a girl of thirteen, both of whom settled in particularly well, the girl feeling compensated by the fact that she had moved from a Senior to a Central School where she felt herself much more on her own level. On the other hand there were cases where children, previously settled and happy, appeared to get restive when their own special school friends returned home to London. Although this problem was not investigated in detail, it seems probable that school friendships played a comparatively important part in the successes and failures of evacuation.

CHAPTER VII

CHILD GUIDANCE IN A RECEPTION AREA

THIS CHAPTER describes what some members of the staff of a Child Guidance Clinic found to do over a period of ten months in a reception area, how they attempted to do it and how they worked with the services already established for dealing with nervous and difficult children. It shows some work that was satisfactory and some that was not and it also bears on the matters discussed in Chapter VI.

Child Guidance is now a recognized community service which aims at restoring and fostering satisfactory development in the less stable child. The Clinic helps to discover his natural gifts and to assist his parents at home and teachers in school to deal with him more wisely. Psychiatrists, educational psychologists and psychiatric social workers are the specialists taking part in the work of diagnosis and treatment for the children who come to Child Guidance Clinics.

Child Guidance in Normal Times. Child Guidance Clinics have been established in this country for just over twelve years. They have set out to deal with that group of children and young people up to the age of about seventeen who show behaviour and characteristics deviating so much from the normal as to be disturbing to themselves and to those with whom they associate. The close interaction between the child and his family makes it, as a rule, unprofitable to deal with him as an isolated unit. He is born into the world with certain inherited trends, but from the moment of birth he is subject to the effects of his parents', brothers', and sisters' feelings and attitudes towards him, and later, but to a lesser extent, to the attitudes of his teachers, his friends, and his employers. He feels safe with them or threatened by them, and he learns gradually to make his adaptations accordingly. Thus character is formed and life-long modes of thinking and feeling are established. Some children adapt more quickly to the outside world;

others appear to be more influenced by forces within themselves.

Most of the children seen in the Clinics are within the normal limits of intelligence, yet by reason of difficulties of an emotional kind, some of them are unable to use their intelligence to the full. Continued failure in learning produces further emotional problems. These children therefore have to be helped to real achievement so that self-confidence may be re-established. This is difficult for the teacher of a large class to bring about in these special cases.

The educational psychologist, therefore, starts off the new learning process, in co-operation with the child's teachers. Sometimes it is personal contact with an understanding adult which in the end achieves success rather than the particular method used. The examination of the child's intelligence in the clinic gives the psychologist the knowledge of where and how to start with remedial teaching.

Other children have from their early years shown signs of anxiety and nervousness either directly as open fears or indirectly, expressed in bad habits, sleeplessness, day dreaming, babyishness, and many other symptoms. Some are remote, friendless children, thwarted in their relationships by their own distrust of themselves. Others again are irresponsible, given to temper outbreaks, quarrelsomeness, defiance, truancy, delinquency. It is for the whole Child Guidance team working together to discover in the child's personality and in his past history and relationships the factors which have caused his unhappy, a-social attitudes, and to work with the child, his parents and the school towards a deeper understanding and a more satisfactory way of living. Some children are so involved in their own inner phantasies that they are unable to make ordinary contacts and to learn by everyday experience. It is for the psychiatrist, then, by his insight and knowledge to help the child to relate his inner experiences to the world about him, and so to integrate both inner and outer resources.

Emergency Child Guidance. At a time when the normal securities of life are continuously threatened and separation from a known environment has to be faced by children, not all of whom are stable enough to meet added difficulties, it is to be expected that help will be wanted in dealing with those who find the strain too great. The known methods of Child Guidance must be modified to meet special needs, but the basic aim remains constant—to discover the child's capacity to meet the demands of life and to make such changes in his environment and in his personality as will help him to do so in the most constructive way.

Since evacuation began, many children have gone through much strain. Some have thriven happily on the new life in the country, but many have felt not only their own insecurity but that of their parents and homes. Some who were difficult even at home in times of peace have become much more troubled. Others have shown signs of strain for the first time. When the burden on the householders is also taken into account, it is easy to see the kind of difficulties which may arise in the foster homes. The foster parents readily feel impatient with the awkwardness or the feelings of resentment and revolt of the older boys and girls, with the homesickness of younger children and the devious and unpredictable ways in which this may be expressed. The foster parents need skilled help to enable them to see the children's unspoken needs and to go on exercising a patience which may be already stretched to breaking point.

The First Days. At the outbreak of war, the Child Guidance Clinic attached to the general hospital in Cambridge was working on a part time basis. At the end of the fourth week of evacuation a Child Guidance social worker offered her services to the billeting authorities. Six weeks later it became possible to establish a small training unit in a house near the hospital and with the co-operation of the Hospital Clinic to undertake there the practical work of seventeen students training for this type of social service in the Mental Health Course at the London School of Economics. Altogether, for most of the session, in the combined unit of the Hospital Clinic and the Training Centre, there were four part-time psychiatrists, with the addition of a fifth for several months, one full-time and two part-time psychologists, a speech therapist, two full-time social workers and one part-time. One psychiatrist and one social worker were involved in training students so that their time was less directly available for work with children.

Before the liaison between the existing Child Guidance Clinic and the training unit was established, the social worker referred to above was asked to deal with many immediate and pressing problems, mainly of billeting difficulties. A bicycle basket carried round the only records, and discussions were held in the billeting offices of the Guildhall and in the schools. Foster mothers were given the chance in their own homes to discuss their anxieties and grievances, children were seen in and out of school, and some readjustments were made in consultation with the billeting officers, i.e. Senior Voluntary Workers. Great difficulty was experienced because for the first months there was no emergency hostel into which children about whom a crisis was pending could be temporarily placed. The numbers of children referred by the Local Authorities to the Hospital Clinic had greatly increased, and a few children were also referred to the hospital Child Guidance Clinic by the Training Centre. Some Court cases were worked jointly with the probation officers. The various social organizations did much work on certain cases, which alas! at the point when everything was converging to make some effective plan possible, were whisked back to London. Some parents were seen when they visited on Sundays and there was much correspondence with L.C.C. Care Committees, children's workers and others.

Later Developments and Work Undertaken. The Hospital Clinic continued its work with the assistance of additional staff, since many evacuated children were referred to it mainly by the Medical Officers of the Local Education Committees of the area, and by the family doctors of the children. A number of cases so referred were made available to the Training Centre in order that the students should have good opportunities both for learning and for service.

After the establishment of the Training Centre the usual

records were kept by its members concerning the children dealt with by them. The material described and the figures used in this chapter refer to the children who passed through the Training Centre, and not to those who were dealt with by the Hospital Clinic.

During ten months 187 cases were referred for investigation to the Training Centre, mainly by Senior Voluntary Workers. Of these 32 were given psychological tests but no sustained treatment. Some returned to London before any plan could be carried out. Of the remaining 155, 121 were referred by Senior Voluntary Workers, 21 by Head Teachers, 5 by School Medical Officers, 3 by private doctors, 3 were transferred from the London Child Guidance Clinic, two were referred by Care Committees, one by a probation officer and one by a foster mother. Work varied widely from one or two contacts over a few weeks to regular clinical treatment with weekly visits to foster mothers, interviews with teachers and Senior Voluntary Workers for six months or longer. Some had infrequent contacts over the longer period, or a short period of intensive work with a 'follow-up' visit after several months. In all cases social work was carried out.

Forty-eight children returned to London while they were still receiving clinic treatment. Many more have returned since the cases were closed, but no accurate details about these are available.

The visits of the social workers numbered 699 to billets and 179 to schools. There were 49 consultations with Senior Voluntary Workers and a great many visits were paid in order to find new billets. The parents of 29 children—namely of 19 per cent of the 155 children for whom social service was used—were seen, either in Cambridge or in London. Some of them were seen several times.

Children and Billets. Three members of the Training Centre staff, dividing all the cases between them, made estimates of the quality of all the billets in which the children had been, or were then staying. Their judgments were not based upon any defined standards, but upon their own personal experience of foster homes for children with special needs in peace time, as well as upon the kinds of homes which were available for these children.

Out of the 234 billets in which 155 children had been placed, the staff was only able to judge 171 homes, as they did not have enough information about the remaining 63. At the beginning there was often no record of *all* the billets a child had been in, and transfers were arranged by all sorts of unauthorized persons.

The billets were classified as follows:

	Number	*Percentage*
A. Very good billets indeed	28	12
B. Good billets	63	27
C. Billets regarded as neither particularly satisfactory or unsatisfactory	37	16
D. Unsatisfactory billets	27	11
E. Very unsuitable billets	16	7
Unclassified (insufficient information)	63	27
	234	100

In eight cases the child was definitely unhappy in a home which seemed on other standards to be good; conversely, a child sometimes found happiness for himself in a household which seemed on the face of it to be quite unsuitable. Such cases, breaking through all generalizations, are of special interest, and a few illustrations will be given.

Case I. Girl, aged nine, unhappy in a billet judged to be moderately good. This child was placed with a kindly and patient foster mother. The reason for unhappiness appears to have been connected with the child's past home-life, where she was the odd-man-out in a large and very poor family. She was a chronic bed-wetter. Unattractive herself, she was placed in this billet with another evacuated child who was particularly charming. At school, too, she seemed rather astray. She was dull and very much inhibited.

Case II. Girl, aged thirteen, lonely and homesick in a billet regarded as excellent. This girl was homesick, and unhappy in spite of being in charge of a kindly and considerate foster mother. She was the middle child at home, and apparently less well loved than the others. In the foster home she was alone, and slept in a large bed. She woke often in the night, and longed for an elder sister or a friend. Her elder sister was quite happy in a good billet with the younger brother, and was inclined to be impatient with this child's homesickness. Later on, after a visit home, this girl was placed in another billet, with a friend.

Case III. Girl, aged six, anxious and unhappy in a billet regarded as very good indeed. This child wetted her bed and complained of stomach pains, for which no physical cause could be found. She was placed in a superior billet, where the foster mother had sound principles of care and management. The home was about the same social level as the child's own home. Nevertheless this child was much happier when she was moved to a home run in a haphazard sort of way. In this large household of grandparents, grown children and their babies, there was much spontaneous affection. It seemed to offer just the kind of reassurance needed by a child who had been distressed at home by scenes of physical violence between her own parents.

Case IV. Boy, aged ten, unstable and depressed in two good billets. This boy seemed to carry over his personal difficulties regardless of the quality of the foster homes in which he was placed. He was dreamy, depressed and unstable, with messy habits. It was at first thought that he would get along better if he was separated from his brother, who was bright and sociable, and monopolized the son of the household. However, when he was separated from the brother and placed in a second, excellent billet he still remained depressed, and the foster home had finally to be changed again. This boy had experienced harsh treatment from his parents. His father was alcoholic. His mother had always worked, and his care had been left to a series of maids.

Case V. Hysterical girl of twelve, placed in a good billet. This girl was excitable and irresponsible. She complained that she was left hungry, and that she had been assaulted. Her foster parents were elderly, and very kind, though being childless themselves they were unused to children. This girl had been brought up in a Public Assistance Home. Her parents' marriage took place after the mother's pregnancy, and she deserted the home when the child was five years old. The father was left with three children and was himself very immature.

Case VI. Delicate boy of eight who did not do well in a good foster home. This child was unhappy, pining, and peaky, and though the foster parents took much trouble to improve his health and to make him feel happier, they could not help resenting the criticism of his poor physique. Transferred to an open-air class where his health improved, this child got along more happily in his billet.

Case VII. Boy, aged ten, who became over-dependent upon his foster mother's affection. This highly intelligent boy became devoted to his foster mother, but was, at the same time, unsettled, sleepless, and difficult to handle. He was precocious emotionally as well as in intellectual development, and the young foster mother found his affection difficult to handle wisely. This boy's family life had been unsatisfactory. His father was unstable, and he was on bad terms with his mother, who was lacking in intelligence.

Case VIII. Brothers, aged thirteen and seven, who improved on being moved from a 'good' foster home to one regarded at first as unsuitable. These two brothers were at first billeted with a middle-aged couple, whose only son was seventeen. It was a home with good standards of care—space to play in, a workshop, and plenty of interesting materials. The foster father and brother were interested in boys and leaders in boys' organizations. Both boys seemed miserably unhappy, and the younger one started pilfering outside. The foster parents were bitterly disappointed that their home was not appreciated, and the boys felt their disapproval. They were rebilleted in a home rather below the economic level of their own home. The foster father was away from home, and there were two other children there. Both boys seemed entirely happy, and the pilfering came to an end. It was discovered that the boys' large family had come in for a good deal of disapprobation from their school in London, and it seemed that they had felt some reflection of this attitude in the superior foster home.

Case IX. Girl, aged ten, who improved on being moved from a 'good' foster home to an overcrowded home of much lower standards. This girl was placed with a pleasant, elderly woman, where she was given much that she had never been accustomed to—varied meals, a pretty room of her own, and special expeditions with her foster mother. She fretted, lost her appetite, and seemed sullen. She was rebilleted in a rather overcrowded home of much lower standards than her own. Here she was an inconspicuous member of a large family of adults and late adolescents. She ate normally, regained her lively expression, and ran the streets happily and without getting into any trouble.

The Need for Trained Visitors. Although the billeting arrangements in Cambridge were probably more adequately organized then in many places, exaggerated reports about the children's difficulties or bad behaviour were often made by the Friendly Visitors to the Senior Voluntary Workers. When such reports led to the child's being referred to the Training Centre, they were investigated by the social workers.

Sometimes it turned out that the reports had been exaggerated, sometimes the foster mother's feelings had changed after her first explosion to the Friendly Visitor. In these cases quite different situations had to be dealt with. For example: One gentle, rather nervous boy of fifteen was reported to be defective, with filthy habits. On further investigation it was found that the boy was merely rather dreamy, with a high average intelligence and rather careless table manners and lavatory habits. He was, however, billeted with middle-aged, highly academic foster parents who had no children of their own and who wanted him to be a fit intellectual companion for themselves.

Again, a thirteen-year-old girl was referred to the Clinic because she was 'beyond control', staying out late at night and being 'involved with boys'. The foster mother turned out to be herself a mere girl, of dullish intelligence, about to have her first baby. The foster child's young sister, a pretty, docile child of seven, fitted into the household easily, but it was a bare and unattractive house and there was nothing for the older girl to do in the long evenings. Billeted with an older woman with growing-up children, a pleasant house, where it was possible to sit round a table and play games and do needlework, this girl was perfectly happy and much liked, and apparently had no desire to go out in the dark with boys.

A boy of eleven was referred for 'filthy habits', i.e. masturbation. It was found that the boy had acute scabies in the pubic region undiscovered for a week or more, and was sleeping in the same bed with two other boys because the foster mother always liked to keep one bed in case her son on service should return.

These and similar instances indicate how important it was to investigate a complaint immediately, since complaints were often made, particularly in the early months, on most flimsy evidence. Some Friendly Visitors did excellent work, but others had comparatively little idea how to approach householders, what to look for, and how to encourage them to go on trying with children who were showing slight symptoms of disturbance.

Symptoms for which Children were referred to the Clinic and the Training Centre. An analysis was made of the complaints for which the hundred and fifty-five children were referred to the Clinic and Training Centre. Many children were said to need treatment for more than one symptom. The total number of symptoms for which these children were referred was two hundred and seventy-nine.

Of the 155 children, 103 (66 per cent) were boys and only 52 (34 per cent) were girls. This disparity is interesting, since there is no evidence that there was a greater number of evacuated boys than girls in Cambridge during the period in which they were seen at the Clinic. The corresponding peace time figures, in one large London Child Guidance Clinic situated in the same borough as one of those from which these children came, show there is little difference in the numbers of boys and girls referred, though when there is any difference there are more boys than girls. Possibly boys' troubles are more difficult to deal with than those of girls; possibly there are more of them, particularly in other people's homes.

The ages of the boys ranged from four to seventeen years, and of the girls, from four to fifteen years.

The symptoms *complained* about did not always correspond with those which were found by the Clinic to need attention; as we have seen, some of the complaints were unfounded, and many were exaggerated. It is likely also that children were referred for those symptoms which were a nuisance rather than for those which might be regarded as signs of anxiety. The list is therefore of interest mainly in suggesting the difficulties most troublesome to local residents and to teachers rather than the true incidence of symptoms amongst children separated from their parents. By far the most frequent problem was bed-wetting, or enuresis. Seventy-five children (48 per cent of all the children referred) were troublesome in this respect. In 40 cases it was combined with other difficulties, but in 35 it was the only difficulty about which complaint was made. Another 19 children soiled themselves, so that incontinence of one kind or another was shown by 94 children (over 60 per cent).

Stealing or petty pilfering was the next most frequent symptom about which complaint was made. This occurred in 25 cases (16 per cent).

These are considerably the most frequent of all the symptoms, and are perhaps amongst the most clearly recognized. Many of the other difficulties are described by words which have no constant meaning, and the divisions between them may be arbitrary and relative to points of view about manners and morals. They will therefore be grouped together more broadly in the order of their frequency.

The following complaints were made in from five to nine per cent of all the children:

Quarrelling: 13 (8 per cent); 'Troublesomeness': 12 (7 per cent); Unhappiness, Homesickness: 12 (7 per cent); 'Dirty habits': 9 (6 per cent); Sex habits (talk and behaviour): 9 (6 per cent); Temper tantrums: 8 (5 per cent).

The following complaints were made in from one to four per cent of all the children:

Disobedience: 7 (4·5 per cent); Backwardness, Lying, Sleep disturbance: *each* 6 (4 per cent); 'Impertinence': 5 (3 per cent); Dreaminess: 4 (2·5 per cent); Crying, Anxiety, Speech difficulty, Destructiveness, Sullenness, Babyishness, Nervousness, Staying out late: *each* 3 (2 per cent); Dirtiness, Nail-biting, 'Shouting and Moaning', Restlessness, Unsettled, Defiant, Roughness, Boasting and Aggressiveness, Hypochondria, Wandering, Worrying, Fearfulness, *each* 2 (1 per cent).

The following complaints were made about less than one per cent of the children:

Friendless, Discontentedness, Bad Table-manners, Tics (nervous movements), Spitefulness, Swearing,[1] Night-terrors, Truanting, Solitariness, Hoarding, Complaints of assault (unconfirmed), Sulkiness, Excitability, Acute pain at menstrual periods, *each* 1 (0·6 per cent.)

Results of Intelligence Tests. Forty children attending the

[1] This complaint was made about a five-year-old.

Training Centre were given tests of general intelligence. The range of intelligence quotients was from 59 to 151. The average intelligence quotient was 97. One child was found to be mentally defective, and three were rated as 'dull'.

TYPES OF TREATMENT AND RESULTS

Type of Treatment	*Re-covered*	*Greatly Im-proved*	*Im-proved*	*Not Im-proved*	*Total*	*Per-centage*
Social Service only	5	1	17	11	34	26
Change of Billet with Social Service only	11	2	9	1	23	18
Psychiatric Treatment with Social Service	1	5	21	15[1]	42	33
Change of Billet and Psychiatric Treatment with Social Service	—	2	6	—	8	6
Placement in Emergency Hostel and Psychiatric Treatment	—	1	14	5	20	15
Transfer to Open Air School only	—	—	3	—	3	2
Totals	17	11	70	32	130[2]	100
Percentages	13	8	54	25	100	

[1] Includes one mentally deficient child.

[2] It is only possible to give results for 130 children out of the 155 who were referred, because 25 returned before they were treated. Out of the 130, 34 children were treated, but returned before the treatment was completed; of these 10 are included in the total of 'improved' and 22 in that of 'not improved'. This makes the results look less satisfactory than they might otherwise have been.

The higher proportion of successes than is usually found in Child Guidance Clinics working under normal conditions is probably accounted for by the fact that some cases were referred for treatment on insufficient grounds, and were found not to be problems.

Improvement under treatment in all types of cases is not as a rule achieved in a quick or spectacular way, although a few difficult cases have been known to clear up after one or two consultations with one or more members of the staff. It is our more usual experience in normal times that regular weekly or twice-weekly interviews with parent and child over a period of about six months are essential in order to make any real headway with fairly long-standing problems, whilst some need as long as two years. But it is not to be expected that foster parents will co-operate in the same way as the child's own parents. It should be noted too that out of the total of 155, only 62 children were fully examined. Absent parents, and the lack of an early history of the child were additional handicaps in diagnosis and treatment.

Social Work and the Time Factor. From the social worker's point of view, there is an immense amount of time spent rather unproductively on Child Guidance in a reception area. So many people are already involved in the child's interest, all of whom have some information to contribute before the clinic examination and treatment can be got under way. The absence of the parents means that there is delay in getting their consent, and that the most direct source of knowledge is lacking, at any rate in the early stages. Those who are teaching the child may not have known him previously. Foster mothers take very divergent views of their responsibility for other peoples' children, and changes in billets make the tracing of reliable information about the child very difficult. For example, one girl of ten years, referred for homesickness, was summarily removed by her mother just after treatment for severe hysterical symptoms had, with great difficulty, been arranged. She was brought for this purpose from the country to the borough. This involved much correspondence and telephoning between various departments. Fourteen visits were made to foster homes and three to schools by the clinic social worker. The assistant organizer of the L.C.C. Children's Care Department did much preliminary work while the child was still in the country. Abortive work such as this is, however, inevitable, and it is counter-balanced by that which is quickly possible and fruitful, and which eases friction all round. The above case need not have involved so much time had an emergency hostel been already available.

The Emergency Hostel. The hostel has been used for a number of children with difficult problems. The children have remained there for periods varying from a few weeks to five months. Regular contact between the superintendents of the hostel and the Clinic and Training Centre has been maintained, and reports on the children exchanged. Mental Health students have been allowed to work there both for purposes of hearing about the children and also for helping with the children themselves, thus enriching their experience. The greatest possible value is attributed to this hostel for unstable children under treatment. Children have made astonishing progress in reaching a greater measure of maturity and adaptability, and this has been largely due to the insight and competence of those in charge.

CHAPTER VIII

CHILDREN WHO WENT HOME

I

WE USUALLY ask the question 'Why?' when something happens which jerks us to attention because it is unexpected. In a country in which it is generally agreed that the family is the greatest source of security and incentive, it seems odd to ask why children go home when there is no obvious reason for their staying away. The more sensible question would perhaps be, "Why did they stay?'

Most parents sent their children away because they expected to be fiercely bombed. It would have been surprising to find the majority of parents public-spirited enough to remain separated for the sake of some slight danger, less, we were told, even in July 1940, than the risks of the road. Still less would one expect people to be affected by a theory of the advantages of dispersal.

Parents could hardly have had any doubts, however, as to what were the views of the authorities on the question. Propaganda had been issued, during the winter of 1939–40, through wireless, newspapers, posters and pictures. Children beamed from a poster in which London parents were urged to 'Keep them happy, keep them safe'. Social workers and teachers must have lent added weight. It did not therefore seem surprising to parents to be asked, during the first six months of evacuation, why they brought their children home.

It might be supposed that they would expect some reproach to be laid at their doorstep and that their explanations would tend to meet this expectation rather than to be a spontaneous expression of their feelings. For this reason we were glad to have skilled interviewers who would be capable of a disinterested weighing of motives and not only of recording what was said.[1] In as many cases as possible, evidence was also obtained from teachers and from the Childrens' Care offices, but most teachers were away from London at the time, and Tottenham had no Children's Care service. The main witnesses, then, in this part of the survey, were the children's mothers and fathers, and the evidence must be looked at with this fact in mind. It was not even possible in many cases to check their statements about the difficulties in foster homes, as the records of the Senior Voluntary Workers in Cambridge were not generally kept, and in any case there had not been time to make more than very brief notes.

Our inquiry in the homes of children who had gone back to Tottenham and Islington covered more than just the reasons for their return. We undertook this study partly in order to check some of our observations about the children in Cambridge, and we therefore included some of the same questions—such as the number of billets they had been in, and the reasons for change; the number of parents' visits, and any special difficulties that the child had shown before and after evacuation. To these we added questions belonging entirely to the child's home and his return to it, financial difficulties, changes in the child's behaviour, his attitude to war dangers, the parents' views about evacuation in general and about the question of sending their child away again.[2]

Brief particulars about the two sets of facts are set out in the table opposite.[3]

In a first glance at the reports from both boroughs certain differences are worth noting.

It has already been said that there were too few young children in the Tottenham groups for it to be taken as representative of all the evacuated children from the borough. This is true also of the children who returned. There was

[1] For this part of the investigation we are indebted to Miss N. M. Lindzell and Mrs. K. Edkins, both psychiatric social workers, loaned for the purpose by the Mental Health Emergency Committee. Miss Lindzell was entirely responsible for the visits in Islington.

[2] The card of inquiry is reproduced in Appendix IV, p. 222.

[3] A table of the distribution of age and sex will be found in Appendix III, p. 216.

no statistical evidence that the age or sex of the children influenced the rate of return home.

	TOTTENHAM	ISLINGTON
Number of children	69	81
Number of households	50	81
Latest date of return of child	December 1st, 1939	March 1st, 1940
Dates between which interviews were held	January 8th and February 12th, 1940	April 6th and June 16th, 1940
Proportion of returned children to those still in Cambridge (approximate only)	One quarter of the Tottenham children in Cambridge had returned	One half of the Islington children in Cambridge had returned
Proportion of all the returned children who were visited (approximate only)	About three quarters[1] (69)	About one fifth (81)
Average length of the children's stay in Cambridge	8·3 weeks	11·5 weeks
Average length of the children's stay in one billet	4·9 weeks	8·8 weeks

In the Islington study we chose the sample on the basis of the proportion of boys and girls of the three different age groups still remaining in Cambridge.[2] In order to get a larger sample of homes we included only one child from each home even when brothers and sisters had been together. It will be noticed that there are more girls than there are boys from both the boroughs, and in the Tottenham study there seems to be an undue proportion of adolescent girls.

The other main difference was in economic circumstances, but this was perhaps less marked than we had anticipated.

The visitors judged of these standards on two different criteria. The first was an estimate of income, judged by the

[1] The only cases deliberately excluded were seventeen which the Director of Education thought, from his previous experience, it was inadvisable to visit. As the Research Committee were unaware of the character of these homes, their exclusion may have affected the findings in some unknown way.

[2] For age groups, see Appendix III, Table X, p. 216.

father's occupation and the general equipment of the household. On this basis homes were rated according to definitions widely used by Child Guidance Clinics, as *comfortable*, *moderate*, *marginal* or *dependent*. The second was the standard of housekeeping, defined as 'care of physical needs', and the interviewers were asked to rate this as *good*, *fair* or *poor*.

In the Tottenham borough none of the children had returned to homes rated as 'dependent', whereas in Islington six of the homes (7·5 per cent) fell into this category.

More reliable evidence as to the economic circumstances of the Islington homes comes perhaps from the assessment of families for billeting payments. Only about three-fifths of the parents had been assessed, as the children of the others had been brought home too soon. Of these 9 (18 per cent) had apparently been excused payment on account of low wages, unemployment, or dependence upon public assistance. In some of these cases allowances were deducted on account of the childrens' absence. It appears therefore as though the poverty of these households may have been somewhat underrated by the visitors. In this small sample of forty-seven households, there is, however, a fairly close correspondence between the proportion of parents paying the full standard charge of 6*s*. a week,[1] and the proportion for the country as a whole, so that the Islington families may perhaps be taken as fairly representative from an economic point of view.[2] A proportion of the parents had however brought their children home in order to avoid making payments, so that although about 45 per cent of those assessed had paid the full 6*s*. whilst their children were away, there would probably be a considerably smaller proportion of all parents who were able and willing to pay this amount.

[1] Parents who could afford more than this were invited to pay the full cost of 9*s*., but there was no legal obligation to do so.

[2] Of some 270,000 parents who have evacuated their children over 40 per cent are paying the full 6*s*. a week or over (*The Times*, January 30th, 1940). The figure for London was 37·3 per cent (*Hansard*, February 6th, 1940).

Number of Islington households assessed: 47/80 (59 per cent).
Number who had actually made any payments: 29/47 (62 per cent).
Number assessed at 6*s*. a week: 23/47 (49 per cent).
Number who had actually made payments at 6*s*.: 21/47 (45 per cent).

Unfortunately we were not able to compare the Tottenham and Islington households in this respect as the Tottenham study was undertaken when there had only been about six weeks for payments to be made. Nevertheless six households out of the sixteen who were making 6*s*. payments stated that they found it a hardship.

At the upper end of the economic scale we found 7 (10 per cent) of the Tottenham children, and 6 (7·5 per cent) of the Islington children came from homes rated as 'comfortable'.

There was some difference between the two boroughs in the standard of housekeeping. In Tottenham over three-quarters of the children returned to homes where the standard of material care was 'good'; in Islington, not quite half. On the other hand, housekeeping was rated as 'poor' in only two Islington homes and one Tottenham home.

It is perhaps worth while noting that in spite of this fairly good standard of physical care in the homes, we found amongst the Tottenham children still in Cambridge a proportion of verminous children which is apparently usual for the country as a whole.[1] Six per cent of the Tottenham children in Cambridge were reported as verminous. On the other hand there was not one case among the sixty-nine children returning to fifty households in Tottenham in which there had been any record of previous attendance at a Cleansing Station. It seems possible either than children were taken back to the homes of better standard first, or that evacuation itself did lead to a spread of this condition. Some of the helpers testified to this from personal experience.

Summarizing then, it may be said that very few of these children came from homes in which the standard of care was extremely low; that about one-twelfth of the Islington and none of the Tottenham homes were very poor indeed; and that about half the children from both boroughs came from households in which weekly earnings must be very carefully laid

[1] Padley, R., and Cole, M., Ibid., p. 99: It is thought that if evacuees from the real East End are excluded, about 5 per cent of the evacuated children were verminous. Reported by Mr. Ede in the House of Commons, March 5th, 1940, *Hansard* 358, Col. 340. (Ed. note. This figure apparently includes cases of scabies and impetigo, which are not included in our figures).

out, and in which savings are almost non-existent. The rest came from households of moderate comfort and security.[1]

Although it is true, in a sense, that the return needs no explanation other than the absence of raids, yet the fact remains that at least half the children remained away. The only method of arriving at reliable conclusions would be to compare the individual children and home circumstances of those who stayed in Cambridge with those who went home, but unfortunately this was not possible.

It could hardly be expected that a clear cut answer could as a rule be found in any given case. Human behaviour is generally determined by a great variety of motives and circumstances. In spite of this it does often seem possible to discover certain 'key' motives or conditions without which a decision would not have been taken, though other influences contributed towards it. This search for key motives has been made in the study of the reasons for return, although there were generally three or four reasons found in each case.

Here are two illustrations of the way in which the reasons were classified as of principal or subsidiary importance in the decision that was made.

Case I. Girl. Aged 14. Returned: Christmas 1939.
Father's Occupation: Civil Service Clerk. *Economic Standard:* 'Comfortable'. *Housekeeping:* Good. *Rate of Payment:* 6*s*. *Parents' Visits:* 6 or 7.

Reasons given by Mother. When Margaret[2] came home at Christmas time, the mother found she had not had a bath for three weeks. She found her clothing very dirty—vest wanted washing, etc., and she was generally dissatisfied with the care given in the billet. As Margaret was fourteen mother asked her whether she wanted to stay at home, and she was finally allowed to do so.

Reasons inferred by Visitor. From mother's account Margaret is an unenterprising girl, who did not help herself at all by suggesting clean clothing, etc., and had not been encouraged to think for herself at home. Reason given by mother probably correct, as mother did not want her home for economic reasons.

Main Reason for Return. Foster home (mother dissatisfied).

Other Reasons. Girl immature, irresponsible. Holidays.

[1] For Tables of Economic Circumstances and Standard of Housekeeping, see Appendix III, Tables XI and XII, p. 217.

[2] All names are fictitious.

Case II. Girl. Aged 7. Returned: November 4th, 1939.
Father's Occupation: Bus Driver. *Economic Standard:* 'Moderate'. *Housekeeping:* Good. *Rate of Payment:* 16*s.* for three children. *Parents' Visits:* 2 or 3.

The request for payment coincided with calling up of two elder brothers of child for military service; these lads had contributed 20*s.* each weekly to household and the sudden reduction in family income led parents to feel contribution asked was impossible. Family moved to cheaper house in consequence of this reduction. Would feel some payment reasonable, but not so much as asked.

Main, and apparently only reason for return: Financial.

An analysis of all the cases[1] from both boroughs brings out quite clearly the three most important reasons for the child's return, other than the absence of danger. Broadly speaking these are the same, whether we are looking for *essential* causes (those without which the child would probably not have returned home at all), or for *all* the causes that contributed to his return. There is, moreover, no marked difference between the two boroughs in this respect. This is in itself an interesting conclusion, since it seems to show that in spite of changes in external events, and of some contrasts in standards of home life, there remained certain steadily operating influences.

The three most important reasons were: (1) family ties, showing themselves either in the anxiety and loneliness of one or both parents without their children, or in the homesickness or persistent desire of the child himself to return home; (2) parents' dissatisfaction with the foster home, or their wish to avoid another change of billet; (3) financial—either the cost of billeting in money and clothes and of their own travelling; or the need to have a child of wage-earning age at home, either to work or to help in the house.

When the records were first analysed the fact of the parents' anxiety and loneliness as a reason for the child's return was kept separately from the child's homesickness. It soon became apparent that this was a rather artificial separation,

[1] One hundred and fifty children from one hundred and thirty-one homes were used for purposes of this study. For detailed statement of figures, see pp. 218-9.

9

particularly as the whole story came as a rule from the mother. When these two causes were grouped together and regarded as 'family relationships', they accounted as a main reason for about one-third of the homecomings. In a good many cases the mother described the initiative as coming from the child, and in a few of these there was evidence that the child had in fact left the foster home and found his own way home.

It is the strong impression of those who talked with the parents that their own loneliness and worry entered particularly into the description of their child's homesickness, and also in various ways and degrees into all the other reasons for return.

The following case, in which a child was brought home mainly because of the mother's need for her, illustrates the combination of influences as described by the mother:

Case III. Girl. Aged 13. Returned to London: September 1939.
Father's Occupation: Chef. *Economic Standard:* Comfortable. *Housekeeping:* Good. *Payments:* Question did not arise. *Parents' Visits:* 1.

Kathleen is an only child. Her mother stated that she was not well (sores on her face), and was also unhappy. It was the visitors' strong impression that the mother was lonely and dependent upon Kathleen for company. 'She does not appear to have a very intimate relationship with her husband, and Kathleen is her main emotional outlet. The father was furious that the mother brought her home.' The mother said that she would not send her away alone again, but thought that she might go with Kathleen if she could bring herself to leave her relatives in the neighbourhood.

Summing up the family, the visitor wrote: 'The father is ambitious and absorbed in his work, which takes him away for long hours. He has not time to return from the West End in his free time in the afternoon, so leaves at 8 a.m. and returns at 11 p.m. Mother appears immature and anxious. No sign of affection between parents—no quarrelling, but mutual indifference. Father is 'a bit old-fashioned', according to mother. . . . Wanted to be strict with Kathleen, but isn't at home much, and thinks mother spoils her. Mother does everything for Kathleen, but is dependent on her.'

Kathleen's teacher described her as 'a very dependable child . . . her teacher's right hand'. Both from the mother's and the teacher's account, she is evidently mature for her years.

The question of the child's homesickness is a subtle one, and conclusions should only be drawn with great caution.

The expression of this kind of anxiety varies widely in different temperaments and at different ages, and the child may not show his pining in any easily recognizable way. This is particularly true of the very young child. We did not feel justified therefore in comparing the age groups in relation to homesickness, though the indications were that the feeling was more often clearly expressed and of course was more easily acted upon by the adolescents.

The following case is an illustration of the older group:

Case IV. Girl. Aged 13. Returned to London: November 23rd, 1939.
Father's Occupation: Tailor. Often out of work. *Mother:* Home piece-work: box-making. *Economic Standard:* Marginal. *Housekeeping:* Good. *Payments:* Deduction by Unemployment Assistance Board. *Parents' Visits:* 2.

Rose is the eldest child in a family of three girls. Her mother, described as 'a very pleasant and quiet woman', said that Rose 'fretted inwardly' whilst she was away. It had been reported to the mother by friends visiting Cambridge that she was looking ill because of homesickness, so she decided to bring her home. Subsequently, she heard from a younger girl that Rose cried herself to sleep every night 'for fear of what would happen to them if father and mother were killed in London'. The mother herself had visited Rose twice in eleven weeks, and she had no complaint to make of the billet, though she is inclined to think that it is best for children to stay with their parents, and would not consider sending this child away again.

Rose had a slight stammer, but the symptom did not become any worse through evacuation. Some time before she went away she had developed twitching movements which it was thought might be chorea, but this had already quite cleared up, and did not recur whilst she was away from home. The mother said that she took after her father, who was 'nervy'. She took a sensible attitude towards the child's stammer.

In order to discover how far the mothers' own nervousness or loneliness entered into her description of the child's homesickness, a separate analysis was made of thirteen cases in which the main cause of the child's return was attributed to the child's fretting or desire to come home. There was no evidence of unusual anxiety on the part of these parents; in fact there seemed only one case of serious worry, which may have led to the mother imputing her own feelings to the child

This was an Italian family in which the father was epileptic. The reasons given by the mother for return ran as follows: 'Child was unhappy, and mother said that as she is 'nervy' and there is a family history of epilepsy, the parents thought it best to bring her home.' Both the father and the younger sister were said to have fits. The mother was described as over-anxious: 'going round frequently to the playground to watch this child and her sister.' The child was described by the mother as excitable and difficult.

In most of the remaining families of this group the family relationships seem unusually close and mutually affectionate, and though in one or two of them the child is described as 'spoilt', 'unduly waited on' or 'indulged', one gets the impression of warmth of affection rather than of over-anxious solicitude. It may be true to say that these parents actually cared for their children so much that they were over-sensitive to their loneliness, but it is impossible to measure degrees of affection.

The second most important reason in order of frequency was the parent's opinion of the foster home. This seemed to account for about one-fifth of the returns. It is difficult, however, to distinguish clearly between this factor and the parents' feelings about changes of billet. In about a tenth of the cases parents seem to have taken their children home either because they had been moved too often, or because they would have to be moved again. In this connection it is worth while noting the special conditions in Cambridge, where many different kinds of demands were made upon local residents for lodgings, and where various types of lodgers and scales of payment could be weighed against one another.[1]

If we put together, then, the parents' attitude towards the foster home and their resentment of the shifting of the child from one billet to another, we find that this accounts for slightly more than a quarter of the returns.

Knowledge of human nature would suggest that parents looking for an excuse to bring their children home would

[1] See Chapter III, p. 41.

tend to blame foster parents for not giving them the proper kind of care. The number of cases in which the foster homes *seemed* to the parents to be unsatisfactory is probably greater than the actual number of poor billets. If this is borne in mind, the proportion of returns due to this cause seems surprisingly low. At an earlier stage in our inquiry it was suggested that perhaps we found a high proportion of satisfactory relationships between the children and their foster parents in Cambridge because most of the boys and girls who did not get along well in their billets had gone home.[1] One answer to this interpretation is that about four-fifths of the children who returned during the first six months did not apparently go home mainly because of difficulties in the foster home, though of course other troubles might have been smoothed out if the foster homes had been of an even better quality than they were.

There have been many interesting accounts of the attitudes of parents towards those who take charge of their children. There is no doubt that jealousy, more or less disguised, is sometimes felt, and a sense of obligation and gratitude may even add to this underlying resentment. Then the mere fact of difference in customs and standards often arouses feelings of anxiety and hostility which may not be formulated as a complaint, or, if they are, may be exaggerated and dramatized.

It was the foster parents themselves who were most frequently criticized by the parents. One comment that recurred often was that the child felt unwanted, or that the hostess seemed to the parents anxious to get rid of the child. Sometimes this was undoubtedly true; but in some cases one gets the impression of parent or child seeking to find a tolerable explanation of their own need for one another. A child crying in the night once fended herself from the comfort of a friend, urging repeatedly, 'I want my mummy. No one else will do,' and there is of course a sense in which this is true for all parents and all children.

The following illustration shows a combination of the mother's need to find an excuse for bringing her son home,

[1] See Chapter II, p. 24.

with what seem to be 'real' reasons for criticism of the foster parents:

Case V. Boy. Aged 9. Returned to London: November 3rd, 1939.
Father's Occupation: Builder of costers' barrows (own business). *Economic Standard:* Moderate. *Housekeeping:* Good. *Parents' Visits:* 3.

Dick was the second child in a family of four, of whom the elder brother, aged fourteen, billeted separately, was not brought home, and a sister, aged eight, had been taken home earlier. A five-year-old brother was not sent away at all.

Dick had had one change of billet, due to overcrowding. He had been placed with four other children, and the hostess said she could not cope with so many for reasons of health.

The mother complained that in the billet the child was not kept clean: his ears were dirty, and his clothing was not properly washed. Every time the parents visited he was unhappy and cried to come home. (The School record confirmed the fact that the child had been homesick.) The mother said that he was obviously not wanted, and both parents felt that this was bad for him. The billet, they said, consisted of an elderly couple of over seventy, and one unmarried daughter. They had been accustomed to undergraduate lodgers, and resented the reduction of income and the increased responsibility of having children.

Summarizing her own impressions, the investigator added: 'Above reasons are in order given by mother with strong feeling. The last point was developed in the course of the interview, and appeared the really important one. Parents resented the attitude of concession on the part of hostess, and "being made to feel like paupers".'

Evacuation was undertaken with some misgiving, especially on the part of the mother, and she was in great need of encouragement and reassurance. The attitude she met tended to increase her initial anxiety. She herself lost her father at the age of three, and was placed in a series of foster homes, so knows what it means to be looked after for profit or on sufferance. She is anxious for her own children to have a happier time, and is particularly sensitive on the subject of foster homes.

The parents in this case had not yet been required to make payments, but the mother said that they would not have minded paying maintenance. They paid what they were asked to (apparently by the foster parents), for extras, e.g. laundry, blacking, etc., but deeply resented the attitude behind the demand for such payments —the phrase that 'some compensation' was required for wear and tear on furniture, etc. (Mother said the arm-chair sagged badly, and she thought the furniture was what the seventy-year-olds had had all their married life!).

The mother stated that Dick seemed unduly quiet when he returned home. He cried often, and had nightmares. Though he had never wet his bed before, he did so in his first billet, where she stated that the children were locked in their room without a chamber.

Her views about evacuation in general were that it was a good thing on the whole for those who wanted it but that it was faulty in method. (Actually it was the father who had insisted upon the children going away.)

'The mother,' wrote the investigator, 'was not anxious for her children to go to an unknown fate. She feels they would be better to perish together; if the children were saved and the parents killed, what sort of a life would they have as orphans? She thinks that schools or colleges should have been commandeered and children put in charge of teachers, matrons, etc., whose job it was to look after children. They should not have been sent to unwilling private homes.'

This mother was obviously prepared for difficulty and acted upon it as soon as it came without seeking further advice.

There is no doubt at all that the expense of keeping the children away was one of the most important influences in bringing them home. The fact that this was true for the Tottenham children, whose parents were less needy, and for whom the problem of winter clothes had not yet arisen in its most serious form, adds weight to its importance for the children who returned later. It is certain that fewer children would have been sent away in the first instance had the scale of payments been made public.[1] But it was not only the scale of payments that caused difficulty. The regular setting aside of *any* sum of money would be a problem in some families not used to planning in this way. The other costs which in many cases were real extras—clothes, travelling, and postage—proved too much of a strain for many households. In round numbers we found that this fact accounted for the return of about one-fifth of the children. Moreover, when it entered at all into their decision it seems, in the majority of cases, to have done so in a way which quite clearly determined the issue. It is true, however, that this 'reason' was relatively easy to state, and might have come to the surface more quickly

[1] The scale of payments was not announced until one month after the main evacuation had taken place.

in an interview with a stranger. Even when allowances are made for this possible over-statement it seems that the proportion of children returning home could definitely have been reduced if the burden of providing for them had been less heavy.

Included in this group of children who returned home for reasons of cost are boys and girls who reached the age of fourteen and who were badly needed at home, either for their wages, or for the kind of help that would add to the earning capacity of their parents. There was actually some uncertainty in the parents' minds as to the position of the child who was due to leave school, and this fact may somewhat have added to the numbers. It might be thought that the proportion of children who returned for financial reasons would be unduly influenced by this age group. This does not appear to have been so, however. The proportion of Islington children above and below the age of twelve who returned for financial reasons is exactly the same, and in Tottenham an even larger proportion of children of under twelve returned on account of the strain on the family income.

Many examples might be given of the bearing of family income, and the difficulties of 'managing', on the return of the children. There seem to be two main types of cases. One is the conscientious family of high standards and moderate earnings, who find that they cannot meet their obligations without falling below the level of home life which they have set for themselves. The other is the poor and sometimes feckless family, living from hand to mouth, unable to set aside a regular sum of money, or dependent upon the support of the children as soon as they reach wage-earning age. As one mother put it, 'At home we can all muck in together.'

One illustration will be given of each of these types of cases.

Case VI. Brothers. Aged 13 and 10. Returned to London: November 19th, 1939.

Father's Occupation: Instalment collector for Furniture Firm. *Economic Standard:* Moderate. *Housekeeping:* Good. *Payment Assessed:* 5*s.* 6*d.* (2*s.* 9*d.* for each of the boys).

John and David were the elder children in a family of three. The whole family was at first evacuated to Cambridge, the mother with a year old baby, and the two brothers together. The mother and baby (for whom fifteen shillings a week had been voluntarily paid), returned to London, leaving the two boys in their billet.

The reasons given by the mother for the childrens' return was, financial stress. The people the two boys were staying with kept asking for clothing, boot repairs, etc. (not unreasonably the mother feels).

'The family' (writes the investigator) 'were at one time in somewhat better circumstances. They are conscientious about payments of all kinds, could not see their way towards meeting all the new expenses, and could not contemplate falling into debt. Mother felt 'an awful sneak' at leaving a doctor's bill unpaid for several months. Family income was reduced by the war, thus making 'managing' more difficult than ever. Mother speaks with enthusiasm of her billet, and that of the boys.'

Were asked to pay 5*s*. 6*d*. for the two boys. Mother feels that this was extremely reasonable, but the combination of circumstances (additional expense plus reduced income) made it impossible for them to meet their obligations.

These parents were full of praise for the arrangements that had been made, though they admitted that they had been more lucky than some people. The family appears to be a self-contained one, with close ties of affection, and mutual feelings of responsibility. The parents are anxious for the children to be out of danger: 'We have lived half our lives, we don't matter so much.' John has a promise of apprenticeship to an engineering firm, and at the time of the visit was helping his father with some of his clerical work in the evenings.

Case VII. Girl. Aged 14. Returned to London: January 1st, 1940.
Father's Occupation: Formerly Horse-keeper. Out of work. *Economic Standard:* Dependent. *Housekeeping:* Fair. *Payment Assessed:* None. *Parents' Visits:* 3. Girl brought home to earn.

This child was the youngest in a family of four, two brothers having recently joined the army. According to the mother the father's unemployment was due to his failing eyesight. The elder brother of seventeen was also out of work. Ellen obtained work in a factory as soon as she returned home, and earned 18*s*. a week.

The record in the Children's Care Department showed that this family had been known to them for years as a source of great anxiety. Home conditions in 1936 reported as 'deplorable'. Father too old and ill to obtain work—used to work with horses and could not learn other work; mother overwhelmed by hopelessness of the position. Parents unable to control any of the children. Both the two eldest brothers (who in 1940 had just joined the army) had

Juvenile Court records, one for sexual misbehaviour with men, and one for assault with intent to rob. Ellen herself, at one time suspected of feeble-mindedness, had been referred to a Child Guidance Clinic for 'dirty habits' and masturbation, and was said by the head teacher to be 'brow-beaten at home, frightened of her father'. The father, however, brought her regularly to the clinic and seemed to take a great interest in her. He actually paid three visits to this child in Cambridge, in spite of the poverty at home.

An interesting sidelight upon this case is that the friend with whom Ellen was billeted in Cambridge came home at Christmas (a month before Ellen), complaining that the foster mother favoured Ellen 'because she had a poor home', and she, Margaret, felt she was not wanted! This is worth noting in relation to Ellen's previous history. The mother acknowledged that she looked well on her return.

These illustrations show that although economic circumstances can fairly clearly be separated out as a reason for bringing the child home, they cannot in fact be understood without regard to the whole standard of family life and to continually changing circumstances. It seems evident that even this aspect of billeting could only be wisely handled by means of individual case work.

Examples have now been given of some of the main reasons for the childrens' return to their homes. These reasons seem to account for about 122 (80 per cent) of all the homecomings. There were, however, other less important influences which it would be important to take into account in making future plans.

Children were quite often taken home on account of illness, or accident—a main reason in 14 (9 per cent) of all the cases. Six had returned on account of infectious illnesses, and six because of skin diseases (almost all scabies and impetigo), apparently acquired in Cambridge. There were several cases in which it appeared that illness might have been prevented if use had been made of the child's previous health record, or if the school nursing service had been properly maintained. There was, for instance, one boy aged ten years who had been regularly under treatment for epilepsy for some years, and whose fits apparently increased in Cambridge because, according to the mother, he was not receiving any treatment. It was sometimes impossible to separate physical illness from family anxiety. Another child was taken home because the parents would not let her go to the local infirmary with an attack of asthma. The teacher said that this twelve-year-old girl was ill and miserable away, and that she was 'the kind of child who ought to be at home'. The visitor reported that the mother's life 'revolved round the care of this child, and that she could not bear to hand over her care to any one else'.

The desire of the members of the family to be together for Christmas played some part in the children's return. This seems to have been the main influence in about 5 (3 per cent) of all the cases, even though the Tottenham children had gone home by December 1st. The general influence of the holidays is clearly shown by the monthly rate of return of the Islington children,[1] though of course the fact of the holidays may only have speeded up the homecoming of those children who would in any case have returned before long. After all, it was perhaps more than could be expected of human nature for the family not to gather round their own hearths for a few days when things seemed pretty peaceful, and then to find it too much of a wrench to part again.

Members of a family who are themselves doing quite well are sometimes taken home because of difficulties with younger or older brothers and sisters, and the child's separation from friends or quarrels with the children in the billet, has played a minor but a not insignificant part.

On the whole judging from *absence* of comment the school situation seems during the first six months of evacuation to have been regarded as fairly satisfactory in Cambridge, and such observations as the 'long distance from school to her new billet', or the lack of facilities for certain kinds of technical education, occur very seldom. It must be remembered that at the time of the return of the majority of these children there were very poor educational facilities in London.

The question of the parents' visits has already been answered in general terms by the comparison between the number of

[1] *Rate of Return of eighty-one Islington Children.*

September	October	November	December	January	February	Total
19 (12%)	10 (22%)	17 (21%)	27 (33%)	5 (6%)	5 (6%)	81

visits each month paid to those who stayed in Cambridge and to those who returned.[1] Individual case studies show, as one might expect, that in a few instances frequent visits were a disturbance both to the child and to the parents. This is not in any way inconsistent with the finding that these family reunions were not on the whole unsettling. Individual examples could equally easily be found of visits that were reassuring to the children and the parents in the families which remained separated.

It is clear from the reports of our investigators that there are all sorts of aspects to parents' visits which may be lost sight of in bare figures. One investigator who worked consecutively in the two boroughs was impressed with the fact that in Islington parents seemed to be much more affected by their neighbours' opinions, and attributed this partly to the closer physical contact of families living in blocks of flats. The motives of parents for keeping their children away or for bringing them back seemed to spread by psychological infection. In some neighbourhoods there grew up a feeling of reproach if you did not care for your child enough to visit him frequently, or even to bring him home. The week-end expeditions became social gatherings, and money was often borrowed to meet the fare. On the station and in the train coming home there was probably plenty of gossip. Grievances sometimes became exaggerated and jealousies fostered. It is interesting to find that among the parents who state that they would prefer camps or boarding-schools for their children, one of the grounds for this point of view is the greater *equality* of treatment that all the children would receive.

There is one feature of the child's return home which has probably been underestimated because of the way in which the evidence was obtained, and because of the fact that it was not possible to get full records of these children whilst they were in Cambridge. This is the influence of the child's behaviour and personality on his return home.

There is no doubt that in some instances what the mother describes as the foster parents, 'not wanting' the child must

[1] See Chapter IV, p. 60.

partly have been due to the fact that he was troublesome. Actually, apart from homesickness, the problems brought about by the child himself only seem to account for about 3 (2 per cent) of all the cases, but they played *some* part in as many as 14 (9 per cent). From an analysis of these problems it appears that the large proportion of those brought home by parents were suffering from what will later be described as symptoms of anxiety or depression; a few were quarrelsome or jealous (unable to get along with the other children in the billet), and two or three were sent home because of delinquency.

It seems probable that in the following case the home was tolerant of low standards and that this boy regarded pilfering as one of the accepted methods of getting his own way.

Case VIII. Boy. Aged 7. Returned to London: November 25th, 1940.
Father's Occupation: Builder's Labourer. Often out of work. *Economic Circumstances:* Dependent. *Housekeeping:* Poor. *Payments:* Assessed at none. *Parents' Visits* (father only): 2.

Jimmy is the eldest child in a family of three. His two brothers, aged five and three, had been evacuated with him, but were not in the same last billet.

During his eight weeks stay in Cambridge, Jimmy was in three billets. The first, which he shared with his brothers, he left, on the suggestion of his teacher, because of suspected pilfering. From the second billet, in which he was very happy, he was taken because of the foster mother's illness.

While in his third billet he brought home some handkerchiefs, a torch and an electric bulb for the torch, on different occasions, and acknowledged that he had stolen them.

He was said to be cheeky to his foster father. To his foster mother he said: 'I shall go on being a naughty boy until Miss X (his teacher) sends me back.'

Apart from the difficulties quoted, his foster mother gave Jimmy quite a good character. He was unusually well mannered, kept himself clean and tidy, got up punctually, and helped in the house. Within the foster home itself, he was absolutely honest, and never touched purse or pennies lying about.

According to his teacher, however, Jimmy was 'an awful pilferer'. She had already caned him for this in Cambridge. She stated that the home was a squalid one (though she admitted that the children were always clean and tidy), and that the father drank. The mother, she said, was a 'dirty, poor, down-trodden creature' who would herself pinch anything she could lay hands on if she thought she would not be found out.

To the social worker who took him to the Child Guidance Clinic in Cambridge, Jimmy spoke wistfully about his second billet where there was a pond in the garden and his foster father made him boats of matchboxes and cork, and took him for long rides in the car. He showed some apprehension about the war, for all his apparent toughness. In his foster home he talked constantly about rationing, and said one day, 'If an Air Raid Warden (warning) goes, I must get my gas-mask and my ration cards and go to school, and stay there until the end of the war.' He was sure that Cambridge would be bombed, but added, 'Our men in the Air Force aren't frightened, are they? Hitler is.' He said that he wanted to be an airman.

According to his teacher, Jimmy was a child of about average intelligence. He was, she said, 'rather a tease, and a bit of a Turk, but no malice, and the others don't dislike him. He responds to kindly treatment and encouragement because he gets none of it at home'.

Jimmy was taken home before another billet could be found for him.

In the Survey interview the mother gave an account of his pilfering in Cambridge, but denied that anything of the kind had happened at home. It was obvious, however, that since his return the child was quite out of hand. He was off with his friends in the streets and his mother found it difficult to get him in at bed-time.

II

Besides the reasons for the child's return to his home, we were interested in discovering how he and his family had been affected by their experiences during the period of separation. Impressions only could, of course, be gained from single interviews, but we felt that conclusions drawn from such visits would at least contain more truth than those based upon the dramatized reports which had been given publicity.

The general view of those who talked with the parents was that although they had brought their children home very few of them harboured any grudge against the authorities or against the foster parents. Even when the foster parents were said not to want the children, it was often felt to be quite natural under the circumstances. There were, of course, some marked exceptions to this, and it was easy to see how one unfortunate incident of bad billeting could spread through a neighbourhood and colour the whole picture. It seems likely that this sort of infectious influence, so easily spread when strong family emotions are aroused, might have been prevented if there had been more skilled service available when things went wrong.

One indication of the parents' attitude towards evacuation was their view as to how it had affected the health and behaviour of their children. Another was their opinion about evacuation in general, and whether they would be prepared to send their own children away again—two attitudes which were found to be by no means consistent with one another.

Parents said that their children's health had been affected in some way in about half the cases. About a quarter of the children were said by their parents to have been very well or to have improved in their health whilst they were away, and about a quarter were not so well or had come back because they had some definite illness. There was no comment about the health of the rest of the children, and it is probably safe to assume that in these cases there was nothing wrong. Although there was no adequate statistical proof, the records gave the impression that girls tended to be taken home more easily on account of their health. This difference was only shown in Islington, where many of the children had returned in the middle of the particularly hard winter, and after an autumn of perfect 'outdoor' weather. It seems likely that mothers tend to be more worried about the health of girls; it is possible also that girls wrote more about the discomforts of the winter in their letters home. Cambridge is a notoriously cold place and 1940 will be remembered for the long frost. There is evidence from the children's essays that they *felt* the cold, both in school and at home. In their own homes they were probably more used to being allowed to play in the room with the cooking going on. It seems a common experience, too, that the increased nervous tension induced by strangeness makes other peoples' homes seem colder. If cold found its way into the children's essays, it is likely that it was described more emphatically in their letters, and this may have made the parents worried about health. There is a further case here for the provision of warm country clothes. Warmth has its psychological as well as its physical aspect.

The change of food also apparently took some getting used to. Both the children and their parents made critical comments about meals, and it is interesting to find that the children's appreciation and criticism is almost always based upon its likeness to or difference from what they have at home.[1]

We asked the parents whether they noticed any other change in their children 'due to evacuation'. Their answers were grouped under changes in happiness, interests, behaviour, attitude to their parents, and attitude to brothers and sisters.

There were very few comments on changes in happiness and in interests. Several parents said that their children were very happy to be at home, but it was difficult to distinguish between this excitement or relief at homecoming, and a more lasting change of mood. Some of the comments upon why children were happier were interesting. Two children were said to be happier because their brothers and sisters were away still, and they had the home to themselves; one because she appreciated the freedom of her home more after a strict foster mother; a fourth because the change had made her more sociable. There were some instances of increased moodiness or depression, which will be discussed later.

Parents noticed changes in behaviour and in attitude towards members of the family in about a quarter of all the children. There is no difference in this respect between the boys and the girls, but there does seem to be some difference between the younger and the older children. On the whole the children under twelve seem to have been more affected by their adventures—or, at any rate, the parents notice the changes in them more than in the older boys and girls.

It will be remembered that in Chapter IV we found that adolescents were apt to get 'up against' their foster parents. It seems likely that at this stage in a child's development difficulties are more often expressed and noticed in terms of relationships, rather than in other ways.[2]

Most of the parents who said that their children had

[1] See Chapter V, pp. 79 and 80.

[2] Cf. Chapter IV, p. 55.

changed as a result of evacuation described these changes in terms of what may roughly be called 'manners' or 'discipline' or in terms of their relationships with other people. Here are a few illustrations:

Case IX. Brothers. Aged 8 and 5. Away ten weeks. Elder boy 'much more pugnacious'. Brother 'restless and quarrelsome'. They fight with one another. (The problem is attributed largely to lack of school on the boys' return.)

Mother most anxious to send the children back to the same billet, where the foster mother is quite anxious to have them. Seems to have forgotten her (the mother's) fear of the river. (These children were brought back because one of the boys tumbled into the river.)

Case X. Boy. Aged 9. Away five weeks. Was very happy in his billet, and his manners and general behaviour were much improved on his return. Mother regrets his return as he is gradually losing his 'lovely manners' (but still cleans his teeth!). 'Does as he likes' at home, but was kept in check in the billet. Mother approves, but cannot imitate.

Case XI. Boy. Aged 14. Away two months. Has developed a sense of responsibility towards mother and sisters. The boy himself decided to come back from his billet. There was nothing wrong with it, but he wanted to come home. Father feels that he did not like the idea of his mother and two elder sisters sleeping alone while father worked at night.

Case XII. Girl. Aged 6. Away three months. More polite. Says 'I beg your pardon'; 'Sorry, Mum', etc.

Case XIII. Girl. Aged 11. Away eleven weeks. More grown up and responsible. More polite. A little less 'I want' and a little more 'Do you think I might have'.

Case XIV. Girl. Aged 11. Away two months. Tendency to be too independent, gradually improving . Has shown less inclination to be controlled by mother—inclined to be 'uppish' and rude.

Case XV. Girl. Aged 13. Away a month. Described as a discontented girl, who became more so after evacuation. She was placed in a 'smart billet' and father seems to have been ready to sympathize with her dislike of this. She would not help in the house when she got home, and the grandmother found her very difficult.

There were more cases of improvement in manners and obedience, judged by the parents, than there were of deterioration.

We had some further evidence of a rather different kind when we asked the parents whether their children had shown

10

any of the symptoms with which Child Guidance Clinics are familiar, either before or after evacuation.

There has been a great deal of discussion as to whether the sudden separation of children from their parents will give rise to serious emotional disturbance, and to undesirable behaviour. The question is far too complicated to be answered in any one study, or after only a comparatively short period of time. We do not yet know enough about the changes which the war may produce in children staying at home to speak with any confidence of the effect of separation. It is possible that apparently good adaptation may be made at some cost to future stability, or that a period of stress may in some children lead to more vigorous development. With all these possibilities in view, it seems worth while to record studies which can throw light only upon one small part of the problem, since at a later stage they may be fitted into a more comprehensive whole.

When we compared the records of the children still in Cambridge with those of the children who returned home, we were given no reason to believe that a large proportion of the nervous or troublesome children were removed by their parents during the first six months of evacuation, for we found roughly the same proportion of children showing some sort of difficulty amongst those who stayed and those who returned. It did seem, however, that children suffering from what we have called symptoms of anxiety tended to be taken home more quickly than the ordinarily troublesome child. Even this conclusion should, however, be accepted with caution. It is well known that teachers and others responsible for looking after other people's children tend to pick out for comment children who are difficult to control, whereas parents become worried about their children's 'nerves'. The difference may therefore be accounted for by the fact that our sources of evidence in Cambridge were the teachers and the Friendly Visitors, whereas in London they were mainly the parents.

We found, then, that the parents spoke much more often about symptoms which indicated anxiety or depression than about any other problem. It was interesting to discover that rather more than half of all the symptoms (many children had, of course, more than one symptom) were shown by the children before as well as after evacuation. In other words, it seems that a large proportion of the children who were fretful and disturbed in Cambridge were children who would have been described as 'nervous' before they were separated from their parents, though their difficulties were probably added to by the strain of parting.

About a third of the symptoms were noticed by the parents only *after* evacuation, though in some of these cases the children had shown other symptoms before. Finally, the parents commented upon improvement in about one-seventh of the difficulties which these children had shown before they left home.

One illustration will be given of each of these three types of cases.

1. SYMPTOMS SHOWN *BEFORE* AND *AFTER* EVACUATION

Case XVI. Girl. Aged 9. Evacuated with elder sister, aged 13. Stayed away for six weeks. Dorothy had always been 'a bit of a worry' to her mother on account of 'nerves'. She had wet herself day and night ever since an attack of scarlet fever, four years since. Before leaving home she was said to be excitable, to have 'nervous movements', and to fidget. These symptoms all persisted in Cambridge.

Dorothy attended a Myopic School in London, and was backward. In Cambridge she had to attend an ordinary school, and was separated from all her friends.

The girls had been placed with a foster mother of nearly seventy, who could not manage the work for both of them. Dorothy was a great anxiety to her elder sister, who had to waken her at intervals during the night in order to prevent her from wetting her bed.

The children's mother was terrified of raids, which she endured in the last war. She would like to go away herself with the two girls, but she cannot afford it.

Other symptoms which were reported by the parents both before and after separation were, in order of frequency: Excitability (7); Frequent crying (6); Fidgeting, or Nervous Movements (6); Shy, or 'Nervous' (6); Sleep Disturbances (5); Food-fads (3); Disobedience (3). No other symptoms occurred as often as three times.

II. SYMPTOMS SHOWN ONLY *AFTER* EVACUATION

Case XVII. Girl. Aged 13. Away fourteen weeks. Eva was said by her mother to suffer from sleeplessness, nightmares, and 'nervous movements' after evacuation. Since returning she has been reluctant to go up to bed alone, and has tossed and turned, sat up in bed, and occasionally cried out. She has started a habit of sucking her fingers and rubbing her mouth.

It appeared that Eva had been separated from her friend in her billet and had shared a bed with another girl whose habits offended her (these were unspecified). The mother was worried by the effect upon Eva, and she felt that the risk of her returning to London was less than the risk of letting her remain and become miserable and nervous.

Eva's elder brother and sister had done extremely well, gaining scholarships, and her teacher thought that she had been put to some strain in competing with them, and in trying to live up to her mother's ambition for her. There was no evidence, however, either from the mother or teachers, of any nervous symptoms before evacuation.

Other difficulties which were noticed by parents only *after* evacuation were: Specific Fears (5); Disobedience (5); Fidgets, or Nervous Movements (3); Sleep Disturbances (3). No other difficulty was mentioned as often as three times.

III. SYMPTOMS SHOWN ONLY *BEFORE* EVACUATION

Case XVIII. Girl. Aged 12. Away six weeks. All previous food-fads are said to have disappeared, and she 'ate heartily whatever was put before her', on her return. Was said to return hungry from her billet.

The parents described Sheila as an excitable girl whose sleep was often disturbed by nightmares. She was said to have been terrified at the prospect of war, and had asked to be sent away. For some weeks previous to the outbreak of war she refused to listen to the wireless.

Her war fears seem to have lessened by the time she returned home. Her parents had never been anxious to send her away, and it was they who decided to bring her back when a change of billet was inevitable.

A somewhat different account of Sheila came from her teacher. She thought her restless and active, but not really 'nervous'. At school she was described as quite normal in her social relationships, and 'a bit fond of the boys'. She was a dancer, and had already taken part in Christmas pantomimes. The prospect of Christmas performances might, it was thought, have influenced her parents in bringing her home.

The Survey visitor thought that the mother was rather proud of the fact that her youngest daughter was 'highly strung', and that she was probably allowed to have her own way at home.

The other problems which seemed to have disappeared or improved after evacuation were: Shyness (3); Disobedience (2). Stealing, Temper, Noisiness, and Nervous Movements are each represented by one case.

It will be noticed that Sheila (Case XVIII) was 'terrified at the prospect of war'. We were naturally interested in the war fears of children, although observations made at this time, when most of the children had only heard two sirens in the first week of the war, and knew them to have been false alarms, could only be speculative, and have long since been superseded by actual observations of children's behaviour under really dangerous conditions. These parents reported fears of raids or other war dangers in 18 (12 per cent) of the children, all except two of whom were under the age of twelve. The parents' report is often guesswork, and is based not only on their knowledge of the child's general response to danger, but also upon their own feelings of apprehension. This comes out very clearly in some of the reports. It suggests that any measures taken to help the child through this experience of fear should be taken in relation to the family, and not only to the children themselves.

This family attitude is illustrated in the following comments, entered under 'Child's Attitude to War Dangers'.

Case XIX. Mother is sure child does not mind them (i.e. air-raids), as 'they won't happen'. Mother herself was in bombed house in last war, and says she now has no fear at all of air-raids.

Case XX. Parents say that child has no obvious fears, while she is with them, but Father refers with anxiety to older sister's St. Vitus' Dance in childhood and chronic facial twitch, because he attributes this to the fact that mother was carrying this baby during air-raids in last war, and is afraid of some effects on this girl if she is in London during the raids.

There were a few children who developed quite specific and articulate fears at the prospect of raids before they had ever experienced them:

Case XXI. Boy. Aged 11. Is very frightened, mother says. 'Can you hear anything?' he says, and wakes up in the night with fears.

On the other hand, some children are able, consciously, at any rate, to take an adventurous attitude towards the prospect of danger:

Case XXII. Boy. Aged 11. Unconcerned. He is dying to use the new air-raid shelter, and is disappointed there has been no warning since his return.

Some of the older boys seem to find in this situation of physical danger an opportunity for chivalry which, rightly used, may even be of value in their development:

Case XXIII. Boy. Aged 14. No fear—feels he must protect mother and sisters, father says.

Case XXIV. Boy. Aged 14. Does not mind war dangers. 'I must take care of you, Mother,' the boy tells her.

We have now learned something of the parents' motives in bringing their children home, and of what they felt had been the effect of temporary separation under war conditions.

It must be remembered that up to the time when all these children had returned home (March 1st, 1940), there had been no bombs dropped either in Cambridge or in London. The second part of this inquiry was, however, carried on until June 16th, and the views that parents gave about the general scheme of evacuation and about whether they would be willing to send their children away again, must be judged against the background of swiftly changing events. The invasion of Holland and Belgium, and the abandonment of resistance in both countries took place between May 10th and 28th, and the retreat from Dunkirk in the following week. On June 4th Mr. Churchill said: 'We shall defend our island whatever the cost may be.' The imminence of mass raids and of invasion was constantly stressed in the Press and on the wireless. Air-raid warnings took place in Cambridge, but not in London, in the week beginning June 3rd. On June 13th newly registered children began to be moved from London, and others were transferred from the coasts. The first bombs to cause death and injury in Cambridge itself fell on June 19th, just after the inquiry had been completed.

We found that there was a larger proportion of Islington parents visited between April 6th and June 16th who were unwilling to send their children away again, than there were of Tottenham parents visited between January and March. Rather less than one-third of all the parents said that they were willing to consider sending their children away again, and most of these would consider it only if their homes became really dangerous.

It was the impression of the investigators that most of those who were completely unwilling to send their children away again felt strongly that in times of danger the family must hold together. This was often combined with the view that you simply could not expect strangers to give motherly care to other people's children for any length of time. For example:

Case XXV. Girl. Aged 12. Youngest of four, and only school-girl. Brought home because another change of billet was suggested, and they felt that as she was 'a bit on the nervous side' this would not be good for her. Also her head became 'dirty' (verminous), and this made her miserable.

The parents see no point in sending the child away again. They cannot see why there should be such a strong dividing line between a twelve-year-old and the rest of the family. Think they would do better to stick together. Father was against it strongly from the beginning. He felt that people couldn't be expected to take in a lot of strange children, and it wasn't in the children's interest to send them where they weren't wanted.

It should be pointed out that the difference of opinion between the parents in this case does not seem to be typical. In cases where the parents differed there were considerably more fathers than there were mothers who had wanted to keep their children away, or who would like them to go away again.

Almost all the parents who said they would be willing to send their children away again were willing to do so only under certain conditions—of which the presence of danger was by far the most frequently mentioned. The better choice of billets was the next most important on the list, and, after this, reduction in payment, keeping members of the family together, and keeping school units together.

We asked the parents to give their views about the evacuation scheme in general, and it was interesting to find that in a very large number of cases there was no correspondence between these views and what they intended to do with their child. This is perhaps a helpful warning to research workers relying upon answers to formal questionnaires, in which problems are generalized. It sometimes seemed, indeed, that the suggestions given for improvement in the general plans for evacuation were just those which might conveniently exclude their own child. Thus, school camps would be better said the parents of two girls, but they should only be used for boys!

About three-quarters of the parents were in favour of some scheme of evacuation, but one-third of these thought it should only be adopted when danger was imminent, another third that it should only apply to young children, and others only to children from poor or overcrowded homes.

A few parents had already made definite arrangements to send their children back to the same billet if danger became more acute:

Case XXVI. Boy. Aged 15. Brought home at Christmas, 'rather than change billets'. Boy in home of Cambridge professor.

Parents would take advantage of the Cambridge invitation at the first sign of danger. They thought the general plan of evacuating children a good one. They had no criticisms and no suggestions.

As to the methods of evacuation, only two-thirds of the parents expressed any views; a good many of them seemed unwilling or incapable of picturing it in general terms. Of the eighty-eight parents who expressed their views, about two-thirds were in favour of private billets, and one-third in favour of residential schools or camps.

A number of the parents qualified their approval, both of billets and of camps. Again the most important qualification of the billeting plan seemed to be the better selection of homes, and a few parents would only have been satisfied if they themselves could have had a hand in the choice of home for their child. The following case illustrates this point of view:

Case XXVII. Girl. Aged 14. Brought home because of conditions in the foster home which parents thought 'indecent' for a girl of her age. Girl had to wash in the kitchen with grown-up sons about, and share meals with garage hands.

Parents would send her away again only 'if danger severe, and they could choose the billet'. They feel the general plan of evacuation is good, and are emphatic as to the need if danger arises.

They suggest that parents should be allowed to choose the billet, receive the Government payment, and give this or more to the billeting mother themselves.

The only other suggestion made by any number of parents about the billeting scheme was that school groups should be kept together, as the parents had been promised they should.

The chief influence in the choice of the parents who would prefer camps seemed to be their feeling that it was more than you could expect of human nature for people to mother strange children. For example:

Case XXVIII. Girl. Aged 11. Had been unhappy in foster home, because the foster mother 'had only taken children on sufferance'.

Mother would not send her away again, though she would not have brought her back, she said, if she had been happy.

Mother thinks camps on the whole a much better arrangement, seeing the question from the foster mother's point of view: 'I can understand it was difficult to have strange children when you did not want them—I should not like it myself.'

It was also the impartiality and the guarantee, as they thought, of better care and feeding that seemed to influence some parents in the choice of camps, as the following illustrations show:

Camps a very good plan: 'all treated alike, and doing the same thing.'

. . . . .

Mother thinks that children should be sent to camps, or if to individual billets, catering should be communal, so that a good breakfast and dinner was ensured for all. This method would make it possible to provide adequately for the children with the money available.

. . . . .

Camps better for children than billets because children would then stay with their teachers, which it was understood would be the case when they agreed to let their boy go ('and then they were separated from their teachers').

It has seemed worth while to describe at some length these records of children who went home during the first six months of evacuation, partly because we had the benefit of the same two skilled investigators for all this part of our inquiry and could therefore place special reliance upon the facts and their interpretation, and partly because the whole scheme of voluntary evacuation is dependent upon the attitudes of parents and children. Unless these are understood any scheme will break down.

This record of one hundred and thirty-one families who became re-united after a comparatively short separation shows first and foremost the strength of family ties. Those who are constantly in touch with family life know that this often does not show itself in the simple expression of affection. It may be that bitter antagonisms exist within the family group but that even so the need for belonging may be stronger than the fear of neglect, anger or even cruelty. Scenes in the Juvenile Court constantly illustrate this truth. In time of danger and uncertainty individuals have even greater need for unity and for the reassurance provided by the familiar background of their lives. It seems that only by understanding these needs, and by helping to provide other means for their fulfilment, could family separation be sustained for any length of time.

These records show that in planning for human beings even on the wide scale determined by national crisis, the community cannot afford to separate material needs from the whole texture of individual experience. It is possible to distinguish causes for the movement of members of the family from one place to another, but in fact all these influences are closely interwoven. General plans can and must be made, but in the long run it is extravagant not to provide personal service to which individuals can turn for understanding and help.

This part of the study suggests that in further plans for evacuation it would be worth while to pay some special attention to what might be called the 'nervous family', as well as to the nervous child. Many of the signs of anxiety shown by the child under these conditions could have been recognized before, and were inseparable from the temperament of the parents themselves and the quality of family relationships.

On the whole, in spite of apparent failure of the scheme for these families, there was little expression of bitterness. The difficulties were often inherent in the situation rather than brought about by individual antagonisms, and many of them might have been overcome by a little patient handling on both sides. The study of the returned children seems in the main to confirm our general conclusion that, in time of grave national crisis, a large number of the citizens of Cambridge have been willing to extend hospitality to other peoples' children, and have for the most part done so with kindliness, with generosity, and with a considerable degree of success.

CHAPTER IX

CHILDREN'S RECREATION IN CAMBRIDGE[1]

IN THE September sunshine of the first weeks spent in Cambridge by London children, it hardly seemed necessary to consider plans for their recreation. The very word is a description of something which becomes necessary for city dwellers. Those who knew the lives of young Londoners watched the children of the countryside with their bulging pockets and their fishing tackle going their independent ways along fen and field and river bank, and hoped that the straggling groups of newcomers, at first only too easily recognized, would soon discover for themselves the delights of the countryside. But river swimming, which to the children's joy was free of charge, had to be stopped when the days grew colder. Shortening evenings brought them home straight from school, and left them to their own resources. In other people's homes even those who knew how to find their own interests seemed to feel lost at first. Many of the old familiar belongings had been left at home; perhaps there were no tools, or no place to mess about in; perhaps messing was discouraged. The streets were dark and silent.

It was soon realized that the future contentment of both children and foster parents would depend upon some provision being made for their leisure time, and that teachers could not take the whole responsibility.

On the whole in the pre-war years the Cambridge people do not seem to have shown much interest in the recreation of children. Social workers and representatives of youth organizations say that they found this general apathy discouraging. Public-spirited persons who appealed for support for a particular scheme, such as the establishment of a Youth Centre in Cambridge, found the response disappointingly slow.

[1] This chapter was written in June 1940.

This lack of public support was illustrated by the difficulties which faced the co-ordinating body for juvenile organizations. For a number of years the Juvenile Organizations Committee, which led a struggling existence under successive secretaries, had made various attempts to put fresh life into the services connected with recreation in the Borough. As long ago as 1934 we find this Council reporting on the need for 'the resuscitation on fresh lines of the Cambridge Federation of Girls' Clubs.' Now, six years later, both a Girls' and a Boys' Federation are being formed by the newly constituted Youth Organization Council, which has replaced the Juvenile Organizations Committee. Little evidence was found of support for voluntary efforts from the Local Education Authority, with the exception of the Juvenile Organizations Committee. They had made comparatively small use of their powers to maintain or aid 'facilities for social and physical training in the day or evening.'[1]

The Effect of the War and Evacuation. The outbreak of war and the evacuation of some 3,000 London children to Cambridge brought to the fore the whole question of the use of leisure, and the response was immediate. The Women's Voluntary Services, already organized and prepared for such an emergency, saw the need and at once offered their services. Both the Billeting Authority and the school teachers realized the urgent need to make some provision for out-of-school activities. The National Youth Organizations set going schemes for linking up evacuated members of troops, companies, etc. with units in the reception area. At the same time offers were made locally by a number of people both resident in and evacuated to Cambridge, particularly by a large body of undergraduates, to help meet the situation.

But the immediate effect of the war on some of the existing local juvenile organizations was disastrous. The commandeering of halls and the black-out requirements meant extinction for some. Boys' groups in particular suffered from the loss of young leaders who joined the forces. The darkening evenings under black-out conditions led to a considerable

[1] Education Act, 1921, Sec. 86C.

drop in numbers, especially where younger children were concerned. Some groups which had previously shown signs of decline could not stand up to these added difficulties, and did not revive: for example, the Bands of Hope. Others, however, began to adjust themselves to the new conditions. Arrangements were made for escorting the children to and from their homes, or times of meeting were altered. In addition, four halls, originally commandeered, were soon made available for use as play centres on Saturdays.

SPECIAL EFFORTS TO MEET THE NEEDS OF EVACUATED CHILDREN

THE MACHINERY OF ORGANIZATION

The Women's Voluntary Services. In Cambridge, as we have seen, the W.V.S. undertook the arrangements, under the supervision of the Local Education Authority, for billeting the evacuated children. They recognized the need for out-of-school activities both in the interest of the children, and for the sake of the occasional relief thus given to the foster parents. One of their members was appointed 'Organizer of Occupations for Evacuees out of School Hours' with the task of organizing help, linking up the various groups concerned, securing halls, and doing whatever was needed in the busy period between the reception of the children and their adjustment to their new life.

While this work was undertaken by the W.V.S. of the *Borough*, the *Regional* branch, in co-operation with the local youth organizations, prepared a scheme 'to amuse the children and relieve the householders by means of competitions which the children could do in their billets or home during the black-out and during week-ends.'[1] Individual and group activities were suggested, and certificates were offered for work reaching the required standard, a special award being

[1] Such activities included making a Christmas or birthday present (material to cost not more than 6*d.*), making a toy or model of a boat, compiling a cookery book containing 100 wartime recipes, taking care of an allotment or piece of garden, writing and illustrating a log-book containing a history of the local town or village.

made to a child who won six certificates. The scheme was worked through the school teachers so that there should be no overlapping with school requirements.

The Cambridge Borough Local Education Authority was immediately concerned with the various efforts made. The Secretary, both through his contact with the school teachers, and with the W.V.S., followed developments closely, and many of the schemes in which teachers and W.V.S. members co-operated were embodied in circulars issued through the Education Department. Permission was given for certain halls, used as school premises during the day, to be open for recreation in the evening. Some schools were used as play centres during the Christmas holidays. Games pitches were available for both evacuated and Cambridge children. Special concessions were made in respect of evening classes, and evacuated children were admitted at the age of 13+.

The school teachers were very closely involved in the leisure time of their boys and girls. In the earlier days of evacuation a valuable step was taken in the formation of a joint committee of evacuated school teachers, local teachers, and the W.V.S., so that schemes might be thought out in relation to the problem as a whole. Evacuated teachers were also represented on the local Games Association. At the same time a number of teachers took responsibility for the recreation of their own school children without calling upon other organized help. It was reported from one school that some of the teachers took it in turns to spend an evening with a group of children in the billets, in order to relieve the householders who wished to go out.

The Undergraduates. The Undergraduates' Council formed an 'Evacuees Care Committee', and students, including those from evacuated colleges, were invited to offer their services for 'recreational activities', 'clerical work', etc. There was a large response, and subsequently several colleges formed their own care committees, and some combined to 'adopt' an evacuated school. The Evacuees Care Committee co-operated closely with the W.V.S.

Juvenile Organizations. The National Youth Organizations

had made special efforts to stimulate local units to meet the new demands. Evacuated members, for example, scouts and guides, were put into touch with groups in the reception areas. The Boy Scouts Association issued a pamphlet on 'Suggestions for Leisure-Time Activities for School Children', and the Girl Guides Association gave its support with an additional leaflet, adapting the suggestions for use by girls. 'The object of this pamphlet is to offer suggestions to teachers and others, who, at this time, have unaccustomed responsibility for the leisure occupations of evacuated school children, . . . ' The W.V.S. co-operated with the youth organizations, acting as the link with the schools, so that all boys and girls who wished to join an existing club or other unit might have the opportunity of doing so.

The Churches. The United Council of Christian Witness set up a committee with representatives of the Anglican and of the Free Churches, of the National Council of Social Service, and of the Y.M.C.A. and the Y.W.C.A., to inquire into the need. As the pamphlet continues: 'This committee felt strongly that centralized activity of any kind would be a mistake involving, as it would, bringing the children through the streets in the dark; they therefore decided to work by stimulating the activities in particular areas to cater for the need through their own Young Peoples' Organizations'. Many of the Churches made a point of welcoming the evacuated children to their Sunday schools, in some cases arranging a special morning or afternoon session for their guests.

Regional Liaison Officers, both for boys' work and for girls' work were attached to the Civil Defence Region. Although they were concerned mainly with young people of fourteen to twenty, it was impossible to make any rigid distinction, and good service was done by bringing Cambridge organizations into touch with National Juvenile Organizations. One result was the organization, from January to March, of a series of lectures on 'Preparation for Leadership', which received a good response. In co-operation with the Cambridgeshire Education Committee, and the Central Council for Recreative Physical Training, special half-day courses in physical training were held, one suitable for men and boys, and one for women and girls.

LEISURE TIME ACTIVITIES THUS MADE AVAILABLE FOR EVACUATED BOYS AND GIRLS

The nature of the activities of Clubs, Troops, Companies and similar units is generally known, so that no details of programmes need be given in this section.

Units of national organization varied in their capacity to absorb the evacuated children into existing groups, or to form new groups.

The Scouts (seventeen Cambridge Troops) linked up evacuated scouts with local troops, but were not able to take in all the Wolf Cubs. Their own difficulties through loss of scouters who had joined up prevented them from recruiting evacuated boys who had not been scouts in London. The London scouts gradually withdrew from the Cambridge troops, partly through the difficulty of leadership, partly because some boys returned to London. The one troop which was formed in connection with an evacuated school did not flourish.

The Guides (nineteen Guide Companies, fifteen Brownie Packs) seem to have been more successful. Apart from welcoming evacuated guides and brownies into existing companies and packs, three new companies and two brownie packs were formed especially for evacuated girls. They were not limited to girls who had been London guides; in fact one company, forty strong, formed in connection with an evacuated school, recruited half its members from those who had not been guides before. The guides were fortunate in having several evacuated guiders from whom to draw, and a vigorous training week-end early in March served to rouse special interest in guiding, and the need for trained leadership.

The Girls' Life Brigade had only one Cambridge unit, and its work was severely curtailed at the beginning of the war by the commandeering of most of its premises. It was thus not possible to welcome evacuees.

The Boys' Brigade (three companies) has, like the Scouts in Cambridge, been hard hit by the war. One company has had to be disbanded, another is working under such difficulty that it cannot absorb evacuees, while the third has been able to welcome a few evacuated boys.

The Girls' Friendly Society with its nine branches, welcomed some evacuees, but it is reported that 'they gradually ceased to attend.'

The Campaigners[1] have five 'clans' for girls and one for boys in Cambridge. Although there were no evacuated Campaigners to join the 'Clans', a special piece of work for evacuees was done by persuading householders to lend a room, preferably with a piano, where small groups of children might meet one evening a week. Some thirty-two of these groups known as 'Clusters' were formed, each with two young people acting as leaders to run the evening's activities as far as possible on Campaigner lines.

The Christian Alliance for Women and Girls (one branch) opened its membership to evacuated girls and this was welcomed in a district where few leisure time facilities were available.

The Junior Y.M.C.A. and Rotary Club, one of the well-supported boys' clubs in Cambridge, made a point of inviting evacuated boys through their school teachers. The leader felt that more use might have been made of the facilities offered by this club, but various factors, including the return of many boys to London at Christmas from the schools concerned, affected such membership. The Y.W.C.A. in Cambridge has no junior members so that evacuated school girls did not join.

Other local clubs included youth groups attached to Churches of various denominations. These were generally open to evacuees, but the majority of boys and girls of school

[1] The Campaigners are a small national youth organization whose clans are modelled in some respects on guide companies and scout troops. Unlike these organizations, the Campaigners have a compulsory rule with regard to Sunday-school attendance.

age were put into touch with the local units of national organizations, many of which were associated with the Churches.

CLUBS OF A SPECIAL CHARACTER FORMED SINCE THE WAR

Club for Evacuated Boys and Girls. An artist, the wife of a local doctor, has thrown open a large room in her house, overlooking the garden, where she, with some occasional helpers, welcomes about twenty children each evening. As many as forty crowd in on Saturdays and the newly formed committee of older children meet on Sunday afternoons. Boys and girls between the ages of seven and fifteen work together, one day making and producing a puppet theatre, another doing woodwork, another painting. Lino-cuts, potato prints and needlework are among the many interests provided for the children. The leader, Mrs. Lynda Youngman, reports: 'The children are allowed a great deal of freedom and all materials are kept so that they can see them and help themselves. The first time this was very extravagant, but they are fast learning to take only what they need. When a new child is wasteful the other children are very scornful. A committee of twelve of the older children has started to run the club and so far has been quite successful. The grown-ups keep in the background as much as possible and take everything the children do very seriously. The object of the club is not only to occupy the children and relieve the foster parents, but to develop the individual and social life of the children through their pleasure in making things, their critical and inventive powers, and in group play such as the puppet theatre, plays and concerts.'

School Clubs. There were several interesting examples of school clubs organized by teachers for their own evacuated children. In one of these, held in a Senior Girls' School, about 70 to 100 girls attend, some of them staying to tea after school, taking their own food and paying a halfpenny for tea. The club is held once a week from 4 to 6.30 p.m. The first hour is given to country dancing, charades and 'noisy games', and the second to a concert. A proportion of the children attend on Saturday afternoons for more skilled crafts, for example, puppet making. It is said that the numbers are smaller because the foster parents often take the girls out on Saturdays. Some of the girls take their Cambridge friends with them to the school club.

Another club for evacuated girls of eight years or more is organized by the wife of the schoolmaster who also acts as Senior Voluntary Worker for billeting in the district. A two-hour programme every week includes country dancing, knitting, sewing, and reed-pipe making. The girls are learning to play the pipes they make. Voluntary workers see the children home.

Play Centres. Four play centres were organized on Saturday mornings by an experienced worker of the London Play Centre Movement soon after the reception of the London children. Equipment was sent down from London and the Centres were run with the help of volunteers including some schoolmasters' wives, some teachers, some undergraduates. Out of two of these centres evening clubs developed, of which the one just described still flourishes. Other successful Play Centres were organized on Saturday mornings and afternoons by the billeting officer, with undergraduate help. They were started in the early days of evacuation, in response to a strongly felt need 'as a relief to the householders, and to provide opportunities for play for children'. These Centres have the advantage of open space for outdoor games and a Church Hall for tea or for play in wet weather. The tea is provided through the generosity of friends of the organizer. Cambridge children are not encouraged, but it is known that a few have crept in.

Special Activities Organized by Undergratuates. Some special plans were started by the Evacuees Care Committee of the Undergraduates' Council. Apart from the work already mentioned, namely, help given by individual undergraduates to existing clubs, companies or play centres, the undergraduates have organized and run their own schemes, and these have proved exceedingly popular amongst the evacuated girls and boys. The distinctive feature is perhaps the invitation to small groups in the 'adopted' school to go along to the undergraduates' rooms and to do, within limits, what they choose. One undergraduate has a play reading, another music; another group makes model aeroplanes from wood. Others meet for stamp-collecting, dancing, debating, engineering and science, chess, drawing and games. A film show at one of the schools adopted is given week by week by the undergraduates. Even this varied list does not include all the resources of the children and the students.

Saturday games in the College grounds have been organized in addition to the small groups in the students' rooms. At Newnham College a hall was lent and the children were also invited to their own rooms by the students. A very popular club for about 56 girls and 30 boys drawn from a wide area in Cambridge flourished here. Undergraduates have also run concert parties to entertain the children; they have led rambles and taken the boys and girls round the colleges, particularly to see rooms once occupied by famous men. ('You see, Oliver Cromwell came to Sidney . . .')

One student of Clare College started a special week-end club. He was convinced that the week-ends were the time when organized activities were most needed. He knew, too, that many undergraduates felt freer at week-ends than during the week. Much preliminary work was done to secure support for the idea of a week-end club, and at length, after Christmas, suitable premises were generously offered rent free, the financial help necessary to start the club was made available from charitable sources, and equipment was provided, largely with the help of the W.V.S. Mr. Frank Tindall, who was responsible for the club, rallied student helpers for the various week-end activities which included indoor and outdoor games, a film show, dramatics and indoor industries and a Sunday school.

The leader reports that while 'the boys should be allowed to follow their own inventions and imaginations and not be subjected to an organized programme or imposed on by the will or character of the leaders' . . . yet 'for all that, it was to be a club, and to foster the club spirit and the rational behaviour of boys towards the rest of the club'. He felt that this could be achieved only if the leader was free to attend throughout the week-end, mornings and afternoons. The helpers were organized for part-time group activities, but the same man was to take the lead in one special interest each week-end. A particular effort was made by the leader to attract 'lone birds' and to bring them into informal games on one of the Cambridge 'Pieces' (open spaces).

The Householders. We could hardly summarize the work of a special character started since the war to provide leisure time facilities for boys and girls without mentioning that of the householders themselves. In the first place the foster parents have in many instances absorbed the children into their family life, their own children and the evacuated children sharing toys, going together to the pictures, or to see the town, etc.

Secondly, householders have invited children billeted elsewhere to come along to a party, or to join a small group for an outing. This was a common practice at Christmas time.

Thirdly, the householders have lent a room for the use of small groups of children, as we have seen in the case of Campaigner 'clusters', and of Mrs. Youngman's club. This practice may be more widespread than is generally known, for example, two groups in connexion with the Crusaders' Movement were found to be meeting in this way, although unknown to many in the district.

Entertainments. Much effort was put into the organization of entertainments for evacuated girls and boys during the first few months after their reception. At half-term the various existing organizations made special efforts; Mrs. Youngman's club was open for the whole week-end; the undergraduates organized rambles, games and tea-parties; and two entertainments were provided through the W.V.S.

In the Christmas holidays, the W.V.S. organized ten parties with entertainments to cover some 3,000 children, a proportion of whom were Cambridge children. Funds were raised locally to supplement the contributions from the

London fund. A pantomime was given by undergraduates of Jesus College, and a Carol Service was held in King's College Chapel. A certain number of schools were meanwhile available as play centres, but fewer children took advantage of this opportunity than was expected, one school reporting more helpers than children.

A local cinema, the Rex, agreed to arrange a special programme open to all school children on Saturday mornings at a reduced admission fee of 3*d.* Some school teachers and a number of undergraduates acted as stewards. This venture had to be discontinued. Not enough children responded to make it financially possible. The reasons for this lack of response have not been studied in detail, but it is thought that the alternative attractions of Cambridge proved stronger for many of the London children. Those who were free were happy to go down to the river, to wander round Cambridge, or to stroll through one of the chain stores. It is known that many, particularly the girls, were busy on Saturday mornings, helping in their billets.

Student concert parties were continued but on a smaller scale, given in most cases to the 'adopted' school.

SOME PRACTICAL DIFFICULTIES

1. *Difficulties of accommodation.* In some parts of Cambridge it has been difficult to find halls and rooms for evening group activities. One or two organizations, e.g. the Girls' Life Brigade, have had seriously to curtail their work through the lack of suitable accommodation. When a hall is used by day as a school it is often not possible to hold an evening activity; caretakers who are willing to clean up and prepare for school the next day cannot be found. Many leaders are finding that insufficient space prevents them from planning their activities for children of different ages as they would like. One hall or one room has to serve all needs.

The lack of room for even simple hobbies in the billet is a very real handicap for many evacuated boys and girls.[1] This,

[1] See Chapter V, p. 82, for the children's comments about their hobbies.

perhaps, goes far to explain the fact that, contrary to expectation, many householders did not welcome the W.V.S. competitions, particularly if they were likely to 'make a mess'.

No difficulty has been reported with regard to *playing fields*. Cambridge is well served with open spaces, and the colleges have responded generously to appeals for games pitches.

2. *Equipment.* The question of financing most club activities has been answered chiefly by support from interested friends, or by special efforts made to raise money. The undergraduates raised funds through the various colleges and banked it jointly on behalf of the Evacuees Care Committee of the Council. One college made a grant through the Students' Union for its own care committee in addition to the general effort. One club received an initial grant from charitable sources and a separate grant for equipment. Certain individual club leaders are bearing the expenses themselves with help from friends. The Play Centres were equipped originally from material brought from the London Play Centres. Some Play Centres and clubs are already finding themselves handicapped for want of fresh material. In all these cases the future is uncertain, and equipment is being used up (especially in the constructive hobbies groups).

3. *Difficulties of Subscriptions.* Clubs and other groups vary in their practice of collecting subscriptions from evacuated boys and girls. Most experienced leaders ask for subscriptions not only towards raising funds but as part of the training in responsibility. One leader of a new club reported, 'With a view to fostering the club spirit we decided to have a subscription of a penny a week-end with the view to eventually establishing some form of self government. . . . The subscription was also intended to make sure that the boys if they came on Saturday would come back on Sunday to get their penny's worth.' But in this case the numbers dropped and subscriptions fell, and it was decided not to exact subscriptions strictly. The difficulty is a real one since some evacuated children

have little or no pocket-money, while others have it in excess. For this reason some leaders have planned other ways of raising funds than by means of members' subscriptions. It was reported from one billeting area that, owing to the variation in the amount of pocket-money, it was thought better not to leave it entirely in the hands of the children. At first the school undertook responsibility but later the foster parents were asked to do so, and to give it to the children at their discretion.

4. *The intermittent nature of much of the help given.* This point is particularly relevant to undergraduate help. With one or two exceptions undergraduate leaders disappeared during the vacations and their activities came to an end. One or two individuals stayed up specially or came back on certain days to help keep their group going.

Another characteristic of undergraduate help is the fact that a large and enthusiastic body can be enrolled at the beginning of a venture, but as the term goes on it becomes more and more difficult for the student organizers to find the required help, particularly as examinations draw near. The organization of this type of help therefore throws an excessive burden on the few. These difficulties are added to at the present time in the case of the men, since the leaders are continually changing as men are called up to the Army. This has led several of the students to suggest the need for 'a central organizing body to co-ordinate the work and especially to deal with the financial side'. But while these drawbacks are recognized by the students themselves, they feel it is worth while to continue their efforts, particularly in view of the success of the small groups in College rooms. That many of the school teachers recognize the value of such help is seen in the close interest they take in the scheme.

IMPRESSIONS AND COMMENTS

1. *Voluntary effort.* A great deal of enthusiastic voluntary effort has been made to meet what were felt to be urgent needs. This effort has had, however, a mixed reception,

some activities have been warmly welcomed, others have been greeted with scepticism, others even openly denounced.

A broad line of criticism comes from those who say: 'There is a danger of over-organization! The evacuated children are being given too much. They will consider themselves privileged persons as compared with Cambridge children. Their self-reliance may be sapped. Leave them to find their own amusements.'

On the other hand there are many who believe that there is not enough opportunity for the evacuated child to amuse himself. Moreover, under conditions of billeting, particularly in a small house with one sitting-room, it often puts a heavy strain on the householder. The club gives opportunity to the child and relief to the householder.

These two groups meet on common ground in the wish to avoid too much organization or too great an emphasis on entertaining the children, as compared with giving them the chance to develop their own interests.

It is important to remember the value to the child separated from his own family of belonging to a group where he will find the personal interest which he needs. It must help to give him a sense of security in his strange new life. The point made by the organizer of the week-end club that a special effort should be made to help the lonely child is a valuable one. It is particularly true of those who may not have fitted in happily in their billets.

2. *Leadership*. The real issue probably lies with the much discussed and vital question of leadership. The skilled leader gets an easy response from the boys and girls, and a measure of discipline gives the opportunity for greater freedom and enjoyment. The inexperienced and unskilful leader is often soon discouraged by 'a rough house'. Training for leadership is now recognized as an important part of the service of youth. Many of the voluntary organizations have run training schemes with help from charitable trusts, and many short courses have had the support of Local Education Authorities. In Cambridge several such short training courses have been held since Christmas, and a valuable step is being taken in

the appointment of a Leader-Organizer responsible to a committee representative of the Local Education Authorities and of the National and Local Youth Organizations. In a University town training is particularly important since many undergraduates may become club leaders. Those club leaders who are scornful of undergraduate efforts, or those who fear that their club members may be 'unsettled' by the intermittent nature of such help, might bear in mind the service which their club could offer in providing a training ground for future leadership. Most leaders recognize that enthusiastic even though inexperienced student help has value, not only for the students themselves, but for the boys and girls who thus make new friends and enjoy fresh and absorbing hobbies.

3. *The Success of Small Groups.* One of the strongest impressions left by this general survey of the provision for the leisure of boys and girls is the outstanding success of small groups. The invitation to 'hobby groups' in the men's and women's rooms of the various colleges has met with enthusiastic response. It is reported that the small 'clusters' organized by the Campaigners have met with a similar success. It is not only the special interest of the chosen hobby which accounts for the keenness of these small groups. There is no doubt that the personal element makes a strong appeal, and both children and adults seem to enjoy the closer relationship.

It has, of course, long been recognized that division into smaller groups has a special value in certain types of recreation, for example in the patrol system of the guides and scouts. But the efforts described above are something more than this. Possibly the home-like atmosphere of a room that is lived in is an added attraction. Whatever the reason, it is noteworthy that while numbers have tended to drop in many of the larger organized units, the small groups are only prevented from expanding not by lack of members, but by the want of facilities.

THE MIXING OF LONDON AND CAMBRIDGE CHILDREN

Indications have been given from various sources that on the whole the children do not mix. Schoolmasters have noted the fact in the playground. Billeting officers have reported it from their observation of children's play in the streets and open spaces. On the other hand single instances of friendship within a household have often been quoted. There were also examples of the necessity of rebilleting children who did not get on with others in the family.

There is not sufficient evidence to show how far London children are being absorbed into Cambridge life. It would be interesting to study the question further, to see which factors act as barriers, and which encourage mutual tolerance and friendliness. Within individual households there is no doubt that many foster parents treat the evacuated children billeted with them as part of the family, sharing with them whatever is provided for their own children. On the other hand the children attend their own London school and take part in London versus Cambridge sports competitions. Special leisure time activities have been organized for London children, small groups within Play Centre or Club usually consisting of a group of friends from London.[1] When evacuated children have joined existing Cambridge units, for example, boy scouts, the result has met with far less success, and it is reported over and over again that very few Londoners are left. Occasionally London children have brought Cambridge children with them, for instance to a Play Centre, but, largely for lack of facilities, this can be no more than a trickle. So far London and Cambridge children tend to remain apart at school and at play.

[1] One reason for the dropping off of children from highly organized groups was suggested by a billeting officer who felt the need for some more informal groups. She argued that leaders are often over-anxious to secure regular attendance, so much so that absence is made to seem an act of disloyalty. The child needs to be able to return after absence without feeling a sense of shame.

THE NEED FOR DEVELOPMENT OF PROVISIONS FOR RECREATION THROUGH THE VOLUNTARY ORGANIZATIONS AND THE LOCAL EDUCATION AUTHORITIES

With the encouragement of the Board of Education there is much greater emphasis to-day on co-operation between voluntary and statutory authorities in provisions for social activities and recreation. It is perhaps more difficult to achieve this in an area where responsibility for Elementary and for Higher Education is divided, as it is in Cambridge. Cambridge Borough, as the authority for Elementary Education, is concerned with the majority of boys and girls under fourteen and for a minority (e.g. those in Central Schools) up to the age of sixteen. It is the authority concerned with the reception of evacuated school children. The County Authority responsible for Higher Education is also charged with the organization of the Youth Organization Council, the emphasis of which is on the welfare of young people of fourteen to twenty. The Board of Education grants for social and physical training strengthen still further the part played by the County Authority, which has to approve schemes submitted by the local youth committee. But grants are also made by the Board of Education directly to National Organzations and these bodies have a considerable membership of children under fourteen. An interesting experiment in co-operation arises when, as in Cambridge, a leader and organizer is appointed jointly by the Local Education Authority for Higher Education and the National Youth Organization concerned. The emphasis will be mainly on development of social and recreational facilities for young people of fourteen to twenty, but they cannot be entirely separated from those of school age, the majority of whom are under fourteen.

Although the present study is concerned with school children, a consideration of plans for recreation is bound to involve a survey of the position as it affects youth generally.

Apart from the special efforts made to meet the needs of evacuated children, it has been suggested that the development desirable for Cambridge as a whole should include the establishment of a Youth Centre for boys and girls, with opportunity for mixed activities, in charge of experienced leaders. This would not only add some of the much needed opportunities for boys and girls, but would be valuable as a training centre for leadership. The Local Education Authority could be invited to provide skilled instructors for special interests such as music and crafts. This co-operative effort would ensure not only the interest and help of the L.E.A., but would take full advantage of the experience of voluntary organizations. These organizations have done much in the past to serve those young people who were not attracted by more formal continued education. Boys and girls who join such a club or centre as junior members are helped to meet some of the difficulties which come at school leaving age. When they become young wage-earners they can still pursue interests already encouraged, and this may lead to a greater appreciation of the opportunities offered by the L.E.A.

As for evacuated boys and girls, it is doubtful whether, as time lapses, separate efforts should be continued. It may be more desirable to provide opportunities which can be shared by all children. It remains true, however, that for the first six months of the war the special efforts made for the London children have proved of great value in helping them to overcome some difficulties, and to enjoy new opportunities.

CHAPTER X

WHAT THE TEACHERS SAY [1]

THE TEACHERS, being evacuees themselves, many of them parents separated from their own children, many more of them foster parents caring for the children of others, have inevitably, and perhaps more closely than all other sections of the community, become linked with evacuation and its attendant problems.

On all occasions and in every place the teachers have been caring for their children, easing their sorrows and sharing their joys. There were days of anxious preparation at the time of Munich, but the days turned to weeks, and the weeks to months, until a year had passed—a year of ceaseless toil in the schools. With September 1st, 1939, the work had not ended but merely begun, for the teachers went out with their children. And during that journey together into the unknown a bond was forged, which has become yet stronger with all the vicissitudes of evacuation.

It was a natural consequence, then, that any inquiry concerning evacuation should give weight to the opinions of teachers, and with this object in view the Cambridge Evacuation Survey Research Committee prepared a questionnaire for submission to teachers who had been evacuated to Cambridge.

About fifty teachers from all types of schools were kind enough to help our work by answering our questionnaire. It had been hoped to obtain information from all those who had been evacuated to Cambridge, but unfortunately many had returned to London before this stage of our inquiry was reached. However, as replies were received from infants', junior, senior, selective central and technical schools, from boys', girls' and mixed departments, from men and women, from heads and assistants, from married and single teachers, and from young teachers as well as those with many

[1] This chapter was written by a teacher.

years of experience, it is thought that the opinions expressed are representative.

The questionnaire (a copy of which is given in the Appendix) concerns itself chiefly with the following points:

A. Changes due to evacuation.
  1. In connexion with the children.
  2. In connexion with the teachers.
  3. In connexion with school routine.

B. Difficulties due to evacuation.
  1. In connexion with the children.
  2. In connexion with the teachers.
  3. In connexion with school routine.

C. Comments on evacuation.
  1. Organization of the present evacuation scheme.
  2. Best type of home.
  3. Suggestions for the future.

An examination of the cards immediately revealed two facts which we consider to be of vital significance.

First, there is no marked division of opinion between the various groups of teachers. For the most part men and women, married and single, old and young, teachers of infants and seniors, heads and assistants, record similar experiences and react in the same way to them.

Secondly, practically all the really serious difficulties mentioned concern human relationships, and are in no way related to routine organization. It may well be that too long was spent in perfecting the mechanics of evacuation, while the personal problems of the evacuee were too quickly dismissed from the mind. A happy settled community in the reception area would surely have been ample recompense for some slight loss of precision during the actual journey out.

A more detailed examination of the returns revealed that there was a substantial degree of agreement among the teachers on the following points, which are given without comment, before they and other matters, concerning which there was a greater division of opinion, are discussed more fully.

A. Changes due to evacuation.

1. In connexion with the children.

(*a*) The health of the children has improved, although there has been more skin trouble than usual.

(*b*) The personal appearance of the children has improved on the whole.

(*c*) The children's relations with their teachers are better and more intimate.

(*d*) The children's relations with their fellows have also improved.

(*e*) The degree of self-reliance shown by the children has increased tremendously.

(*f*) The general outlook of the children has broadened and their interests have become more varied.

(*g*) There appears to be a slight lessening in the response to external discipline.

(*h*) The power of concentration has become noticeably less.

(*i*) Progress in normal school work has declined.

(*j*) There has been a slight tendency for the children, especially the younger ones, to acquire a Cambridgeshire accent.

2. In connexion with the teachers.

(*a*) The breaking up of family life was the change which affected the majority of the teachers most seriously.

(*b*) There is a much closer bond of sympathy and understanding between teachers and children.

(*c*) The teachers' relations with their colleagues have also improved.

(*d*) There has been a slight tendency to take school work less seriously.

(*e*) The financial position of nearly all teachers deteriorated in the early days of evacuation.

(*f*) There has been for many teachers a marked increase in extraneous duties and responsibilities both in volume and variety.

(*g*) Many teachers note with regret the loss of privacy in their home life.

3. Changes in school routine and conditions.

(*a*) School buildings placed at the disposal of evacuated schools are considered to be inferior to those in London.

(*b*) Laboratories and handicraft rooms are not up to the standard of those at home.

(*c*) Staff rooms, in particular, are considered inadequate.

(*d*) The number of rooms available for classes is inevitably smaller than it had been.

(*e*) Library facilities are considered to be not so good on the whole as in London.

(*f*) Classes are smaller in most cases than they were in London.

(*g*) There is a wider range in age and ability among the boys and girls in the same class.

(*h*) Facilities for recreation have improved for most schools.

(*i*) In most cases schools or departments have shared a building with a local school, but in nearly all cases normal school hours have been worked.

(*j*) Holidays have been curtailed, while staffs have had their holidays on a rota system.

(*k*) When numbers have become small the children who remain have been absorbed into the local schools.

B. Difficulties due to evacuation.

1. In connexion with the children.

(*a*) The difficulties connected with the billeting of children have been outstanding.

(*b*) At first there were minor difficulties connected with the supply of clothing, and washing and mending, but most of these troubles soon disappeared.

(*c*) Homesickness caused a certain amount of difficulty, but was not considered to be one of the major problems.

2. In connexion with the teachers.
   (*a*) Many teachers experienced difficulties connected with the billeting of themselves.
   (*b*) Financial difficulties were of great importance in the early days of evacuation.
   (*c*) Most of the teachers, including many who are unmarried, found difficulties due to their removal from home.
   (*d*) One of the most important causes of difficulty was the uncertainty of the teachers' position, and the fact that this rendered it impossible to plan ahead.
3. In connexion with school routine and conditions.
   (*a*) Constantly changing numbers of children on roll caused a great deal of difficulty.
   (*b*) Staff changes also constituted a major difficulty in many schools.
   (*c*) Shortage of stock in the early days of evacuation caused some inconvenience.
   (*d*) The sharing of buildings with other schools has rendered it impossible to use those buildings to the best advantage.

C. Comments on evacuation.

1. Organization of the present evacuation scheme.
   (*a*) The actual movement of the children was well planned.
   (*b*) Failure to ensure stability was a grave defect.
   (*c*) Failure to establish previous contact between evacuation and reception areas caused failures which might have been avoided.
   (*d*) Too little regard was paid to the requirements of individual schools.
   (*e*) Failure to make immediate financial adjustments was responsible, either directly or indirectly, for the return of many children and teachers to London.
2. Best type of home.
   (*a*) The majority of teachers feel that children should be in homes of similar economic status to their own.

(b) Many teachers suggest that camps or hostels may provide the solution to many of the problems of evacuation.

(c) It is agreed that special homes should be provided for difficult children.

3. Suggestions for the future.

(a) Movement should be in units based on schools or groups of schools.

(b) Steps should be taken to ensure reasonable stability.

(c) There should be a greater degree of co-ordination of the work of the various groups of people concerned with evacuation.

Lest it be thought that in the foregoing summary there are many surprising omissions, it should be made clear that it does not include many things dealt with in other sections of our inquiry, nor does it record all the expressions of opinion of individual teachers. We feel, however, that some of the suggestions made by the few are so obviously right that they will be readily accepted by the many, and therefore we include them in the discussion which follows.

Changes due to Evacuation. It has been evident that on the whole the health of the children has greatly improved, and this is ascribed to more sleep, more fresh air, better feeding, a quieter life, and less 'potted amusement'.

Possibly next to the general improvement in health the change in the attitude of the children to teachers and school is of the greatest significance. Those who had shared a great adventure naturally drew closer together, and in times of trouble the child turned naturally to the teacher for sympathy, feeling that they were fellow-sufferers in a hard world. Children and parents alike acquired a more conscious realization of the value of school, and in the early days our boys and girls came eagerly to school to discuss their adventures. For a time school was their home, the place where they could be themselves, the place where they could relax, and, above all, the one place where they might re-establish contact with the world they knew. Teachers record that children confided in them in a way which was unusual before evacuation. The holiday atmosphere deliberately fostered in order to allay fears in the pre-evacuation period tended to persist, and this led to plenty of goodwill, but a much slower response to orders, although with the passing of time a tendency to return to a more normal response has been noted.

The way in which they have been thrown together has led to a similar increase in the comradeship not only of the children and their fellows, but also of teachers and their colleagues. Many teachers have felt that the fact that they are able to meet socially out of school is largely responsible, but others believe that the better understanding is due to mutual sympathy in the matter of separation from home amenities. While there has been this increase in good feeling among fellow-evacuees, it has been noted that many of the London children have to a large extent ignored the Cambridge children, and it is certain that evacuees and local children in the same playground have not mixed. Towards the end of the first year of evacuation a natural convergence of interests seems to be appearing, and a mutual understanding is beginning to emerge, but the process has been slow. Recently the prefects from a local school were invited to the farewell party of the boys and girls of a visiting school, and when it was over the guests approached the teacher in charge, thanked their hosts with obvious sincerity, and after a pause their leader added, 'And we have learned too, sir, that the London boys and girls do know how to enjoy themselves—after all.'

Another notable change in the children is in their self-reliance. Pampered and nervous kiddies have gained in assurance, have learned to think and act for themselves, and in every way have become free to develop their own individuality. There has been a widening of interests, and as a consequence a broader and more mature outlook on life has developed. Once again the process was slow and many teachers were disappointed to find that after several months the real interests of the children were still those of the town—the cinema, the speedway, trams and the noise of traffic.

Many children were soon taken to see some of the glories of Cambridge only to report on return, 'Please, sir, there's a lovely Woolworth's in the town.' However that phase has passed and boys and girls are to be seen everywhere really enjoying the things that Cambridge has to offer, but which London knows not.

And when we ponder on some of the things that follow we may do well to remind ourselves of this enjoyment, and any who pause to ask, 'Was it all worth while?' will know that there is only one answer. What does it matter that the power of concentration of the children in the classroom was lessened, for were they not learning in a wider field of experience? Why should we worry that their progress in book-learning was retarded, when we know that they have learned things that are not to be found in books? The development of character will ensure the concentration when it is really essential, while the increase in initiative will in course of time stimulate a desire for further knowledge, and it will come from within and not be enforced from without. Indeed, in recent months the children in one school at least have been working for examinations with a degree of enthusiasm and concentration certainly above the average. While bombs have fallen near them, while their parents have pleaded with them to go home, and while their teachers would have regarded with sympathetic understanding a slackening of effort, they have worked through it all with a calmness and deliberation which has won the admiration and respect of all those who have had the good fortune to be in close contact with them.

The teachers on the whole appear to have accepted the conditions of evacuation with resignation, and many say that their patience has increased. They ascribe this to the smaller classes, and a tendency to treat school less seriously. There is a feeling that on the whole the buildings, craft-rooms, and library facilities are not so good as at home, but there are no complaints on this score, for it appears to be recognized that such things are inevitable. Many teachers have, however, become worried by the continually changing conditions, and feel that as a consequence their efforts are largely wasted.

When children return to London, classes become smaller, until eventually children of widely differing ages and ability are put together in one class, a thing which teachers feel is good neither for them nor their pupils. Then members of the staff are recalled to London, and once more there is a change. In the schools with specialist teachers this has become a tremendous nuisance, for with decreasing numbers it has become increasingly difficult to cover the syllabus satisfactorily. This is the one change in school conditions which teachers in Cambridge do not appear to regard with equanimity, and they are agreed that for a really successful evacuation scheme some means must be devised to secure stability. It is suggested that parents should be asked to agree to leave their children, at any rate, until the end of a term, as this would in some measure help to solve a very serious problem.

Difficulties due to Evacuation. During the course of evacuation many little troubles have arisen, most of them cured quite easily, but one problem has remained insoluble throughout a while year. No one who has been with the children in the reception areas will need to be told that it is billeting which has caused so much worry and so many anxious consultations. Right at the word 'go' the troubles started, and even now at the very end of the first year of evacuation they still continue. At any one time there is a high percentage of contented evacuees, thanks to the kindness and understanding shown by the great majority of the foster parents, often in very difficult circumstances, but in spite of this children continue to leave their billets and return to London through some misunderstanding. Recently a girl who had been happily billeted for the whole year, and who was about to leave school, wrote home to say how extremely unhappy she was in her billet. Before the matter could be adjusted the parents took the child home, a most unfortunate end to what had been considered a good example of successful billeting, for not only did the child leave with a sense of grievance, but the foster parents were very hurt at what they felt to be the ingratitude which had followed their kindness and self-sacrifice.

Many of these things have been unavoidable, but the

teachers consider that many more of them might have been avoided with more careful planning. The great majority of the teachers contend that they could have told in advance that certain billets in which children were placed would be unsuitable for those children, and that consultation between evacuation and reception areas would have prevented such mistakes being made. However, these misfits were soon discovered, and steps taken to put things right, but no sooner had this happened than it was discovered that undergraduates were coming to occupy many of our billets. Children who had been happy in homes where the mother was used to dealing with rather boisterous young people were uprooted and in many cases entered their new homes with a feeling of resentment, while in some cases parents took their children back to London rather than allow them to make another move. Foster parents and children alike have regretted the necessity for the change, while teachers feel that all possible measures should be taken by the authorities to avoid the necessity of removing a child from a happy billet. Later still some householders became rather weary, and this feeling of weariness was accentuated by the fact that the idea became prevalent that some of their more fortunate neighbours had dodged their obligations. To a small extent teachers and helpers were able to give some relief, but the teachers feel that possibly more might be done in this direction, while they believe that the principle of compulsion should be applied in billeting. They realize that in the first instance the volunteers were likely to provide the better homes, but at the same time they feel that the vast majority of the populace would deal kindly with children if they were told they must have them. Finally, of course, there was the absence of bombs on London, coupled with the presence of German bombers over some of the reception areas. This worried parents, who thought themselves to be safe while their children were in danger, and unsettled foster parents who became unwilling to shoulder the responsibility. Ultimately this too led to the return of many children to London.

Teachers as well as children have found their own billeting

problems to be one of their major difficulties. One teacher records seven billet changes, while another who had three changes said that with each change there was a rise in price and a lowering of the standard of accommodation. Many teachers eventually solved the problem by renting houses of their own, although in the early days of evacuation this appeared to be discouraged by the authorities, and, moreover, the uncertainty of the position made many teachers hesitate before increasing their already heavy expenses. And this brings me to the second of evacuation's major problems—financial matters.

Nearly all the teachers have expressed very strong views on financial arrangements connected with evacuation, and it is with great satisfaction that we note that steps have already been taken to remedy most of the evils. Teachers were agreed that allowances for the older boys and girls should be increased, for many good but poor homes were forced to get rid of their children because otherwise they were faced with the necessity of losing money, which was impossible, or alternatively with under-feeding the children, which to kindly folk was equally impossible. However, this has now been remedied, but unfortunately not before a great deal of unnecessary disturbance had been caused.

Many teachers are of the opinion that the authorities do not recognize sufficiently the extra expenses incurred by parents when their children are away from home, and it is thought by some that, if the Government had waived its claim to payments by parents, the comparatively small financial loss would have been more than counterbalanced by the gain in enthusiasm for evacuation and the greater stability thereof. The teachers' own claims have been met, but very many teachers were very worried before Christmas, up to which time there had been no recognition of the greatly increased expenses of those who had continuing liabilities. There is a feeling too that a standard billeting charge for teachers should have been fixed, for although the majority of them found that charges were reasonable, a number had most unfortunate experiences. Furthermore, many teachers, being out of their own homes, found themselves spending more on entertainment, while regular visits to their families were expensive. It is worth noting that all teachers who were separated from their children desired to see them at regular intervals, and it would thus appear that parents, at least, feel very keenly any tendency to isolate their children from them. In spite of the fact that visits of parents may cause slight homesickness the majority of the teachers would agree that such visits are beneficial and should be encouraged within reasonable limits.

Most teachers welcomed the new extraneous duties, and the greater responsibilities involved, while a few whose duties were comparatively light stated that they would have enjoyed having something more to occupy their minds. Almost without exception the teachers who were evacuated with the children had given personal undertakings to parents to keep a watchful eye on John or Mary, and those who came to Cambridge were not unmindful of their promises. Many an anxious mother was reassured, often a tearful child sent smiling on her way, more than a few foster parents dissuaded from precipitous action, while on at least one occasion consultations concerning an errant child lasted far into the night. Throughout the long dark winter evenings teachers received tremendous help from undergraduates and voluntary organizations in Cambridge in keeping the children happy. Many pleasant contacts were made both by children and teachers, and we hope that our many friends in Cambridge will carry away memories as happy as ours of those evenings together. There were difficulties, however, to be overcome, and once again they concerned the billets. Many foster parents, quite rightly, were unwilling for their children to be out after black-out, and the task of seeing them home mainly devolved upon the teachers, no light task when children were billeted at opposite ends of Cambridge. One teacher at least would plead that next time children in the same school should be billeted near to each other.

Then meals caused a certain amount of trouble, for often the normal meal-times of a billet were inconvenient for the evacuee. Teachers think that communal meals would solve this problem and with the co-operation of the W.V.S. and a local catering firm, one Tottenham school was able to institute a very successful communal midday meal.

Travel to school was at one time a source of difficulty where billets were scattered, for the local education authority was unwilling to pay the children's fares, and few of the evacuees possessed bicycles. However, since that time bicycles have appeared almost miraculously, and our children dash round Cambridge with almost native assurance.

Holidays have caused a certain amount of discontent, for although it was realized that curtailment was unavoidable, and that cancellation might even be necessary, it was felt that provisional arrangements might have been made earlier than actually happened in some cases.

Comments on Evacuation. It is agreed that the arrangements for the transfer of the children from the evacuation to the reception areas were extremely good, but it is felt that previous contact between the two authorities would have ensured that subsequent problems would have been greatly eased. It is believed that too little thought was given to the educational side of the problem and that the needs of individual schools were not considered sufficiently. It is recorded that one class had half a hall, while the other half was occupied by A.R.P. members who consoled themselves with wireless, ping-pong, and billiards all day long. When it was explained that in the circumstances teaching was very difficult these things stopped, but the teachers concerned felt that it was very unfortunate that harmless recreation should have to be denied to those who at the time were engaged on a very dull job. In another instance most of the boys belonging to a technical school returned home because facilities for their highly specialized studies were not available.

As previously mentioned, those who accompanied the schools to Cambridge speak with one voice on the effects of the instability of conditions in the present evacuation scheme, and they are agreed that stability is a *sine qua non* of any successful venture of this sort.

On the question of the homes which should be chosen for the children there is a certain division of opinion, although in most cases opposing points of view appear to be easily reconciled. Some teachers state definitely that they believe that billeting in private houses is not only right, but that it has been successful, while most of those who believe that it has not been a complete success agree that most of the troubles could have been avoided. It is certain that provision of homes for difficult children, and more adequate financial arrangements would certainly have eliminated many troubles, and it is noteworthy that requests for both of these things have already been answered by the authorities. It is considered by many teachers, but by no means all, that for successful billeting, children should be in homes of corresponding economic standards to their own, and if this be so it is fairly easy to accomplish. It should be noted, however, that many children in Cambridge have, in fact, been happily billeted with families on a higher social level than their own, and surely these new contacts must be for the ultimate good of the community. The more complete the understanding between various classes of society, the more united is the community likely to be, and the more readily will all our folk move forward together to the attainment of common ideals, and it may well be that once again in the history of mankind, 'a little child shall lead them'.

Those teachers who feel that the present venture has not been altogether successful advocate camps or hostels, while some of those who feel that billeting in homes has been a useful social experiment agree that an attempt to establish a self-contained school community should, at any rate, receive careful consideration. Teachers realize that they would be involved in much work and would assume even greater responsibilities, but they are prepared to accept these things should they render possible a successful solution to the problems of evacuation. Teachers have not differentiated between camps and hostels, but there are indications that they have hostels in mind, rather than camps; while one teacher goes so far as to recommend the establishment of permanent elementary boarding-schools in the country. Many arguments have been brought to bear on the question, and while most of them will be familiar, some of them we believe to be new. It is contended that bedroom accommodation in a billet may be unsatisfactory, although the children may be happy, while baths are often a difficulty. It is stated by some that feeding in hostels is better, while treatment is more uniform, and thus jealousy is eliminated. A few teachers, while agreeing that camps would overcome billeting problems, feel that they would tend to too much regimentation and mob influence. It is suggested that an increase in delinquency such as that which followed the first evacuation might be prevented, for it is thought that it occurred after the parental authority had gone, and before the foster parents had asserted themselves. One teacher has stated a very good case for camps in a rather poignant statement, in which she says, 'For two quite different reasons I should advocate the camp scheme for senior children in any future evacuation: first, because a billet can be a good one without necessarily being a happy one; and, secondly, because the children must always feel an obligation to behave properly and to be grateful. In their own homes they are part of the household, they share things by right and not by privilege, and if they are in a bad mood they behave badly at the time, but once it is over they are just as dear to their parents as before. The incident may not be forgotten, but it does not make any difference to the real feelings between parent and child. In a camp they would not feel the same gratitude for their food and shelter, as they would all be treated in the same way, and services would be done by people paid to do them, and not by householders who are doing "extra". I don't think children ever relax in their billets. In a camp there might be facilities for keeping pets—every evacuee has missed his or her pet animal, and there is no chance of having any in a school shared by too many people.' We feel that we cannot do better than to leave the case for the camp there, in the hands of such a doughty protagonist, and one whom we feel sure must both understand and love the children with whom she has to deal.

There still remains the problem as to whether there should be evacuation at all, and the teachers who discuss this point feel that the family unit is so much an essential part of English life that the removal of the children should be avoided if possible. They suggest that all buildings, homes, and schools alike should be provided with safe shelters, but they realize that this is not capable of immediate accomplishment, and that meanwhile evacuation should continue. It is considered, moreover, that those in control should begin to plan even further ahead and begin to institute a policy of decentralization on a permanent basis. Such a policy would of course obviate the need for the separation of children from their parents, and the comparative ease with which the present partial decentralization has been accomplished should do much to remove the fears of those who feel it to be incapable of successful achievement. All are agreed that, in any later scheme of evacuation, there should be those facilities for co-operation, those financial adjustments, and those special provisions for difficult children which have already been mentioned. Teachers are of the opinion, too, that it is necessary for trained workers to be with the children, and that a band of helpers working jointly with the schools and the billeting authorities would do much to render the scheme successful. They claim that any further scheme in which the children are not sent with their teachers will be a fiasco, and they feel, moreover, that children should not be absorbed if it can reasonably be avoided. From time to time many children return to town rather than face separation from their own school and their own teachers.

Certain minor recommendations are made which might help. It is thought that water should be provided at all distributing centres, and that helpers should be present to carry parcels for the tired children. School banks are suggested, to which parents should forward all money, and we believe they might do something to help to remedy certain existing evils. Teachers and foster parents alike have felt that some children have had a great deal of pocket-money, which they have spent wastefully, while at the same time they have been short of necessities. Some teachers say that canteens should be provided for visiting parents, but it must be recorded that when such provision was actually made in Cambridge there were very few visitors, and we have the impression that, although some parents demanded the hospitality of the foster parents as a right, on the whole the visits were carried out with every consideration for those who had welcomed their children, and that very many valuable friendships have been established thereby. Canteens, if they are provided at all, are probably of greatest value in the early days of evacuation before parents and foster parents have learned to know each other.

The task of collecting and co-ordinating the opinions of my colleagues has been long, and now at last that it is finished I hope it may be permitted to me to end upon a personal note. There have been times when I have been unhappy, when I have pondered on the wisdom of it all. I have been grieved by the ingratitude I have seen, I have been amazed at the inconstancy of purpose I have so often met, and there have even been times when I have doubted our resolution and the will to endure, but in my quieter moments I have known that the gratitude outweighs the ingratitude, that the inconstancy has been more apparent than real, and that the resolution is always to be found when the need for it is realized.

I remember, with admiration, the bravery with which children and parents alike parted from each other in the early hours of last September, not knowing what the future might hold for their loved ones, and I am still conscious of the pride with which we teachers received the children from their parents. Here was a compliment more real than any words could bring, and I believe that it marked the beginning of a new era of co-operation between parents and schools.

The memory of the surprising smoothness with which the actual movement was accomplished, and the kindliness with which we were received, still lingers. Many of us were in our billets by midday, and before tea we were out shopping with our foster mothers, out fishing with our foster brothers, and even swimming, for some of us had managed to hide a costume in our all too heavy packs, for had not teachers spoken of the possibilities of a glorious seaside holiday? A happy chance led me to my billet, an ivy-covered cottage, a kindly lady welcomed me, and I knew that I had found a home. Within a week I had brought my wife and child, and at the end of a year we are still there. Every consideration we could ask we have had, and more. I have been happy, and I know many of my boys and girls have been happy in similar homes. I recall with pride the good impression created by our youngsters, and I have been privileged to make many friends through them. Wherever I have been I have been received with kindness in the foster homes, and many have sought me out to say pleasant things about our children.

The long winter evenings brought us even more friends, and I am sure that those happy hours spent at Newnham will live for ever in the memories of those who were fortunate enough to be there. And later we were privileged to see 'our undergraduates' distinguish themselves in the world of sport, for we had running, hockey, tennis, and cricket blues in our little group, and, possibly greatest thrill of all for our boys, our cricketer has this summer made three centuries in succession. We are familiar with Fenner's and we ourselves play cricket on Parker's Piece with its memories of Jack Hobbs. Then there were those escort duties in the darkness of the black-out, with the amazing confidences, which in themselves would fill a book, and at the end the inevitable, 'Thanks ever so much, sir. Good night.' There were those Christmas parties, and more than one invitation to Christmas dinner when it was known that I would be in Cambridge. Amid such kindness and good fellowship, can there still be any doubt as to whether it was all worth while?

And when the summer came again we went into the fields together; we cast from us the restrictions of winter, and felt that at last we were a part of Cambridge. London for me holds little beyond my work and my friends. Now my work lies near to the countryside. The birds and the flowers are never far away, there's a freshness over everything, and I am content. Yet there is one thing I still miss. My own home is on a hill with green meadows and wooded valleys below. How I miss those hills, and long for them, as I tramp the flat roads of Cambridge. They say the fen country eventually casts a spell over you, but I still want the hills, and the woods, and the pastures I love.

APPENDIX 1

MEMBERS OF RESEARCH COMMITTEE

Mrs. Adrian	Mrs. Melanie Klein
Mr. W. W. Ashton	Dr. C. M. Lloyd
Mrs. Bathurst	Dr. H. A. Mess
Dr. John Bowlby	Mr. N. S. Mercer
Mr. G. A. Bullen	Dr. W. Paterson
Miss C. N. Fairbairn	Dr. R. H. Thouless
Dr. Lucy Fildes	Miss S. M. Wortman

Chairman: Dr. Susan Isaacs

Hon. Secretaries: Miss S. Margery Fry and Miss S. Clement Brown

The following also attending meetings from time to time and gave help and advice:

Dr. W. J. Barry	Miss E. Horder
Mr. Bolitho	Miss K. Davies
Mr. Aymeric Straker	Mr. J. W. Whitfield
Miss R. M. Fletcher	Miss M. Rooff

CONSULTATIVE COMMITTEE

In addition to the members of the Research Committee, the following consented to serve on the Consultative Committee:

Professor F. C. Bartlett	Mr. G. H. McKay
Professor A. M. Carr-Saunders	Dr. R. Noble
Miss Clay	Dr. F. B. Parsons
Miss D. M. Cunliffe	Mrs. Rackham
Miss Ruth Darwin	Mrs. Rootham
Miss H. Dent	Professor Ryle
Miss R. M. Fletcher	Miss H. H. Skillicorn
Mr. T. F. Foreman	Miss E. Smith
Professor M. Ginsberg	Dr. A. J. Smyth
Mr. S. N. Godfrey	Mrs. Stevens
Dr. C. A. Mace	Mr. M. J. Vine

The Consultative Committee met as a whole on two occasions, and many important points were discussed. It was not, however, responsible for the detailed planning and carrying out of the Survey, and was not (owing to exigencies of time and circumstance) called upon to consider this report before publication. It is thus in no way responsible for the conclusions or opinions expressed in this volume.

APPENDIX II

The following recommendations were circulated among Public Authorities and interested persons in the spring of 1940.

CAMBRIDGE EVACUATION SURVEY

MEMORANDUM ON PRACTICAL RECOMMENDATIONS

The following recommendations are based upon evidence from two sources.

The first of these is a survey of about four hundred children from the borough of Tottenham. Roughly three-quarters of these children were still in the Cambridge borough at the time of the survey, and about one-quarter had returned to Tottenham, where their homes were visited.

The other source of information is the considered evidence of the Research Committee of the Survey. This committee has held about fifteen meetings during the past five months. Members of the committee include the chairman of the Cambridge Reception Committee, teachers, educational psychologists, psychiatrists, and professional social workers, most of whom have been directly concerned with evacuated children in this area.

The Research Committee is aware that certain plans for further evacuation have already been made. The following recommendations have therefore been drawn up with these plans in mind. This does not imply that the committee is in complete agreement with the scheme put forward in Government Evacuation Scheme, Ev. 8, 1940.

MAIN RECOMMENDATIONS

1. Members of the same family should be sent to the same district.
2. School units should be maintained as far as is practicable. This provision is particularly desirable in the case of selective central, secondary, and technical schools.
3. Certain facts should be obtained about each child before evacuation, and these should be conveyed to the receiving authority.
4. Parents' visits to children should be encouraged by granting special facilities for travel.
5. In all evacuating areas, centres should be available where parents whose children have been sent away should be able to consult social workers about the welfare of their children and about other family matters connected with evacuation.

6. Two types of helpers should be appointed by and responsible to the evacuating authority.
7. Two types of professional social workers should be appointed by and responsible to the receiving authority.
8. The Billeting Officer should in every case be an individual who has special knowledge of the needs of children, and of local social conditions, and the method of appointment should be regularized to meet this requirement.
9. In reception areas certain additional facts should be obtained about prospective foster homes.
10. In addition to foster homes, there should be provided in each reception area: (*a*) a temporary hostel; (*b*) emergency and observation homes; (*c*) a home or homes for difficult children.
11. Billeting Officers should be advised of certain considerations to be borne in mind when placing individual children in foster homes.
12. Receiving authorities should provide a place where parents can meet their evacuated children.
13. Preparation for the recreation of evacuated children should be made by the appropriate organizations before their arrival.
14. Prospective foster parents should be informed of their rights in regard to compensation for dilapidation.

I. GENERAL PLANS (1 and 2)

The Research Committee regard with concern the prospect of the separation of children from their school units. In their view it would have been preferable to evacuate schools in groups, and thus to maintain both family and school units. This has obvious advantages from the educational standpoint.

If it were possible to keep only some school units together, the Committee would recommend that this provision should be made in the case of selective central, secondary, and technical schools.

There is, moreover, clear statistical evidence from the Survey that a greater number of difficulties in the relationship between children and foster parents occurs after the age of twelve. This being so, it seems particularly important that these children should be given the reassurance of being with their own teachers and friends.

II. PREPARATIONS IN THE EVACUATION AREAS (3 to 6)

3. The problem of finding suitable foster homes for different types of children would be greatly eased if certain facts were made known to the receiving authority on the children's arrival by means of a duplicated card.

These cards should be handed to the receiving authority by the person responsible for the party so that the facts may be used in billeting.

The facts entered upon the cards should include the following: Name; Date of Birth; Sex; Home Address; Home School; Health (any special handicaps); Soiling or Wetting; Behaviour (any special difficulties). Special blanks should be left to be completed by the receiving authority. (For form of card, see p. 202.)

4. The visits of parents to their children should be encouraged. The survey yielded statistical evidence of the fact that regular visits from parents are not a disturbing influence in the relationship between the children and their foster parents, and there were indications that in the majority of cases they contributed towards the satisfactory adjustment of the child in his foster home.

It is therefore recommended that arrangements should be made by the Government to offer parents a special low *flat-rate* fare for visits to their children in whatever part of the country they happen to be.

5. The Research Committee was impressed with the need for preventing the casual drifting back of children to their own homes. Both educational and social plans in the reception area are dependent for their smooth working on the constancy of the number of children to be cared for.

All possible measures should therefore be taken to keep the parents fully informed about the welfare of their children, to give them opportunities for talking over difficulties, and to encourage easy communication between parents and children.

The Committee suggests that, in areas where they do not already exist, centres such as those offered by the London Children's Care Offices and the Citizens' Advisory Bureaux should be available, where parents may consult social workers about their children, or about other family matters connected with evacuation. It would be helpful if each of these centres could be supplied with a list of children evacuated from the district. The parents should be informed of the existence of such centres before they send their children away.

6. Two types of helpers should be appointed by the evacuating authority:

(*a*) *Escorts:* To return as soon as evacuation has been completed. The enlistment of such helpers may well be left to the head teachers with the assistance of local social agencies.

(*b*) *School Helpers:* To remain attached to the school in which the children are received, and to co-operate with the social workers employed by the receiving authority in maintaining a link between the school, the foster homes, and the Billeting Officer.

There is clear evidence that an undue burden of duties which should properly belong to social workers has been laid upon the teachers, and that in some cases there has been a lack of close co-operation between the teachers and school helpers on the one hand, and the local voluntary workers on the other.

In the view of the Committee the remedy lies in the more careful selection of school helpers, and in the appointment by the receiving authority of some full-time trained social workers who could devise a satisfactory plan of co-operation (see below).

There should be available for each head teacher an experienced and responsible school helper. This helper should be attached to one school or to a group of schools, depending upon the number of children, and should be constantly available to deal with questions of the welfare of individual children. These problems are inevitably brought to the head teacher, and at present occupy far too great a proportion of his or her time.

(For details of functions, qualifications, and recruitment of school helpers, see p. 202.)

III. PREPARATIONS IN THE RECEPTION AREA (7 to 12)

The Committee is strongly of opinion that many of the problems, including the return of a proportion of the children to their own homes, would have been avoided if a sufficient number of full-time trained social workers had been available to work under the direction of the receiving authority, and to help in organizing voluntary service.

Two types of trained social workers are needed:

(*a*) Those with general training in social service, accustomed to family case work, and prepared to deal with the ordinary difficulties of foster home placement.

(*b*) Those with special training and clinical experience of the child showing nervous symptoms or difficulties of behaviour.

It is estimated that the number of *general* social workers required would be about one to every five hundred evacuated children, provided that a sufficient number of voluntary helpers were available.

Wherever possible a psychiatric social worker (see III (*b*)) should be available for consultation with the general social workers of the district about specially difficult children.

Most of the actual visiting of the foster homes may safely be left to local voluntary workers, but it has been found in practice that these workers have home responsibilities which prevent them from being constantly available to deal with emergencies.

This difficulty would be remedied if, in the first place, the school staff had a responsible helper easily available, and, in the second place, this helper could always communicate with the trained social worker responsible for the district.

The school helpers and the voluntary visitors of the neighbourhood should by local arrangement divide between them the supervision of the children in their foster homes, under the general direction of the trained social workers of the district.

(For details of the functions, qualifications, and recruitment of trained social workers, see p. 204.)

9. When the new roll of suitable foster homes is made it is suggested that it would be of value to note the following facts in addition to those already required by the Ministry of Health:

(*a*) The number of *bedrooms* in the houses.

(*b*) A special note of those oster parents who are likely to be particularly skilful with children.

The survey figures demonstrated the fact that some children who were troublesome in several homes eventually settled down satisfactorily in well-chosen billets.

Whilst this selection of homes must to some extent be a matter of trial and error, the Committee think that some difficulties might be avoided if certain homes were selected in the first place.

IV. RESIDENTIAL CARE OTHER THAN IN FOSTER HOMES

10. The Committee consider it desirable to have three types of Homes available in any area receiving a considerable number of children:

(*a*) *A Temporary Hostel*

This should serve as a provisional shelter for children who are unsuitable for immediate billeting by reason of health, cleanliness, or behaviour.

An adequate staff of voluntary workers and school helpers should be temporarily available at this hostel to assist the trained social workers.

The hostel could be furnished simply with camp beds, mattresses, etc.

The Committee agree with the estimate of 5 per cent laid down in Ev. 8, p. 14, as the proportion of children who are likely to be in need of this temporary care.

(*b*) *Homes for Emergency and Observation*

These are required for the whole period of evacuationf or a small proportion of children who need quick removal from their billets. The need may arise because of illness in the household or other family vicissitudes, as well as on account of problems created by the child. They would also be useful for temporary observation before finding a new billet.

The Homes could only meet these needs effectively if they were within convenient distance of the foster homes. The turnover would be fairly rapid, and, in a small compact area accommodation for about thirty children should be adequate for a population of about four thousand evacuated children. In country areas, where the children are more scattered, it would be preferable to have several smaller homes conveniently situated.

(c) A Home for Difficult Children

It is estimated that at least 2 per cent of the children will be permanently unsuitable for foster homes on account of nervous symptoms or difficulties of behaviour.

These types of children can best be cared for in small groups of ten to fifteen.

If there were opportunities for taking over one or two small houses in different parts of a borough, or in small towns in a country area, it would be better to open several small homes rather than one large one.

It may occasionally be possible to find local householders with special experience who would be competent to run homes of this type if they had the advice of an educational psychologist or a psychiatric social worker, but it will usually be necessary to make a special appointment.

V. PLACEMENT OF CHILDREN IN FOSTER HOMES

11. There is statistical evidence in the survey:

(*a*) That it is *generally* best to place members of the same family together in the foster homes.

(*b*) That it is particularly important for girls of over twelve to be placed with other children.

VI. OTHER RECOMMENDATIONS FOR SUSTAINING EVACUATION (12 to 14)

12. Provision should if possible be made for a place to which parents can take their children when they visit, and where they can obtain cheap refreshments.

Parents should be clearly informed in writing of the name and address of the local social worker responsible to the billeting authority for the supervision of their children, and of the hours during which she will be available for consultation.

Arrangements should be made for a worker to be on duty when the parents visit their children at the week-end.

13. It would be helpful if, before evacuation takes place, a meeting could be called by the receiving authority of all those organizations and individuals interested in the provision of recreation for local children. Plans could then be made to extend facilities to meet the needs of evacuated children.

It would be of great assistance to teachers, school helpers, and social workers if a list of the main organizations, their leaders, their activities, and the numbers of new members they would be prepared to receive, could be supplied during the first few days of evacuation.

14. It has been brought to the attention of the Committee that

in some areas foster parents have suffered seriously from dilapidation of their homes. The prospect of such loss without redress apparently deters some householders from offering to have children.

The Committee therefore recommends that foster parents should be informed of their rights in this matter.

NOTE 1

Draft for card to be completed for each child by the evacuating authority, and handed over, in duplicate, to the receiving authority.

B or G

Date of Birth .... Name (Blocks)............

Home School .... Address ....

....

Health (Any special handicaps) Soiling or Wetting

Yes	No

Behaviour (Any special difficulties)

Receiving Authority

Receiving School .... Foster Parents' Name......

Head Teacher .... Address ....

NOTE 2

DUTIES, QUALIFICATIONS, AND METHODS OF APPOINTMENT OF SCHOOL HELPERS, TRAINED SOCIAL WORKERS, AND SUPERINTENDENTS OF HOMES AND HOSTELS

1. APPOINTMENTS BY EVACUATING AUTHORITY

The following duties are suggested for school helpers:

1. To maintain an effective link between the teaching staff of schools

and the trained and voluntary social workers employed by the billeting authority.

2. To assist, for as long as they are needed in the temporary hostel during the first few weeks of evacuation, in such matters as cleansing, clothing, and acting as escorts to children.
3. To help during the whole period of evacuation in dealing with the material needs of the children (e.g., clothes, school meals, etc.).
4. To give such assistance as is found to be needed after local consultation:
   (*a*) In visiting foster homes to supervise the welfare of the children.
   (*b*) In giving occasional relief to foster parents by supervising the children in the evening.

It is important that there should be no visiting of foster homes by school helpers without the express knowledge and co-operation of the local trained and voluntary social workers.

a. It would be an advantage if the school helpers could be drawn as far as possible from the children's home district.

b. While it is not desirable to insist upon any formal qualifications for school helpers, they should in every case be individuals who have had experience of looking after children or of visiting homes.

c. Experience has shown that it is undesirable to give this kind of responsibility to mothers who have been evacuated with their own children.

d. Some salary besides a billeting allowance should be made to a proportion of school helpers who would be capable of taking more responsibility and would be expected to arrange their times so as to be available outside school hours.

A senior helper should be able to deal with about 150 children if she had two or three assistants.

School helpers should be appointed by head teachers in consultation with local social agencies, such as the L.C.C. Children's Care Department.

Information about salaries paid to individuals with comparable experience and responsibility could be obtained from the National Association of Local Government Officers.

2. APPOINTMENTS BY RECEIVING AUTHORITIES

The following duties are suggested for the general social workers to be appointed by and responsible to the receiving authority:

1. To help in the first billeting of the children.
2. To assist in the co-ordination of voluntary and professional social service.
3. To help the reception authority in correspondence with parents about their children.

4. To be available for consultation by the voluntary workers in any case presenting difficulties.
5. To consult the psychiatric social worker about any child who is outstandingly difficult.

The qualification of general social workers should be a Social Science Certificate or its equivalent.

The number required is estimated at about one social worker to every five hundred children, provided the straightforward visiting could be undertaken by local voluntary workers, and by school helpers.

As far as possible the evacuating and receiving authorities should reach agreement before evacuation takes place as to the number of trained social workers who will be needed, and whether they will be available locally, or could be sent down from the evacuation area.

Lists of eligible candidates can be obtained from the special register of the Women's Employment Federation, Bedford College, Regent's Park, together with rates of salary. Information can also be obtained from the British Federation of Social Workers.

As far as possible a psychiatric social worker should be available in each reception area.

a. To advise in the choice of billets for children who present outstanding problems.
b. To select children who are likely to be permanently unable to settle down in any foster home, and to arrange for their admission to the emergency home, or to the home for difficult children.
c. To refer cases in need of medical or psychiatric treatment to the School Medical Officer with a view to consultation at a Child Guidance Clinic if such exists.

Her qualification should be a Mental Health Certificate.

The psychiatric social worker should be appointed by the receiving authority, or by a combination of receiving authorities.

Particulars about qualified persons and rates of salary may be obtained from the Mental Health Emergency Committee, 24, Buckingham Palace Road, S.W.1, or from the Association of Psychiatric Social Workers.

Advice about qualifications, salary, and recruitment of individuals suitable for superintending homes and hostels can also be obtained from the Mental Health Emergency Committee.

(*Signed*) SUSAN ISAACS, M.A., D.Sc.
(Chairman: Research Committee)

S. CLEMENT BROWN, MA..
(Honorary Secretary: Research Committee)

APPENDIX III

STATISTICAL TABLES

SINCE THE average reader of this book is more likely to be interested in the broad outlines of the conclusions reached by the Survey than in the detailed figures on which these conclusions were often based, it has seemed better to the Editors to relegate the tables of figures to this Appendix where they will be available to critical readers who wish to examine the foundations of the Survey's conclusions.

In all cases when conclusions are to be drawn from numerical data, it is necessary to use statistical methods for determining whether any differences which appear within the figures indicate a real difference between what the figures measure or whether they are only such differences as might arise by chance between measurements of really equal things. In other words, the 'significance' of the figures must be determined. In most of the data given below, the figures take the form of contingency tables. If conclusions are legitimately to be drawn from them, the significance of any departures from randomness must be tested. The standard method of doing this is the calculation of the quantity χ^2 and the determination from appropriate tables of the probability (P) that a value of χ^2 as high as that observed would be found in a set of figures randomly distributed (that is, without any real tendency to be grouped in some parts of the table rather than in others). We shall adopt the usual convention of taking a value of P less than ·05 as sufficient evidence of a departure from randomness, that is, of the presence of some real cause tending to bias the figures in the observed direction.

For example, in Table 1a (p. 207) the question which naturally arises is whether there is any tendency for either boys or girls to show a greater proportion of maladjustments. If there were such a tendency, its result would be to bias the figures in the direction of piling up a greater proportion of either the boys or the girls in the − 1 and − 2 classes.

At first sight, the table appears to indicate a slightly greater proportion of maladjustments to billeting conditions amongst the boys. The boys have 14 (9·7 per cent) in the classes − 1 and − 2, as against 11 (6·9 per cent) amongst the girls. For the proportion to be exactly the same amongst boys and girls, the figures in these classes for boys and girls should be 11·9 and 13·1 respectively. These facts can be conveniently expressed in the fourfold table below in which the figures without brackets show the actual numbers found in the two classes and the figures in brackets show the number to be expected if the proportions of maladjusted were exactly the same for boys and girls.

	+2, +1, & 0	−1 & −2	Totals
Boys	131 (133·1)	14 (11·9)	145
Girls	148 (145·9)	11 (13·1)	159
Totals	279	25	304

In each cell the deviation from expectation is 2·1; there are 2·1 more unhappily adjusted boys and happily adjusted girls, and 2·1 fewer happily adjusted boys and unhappily adjusted girls than there would be if there were the same proportion of happily to unhappily adjusted individuals in each sex. The problem is to determine whether this really indicates a greater likelihood of unhappy adjustment amongst the boys or whether it is such a deviation from expectation as might occur by chance if the likelihood of unhappy adjustment were the same in both sexes.

The quantity χ^2 is, in general, calculated as the sum of the deviations in each cell squared and divided by the expected number in that cell. In a fourfold table, however, a better estimate is obtained by taking half less than the deviation as the amount to be squared. χ^2 is thus $1{\cdot}6^2 \times (1/133{\cdot}1+1/145{\cdot}9+1/11{\cdot}9+1/13{\cdot}1) = {\cdot}45$. The number of degrees of freedom (n) (i.e. the number of cell values which can be independently varied while retaining the same marginal totals) is 1, since although any of the four quantities (131, 148, 14, and 11) might have had a different value, any change in the value of one will necessitate changes in all the others. By reference to the appropriate tables, it is found that the probability of a value of χ^2 as large as this occurring by chance from a group of figures with one degree of freedom is about ·5. That is, a deviation from expectation as great as that observed is as likely as not to be found if there is no real difference between the two sexes in ease of adjustment to the foster home. There is, therefore, no ground whatever for concluding from these figures that boys are less likely than girls to be able to adjust themselves satisfactorily to the situation of being billeted on foster parents.

Instead of reducing the figures to the form of a fourfold table, it would have been possible to apply the χ^2 test to the original 5×2 table which is a contingency table with four degrees of freedom. This gives the same result that there is no significant deviation from the distribution to be expected on the hypothesis that boys and girls adapt themselves equally well to the conditions of billeting ($\chi^2 = 1{\cdot}5$,

P=·8). In the treatment of the tables which follow, the device has generally been adopted of reducing the contingency table to a four-fold table and applying the test of significance to this. This procedure has certain theoretical advantages in addition to the important practical advantage of saving labour in calculation. The theoretical advantages are: (1) that it is possible by this means to test the particular hypothesis under consideration instead of the general characteristics of the table, and, (2) that the properties of the χ^2 distribution are known more precisely for the condition of one degree of freedom and in doubtful cases (such as those of unsymmetrical distribution and of cells containing very small numbers) it is possible to apply more exact tests as explained in Fisher's *Statistical Methods for Research Workers.*

The distribution of the different assessments amongst boys and girls in the Tottenham and Islington groups are shown in the following tables.

TABLE I

(a) Tottenham Children

Assessment of satisfactoriness of relationship in foster home	+2	+1	0	−1	−2	Totals	Percentage −1 or −2
Boys . . .	54	57	20	9	5	145	9·7
Girls . . .	63	59	26	6	5	159	6·9
Totals . .	117	116	46	15	10	304	8·2

(b) Islington Children

Assessment	+2	+1	0	−1	−2	Totals	Percentage −1 or −2
Boys . . .	91	35	16	14	1	157	9·5
Girls . . .	127	39	15	13	1	195	7·2
Totals . .	218	74	31	27	2	352	8·2

When reduced to the form of fourfold tables (as explained above) and tested for significance, these yield:

(*a*) $\chi^2 = \cdot 45$, $P = \cdot 5$
(*b*) $\chi^2 = \cdot 39$, $P = \cdot 5 - \cdot 6$
(*a*) and (*b*) added together, $\chi^2 = 1 \cdot 05$, $P = \cdot 3$

Neither separately nor together, therefore, do these figures provide any evidence of a relationship between sex and difficulty of adjustment to the foster home.

Tables IIA and IIB show the distribution of the different assessments of satisfactoriness of foster home relationship amongst the different age groups for the Tottenham and the Islington children respectively.

TABLE IIA. *Tottenham Children*

AGE AND SATISFACTORINESS OF ADJUSTMENT TO FOSTER HOME

Age	*Total Number*	+2	+1	0	−1	−2	*Percentage −1 or −2*
5–6	12	3	5	4	–	–	0
6–7	12	7	5	–	–	–	0
7–8	20	12	4	3	–	1	5
8–9	30	12	12	6	–	–	0
9–10	26	11	10	5	–	–	0
10–11	26	9	13	3	–	1	4
11–12	25	10	6	8	1	–	4
12–13	32	16	13	1	2	–	6
13–14	53	14	25	7	3	4	13
14–15	33	12	9	4	4	4	24
15–16	22	8	5	4	5	–	23
Totals	291	114	107	45	15	10	8½

The significance of the rise in percentage of unsatisfactory adjustments in the higher age groups may be tested by rearranging this as a 3 × 2 table as below:

Ages	*Total Number*	+2, +1, 0	−1, −2
5–8	44	43	1
8–12	107	105	2
12–16	140	118	22
Totals	291	266	25

For this table $\chi^2 = 17{\cdot}6$, and P is less than ·001. The excess of difficult adjustments amongst the children is, therefore, unquestionably significant.

TABLE IIB. *Islington Children*

AGE AND SATISFACTORINESS OF ADJUSTMENT TO FOSTER HOME

Age	*Total Number*	+2	+1	0	−1	−2	*Percentage* −1 *or* −2
3–5	12	9	2	0	1	0	8
5–6	17	10	4	1	2	0	12
6–7	29	17	8	2	2	0	7
7–8	35	25	6	4	0	0	0
8–9	41	20	8	8	4	1	12
9–10	49	34	9	2	3	1	8
10–11	51	27	14	6	4	0	8
11–12	39	26	8	3	2	0	5
12–13	36	23	8	1	4	0	11
13–14	35	21	7	4	3	0	9
14–15	8	6	0	0	2	0	25
Totals	352	218	74	31	27	2	8·2

Arranged in three age groups (3–8, 8–11, 11–15) and into two classes of assessments as in Table IIA, $\chi^2=1{\cdot}5$, $n=2$, and $P>{\cdot}3$. There is no significant relationship between age and assessment for satisfactoriness of billeting adjustment.

If, in order to test the specific conclusion emerging from IIA that children are less happily billeted after 13 years, we arrange a fourfold table comparing the 13+ group with all the others, we find $\chi^2={\cdot}35$, and $P={\cdot}6$. There is no significant relationship.

Tables IIIA and IIIB show the distribution of the different assessments for satisfactoriness of relationship between foster parent and child for foster mothers of different ages.

TABLE IIIA. *Tottenham Children*

Age of foster mother	*Total No. of cases*	+2	+1	0	−1	−2	*Percentage* −1 *or* −2
Below 40 . .	122	47	46	17	6	6	10
40–60 . .	93	46	26	12	7	2	9
Over 60 . .	27	12	11	4	0	0	0
Totals . .	242	105	83	33	13	8	8·7

TABLE IIIB. *Islington Children*

Age of foster mother	*Total No. of cases*	+2	+1	0	−1	−2	*Percentage* −1 *or* −2
Below 40 . .	199	118	41	24	15	1	8
40–60 . .	116	79	25	6	5	1	5
Over 60 . .	27	13	6	1	7	0	26
Totals . .	342	210	72	31	27	2	8·5

The most striking apparent deviation from expectation in IIIA is the total absence of children showing an unhappy relationship with foster mothers of more than 60. This deviation is not, however, significant. If a 3×2 table is constructed by taking the three age-groups of foster mothers and dividing the cases in the two classes (+2, +1 or 0) and (−2 or −1), we find $\chi^2 = \cdot 28$ which (with two degrees of freedom) gives $P = \cdot 2$ approximately. If we test the particular hypothesis that foster mothers of over 60 are more successful by dividing the foster mothers into two groups of over and below 60, we get a 2+2 table. Since one of the cells is zero, we may conveniently use the exact criterion for determining P as $|\underline{a+b}.\ |\underline{c+d}.\ |\underline{a+c}.\ |\underline{b+d}/\ |\underline{a+b+c+d} \times 1/\ |\underline{a}.\ |\underline{b}.\ |\underline{c}.\ |\underline{d}$ (where a, b, c, d are the numbers in the four cells). This gives $P = \cdot 15$. Since, however, there is no *a priori* reason for expecting the hypothesis tested, it would be more correct to ask what is the probability of the most striking of the three comparisons which might have been made showing such a deviation from expectation if chance alone had been operating. P will then be $1 - (1 - \cdot 15^3) = \cdot 6$. The observed deviation is as likely as not to occur if there is no real difference between the foster mothers of over 60 and those below 60.

IIIB also shows a deviation from expectation in the foster mothers over 60. This is in the opposite direction and is significant. If the table is converted into a 3×2 table as above, it is found that $\chi^2 = 12 \cdot 2$ and $P < \cdot 01$. If it is converted into a 2×2 table in which the foster mothers above and below 60 are directly compared, $\chi^2 = 9 \cdot 11$, $P = \cdot 0026$. If we take into account the fact that this is the most striking of three comparisons which might have been made, P becomes ·01. The deviation from expectation is still clearly significant.

Table IV shows the relationship between permanency of occupation of billet and assessment for happiness of relationship with the foster parent. Since both Tottenham and Islington children here show the same tendency, the two groups are shown in a single table.

TABLE IV. *Tottenham and Islington Children*

CHANGES OF BILLET

	Total Number	+2	+1	0	−1	−2	*Percentage −1 or −2*
No change in billet	294	173	79	28	11	3	5
One or more changes . .	327	148	96	44	30	9	12
Totals .	621	321	175	72	41	12	8·5

When Table IV is reduced to a 2 × 2 table comparing cases in the −1 or −2 classes with all the others, it is found that $\chi^2 = 9{\cdot}3$ and P = ·002. The excess of unhappy relationships with foster parents amongst children who have changed their billet is therefore significant.

Table V shows the relationship between frequency of parental visits and satisfactoriness of relationship with foster parent. Since the same tendencies were shown in the Tottenham and the Islington groups of children, the two groups are here shown together.

TABLE V. *Tottenham and Islington Children*

PARENTS' VISITS

	Total No. of cases	+2	+1	0	−1	−2	*Percentage* −1 *or* −2
No visits . .	18	11	2	1	4	0	22
Occasional visits (less than monthly)	308	146	99	35	22	6	9
Frequent visits (more than monthly)	233	133	63	25	10	2	5
Totals . .	559	290	164	61	36	8	8

When the number of minus assessments amongst those children with no parental visits or only occasional ones are compared with those amongst the children with frequent parental visits by means of a fourfold table, we find that $\chi^2 = 3{\cdot}4$ and P = ·06. The difference in favour of the children with frequent visits is, therefore, on the horder-line of significance.

Tables VI and VII show the results of the inquiry into how far satisfactoriness of adjustment to the foster home was determined by the presence of other children. These other children might be the evacuees' own siblings (brothers or sisters), fellow-evacuees, or Cambridge children. The possibility of the presence or absence of any or all of the children of these three groups give eight possible combinations which are shown in the eight lines of Table VI.

TABLE VI. *Tottenham and Islington Children*

EFFECT OF PRESENCE OF OTHER CHILDREN ON HAPPINESS OF BILLETING RELATIONSHIP

Other children in billet	*Total No. of cases*	+2	+1	0	−1	−2	*Percentage* −1 *or* −2
S+ E+ C+ .	28	17	8	2	0	1	4
S+ E+ C− .	27	13	7	5	2	0	7
S+ E− C+ .	100	45	36	12	6	1	7
S+ E− C− .	74	44	22	6	2	0	3
S− E+ C+ .	70	38	17	10	5	0	7
S− E+ C− .	54	25	16	3	9	1	18·5
S− E− C+ .	144	76	36	19	11	2	9
S− E− C− .	90	46	29	6	6	3	10
Totals . .	587	304	171	63	41	8	8·4

S+ means that one or more of the child's own brothers or sisters were present in the billet; S− means that there were none of the child's brothers or sisters in the same billet. E+ and E− refer similarly to the presence or absence of other evacuees, and C+ and C− to the presence or absence of Cambridge children in the billet.

The most general indication of this table is that the presence of other children in the billet is favourable to a happy adjustment; the percentage of unhappy adjustments is low in the first line when children of all three groups are present in the billet and is high when no other children are present (in the last line). More specifically it appears that the presence of the child's own brothers and sisters is favourable to adjustment since the percentage of unhappy adjustments is lower in the first four lines than in the last four.

In order to test the significance of the effects of the presence of other children, the whole group may be subdivided in three ways according to whether siblings, fellow-evacuees, and Cambridge children respectively are present in the billet or not. Each subdivision may then be further subdivided as before into the two classes of those not unhappily adjusted (+2, +1 or 0) and those unhappily adjusted (−1 or −2). We then get the three 2×2 tables below.

TABLE VII. *Tottenham and Islington Children*

EFFECT OF PRESENCE OR ABSENCE OF SIBLINGS, FELLOW-EVACUEES, AND CAMBRIDGE CHILDREN ON HAPPINESS OF ADJUSTMENT TO FOSTER HOME

	1. *Siblings*			2. *Evacuees*			3. *Cambridge children*		
	+2, +1, 0	−2, −1	*Percentage* −1 *or* −2	+2, +1, 0	−2, −1	*Percentage* −1 *or* −2	+2, +1, 0	−1, −2	*Percentage* −1 *or* −2
Present in billet	217	12	5	161	18	10	316	26	7½
Absent from billet . .	321	37	10	377	31	7½	222	23	9½
Totals . .	538	49	8½	538	49	8½	538	49	8½

The value of χ^2 and of P for the three parts of this table are: 1. $\chi^2=4{\cdot}1$, $P={\cdot}04$. 2. $\chi^2={\cdot}65$, $P={\cdot}4$. 3. $\chi^2={\cdot}37$, $P={\cdot}6$.

The superiority of the children with their own brothers or sisters in the billet is, therefore, alone significant. The deviations from expectation in the case of fellow-evacuees and of Cambridge children are only such as are to be expected by chance if the presence of these children makes no difference to the likelihood of successful adjustment to the foster home.

For the Islington children alone a comparison was made between the social and economic status of the child's own home and his foster home. Table VIII shows the figures for various degrees of satisfactoriness of adjustment when the foster home was superior in this respect to the child's own home, when they were of approximately equal status, and when the child's own home was the superior one.

TABLE VIII. *Islington Children*

RELATIVE ECONOMIC AND SOCIAL STATUS OF FOSTER HOME AND OWN HOME

	Total	+2	+1	0	−1	−2	*Percentage* −1 *or* −2
Foster home superior to own home	133	78	34	10	10	1	8½
Foster home and own home of equal status .	181	119	29	17	15	1	9
Own home superior to foster home .	10	5	2	2	1	0	10
Totals . .	324	202	65	29	26	2	8½

If, as in other cases, we make a division into children assessed as +2, +1 or 0 and those assessed as −1 or −2, we have a 2×3 table with $\chi^2 = \cdot 06$, and $P = \cdot 97$. It is obvious to inspection, as this calculation confirms, that there is no difference between the incidence of maladjustments in these three cases.

The details of the figures for the Intelligence Quotients of 40 children badly adapted to foster homes and of a comparison of 40 well adjusted children (referred to in Chapter VI, p. 91) are as follows:

TABLE IX

	Mean I.Q.	*Standard deviation*	*Standard error*
40 children badly adjusted	113·7	14·8	2·4
40 children well adjusted	112·6	13·8	2·2
Difference . . .	·9	—	3·2

Since the difference between the two groups is ·9 and the standard error of this difference is 3·2, it follows that P is about ·8. There is no evidence whatever of any difference in average intelligence between the children happily adjusted to their foster homes and those unhappily adjusted.

CHAPTER VI

TABLE X

THE CHILDREN WHO WENT HOME

AGE AND SEX DISTRIBUTION OF THE RETURNED CHILDREN IN THE TWO BOROUGHS

Tottenham

Age	5–7	*Per-centage*	8–11	*Per-centage*	12–15	*Per-centage*	*Total*	*Per-centage*
Boys	5	7	13	19	11	16	29	42
Girls	6	9	12	17	22	32	40	58
Total	11	16	23	36	33	48	69	100

Islington

Age	5–7	*Per-centage*	8–11	*Per-centage*	12–15	*Per-centage*	*Total*	*Per-centage*
Boys	10	12	16	20	9	11	35	43
Girls	11	14	20	25	15	18	46	57
Total	21	26	36	45	24	29	81	100

TABLE XI

ECONOMIC CIRCUMSTANCES IN THE HOUSEHOLDS OF CHILDREN WHO RETURNED TO TOTTENHAM AND ISLINGTON

Economic Standard	Comfortable		Moderate		Marginal		Dependent		Total	
	No.	*Percentage*	*No.*	*Percentage*	*No.*	*Percentage*	*No.*	*Percentage*	*No.*	*Percentage*
Tottenham .	7	10	28	41	34	49	0	0	69	100
Islington .	6	7·5	28	35	40	50	6	7·5	80	100
Total . .	13	9	56	38	74	49	6	4	149	100

TABLE XII

STANDARD OF HOUSEKEEPING ('CARE OF PHYSICAL NEEDS') IN THE HOUSEHOLDS OF CHILDREN WHO RETURNED TO TOTTENHAM AND ISLINGTON

Standard of Housekeeping	Good		Fair		Poor		Total	
	No.	*Percentage*	*No.*	*Percentage*	*No.*	*Percentage*	*No.*	*Percentage*
Tottenham .	53	77	15	22	1	1	69	100
Islington . .	38	48·5	39	49	2	2·5	79	100
Total . .	91	61·5	54	36·5	3	2	148	100

Notes. 1. In Tottenham there were 69 children from 50 households. In Islington only one child was studied from each of 81 households.

2. Economic circumstances were not rated in one household, and standard of housekeeping in two—both Islington.

TABLE XIII

REASONS FOR RETURN

	Numbers					*Percentages*				
	Principal reasons		*All reasons, principal and subsidiary*			*Principal reasons*		*All reasons, principal and subsidiary*		
	Tot-ten-ham	*Is-ling-ton*	*Tot-ten-ham*	*Is-ling-ton*	*Both Boro's*	*Tot-ten-ham*	*Is-ling-ton*	*Tot-ten-ham*	*Is-ling-ton*	*Both Boro's*
I. FAMILY RELATIONSHIPS	**23**	**33**	**44**	**64**	**108**	**33**	**41**	**30**	**38**	**34**
1. Parents anxious or lonely	8	17	18	26	44	11	21	12	15	14
2. Child homesick or eager to return (see 11)	11	11	22	23	45	16	14	15	14	14
3. Parents' visits disturbing	—	1	—	9	9	—	1	—	5	3
4. Returned because of brother or sister	4	4	4	6	10	6	5	3	4	3
II. ECONOMIC	**9**	**16**	**24**	**30**	**54**	**13**	**20**	**16**	**17**	**17**
5. Billeting cost (actual or prospective)	7	12	20	22	42	10	15	13	12	13
6. Childs' wages or help needed	2	4	4	8	12	3	5	3	5	4

III. RECEPTION CONDITIONS	**27**	**18**	**46**	**41**	**87**	**39**	**22**	**31**	**24**	**27**
7. Billet unsatisfactory	18	11	32	26	58	26	14	22	15	18
8. Change of Billet (actual or prospective)	9	7	14	15	29	13	8	9	9	9
IV. THE CHILD	**10**	**9**	**27**	**21**	**48**	**14**	**11**	**18**	**12**	**15**
9. Illness or accident	8	5	11	11	22	11	6	7	6	7
10. Nervous or difficult	2	2	9	5	14	3	2·5	6	3	4
11. Homesick (see 2)	....	....	....	....	....	....	....	....	....	....
12. Companions: misses or quarrels	—	2	7	5	12	—	2·5	5	3	4
V. OTHER REASONS	**1**	**5**	**8**	**16**	**24**	**1**	**6**	**5**	**9**	**7**
13. School unsatisfactory or inaccessible	—	—	6	2	8	—	—	4	1	2
14. Returned for holidays	—	5	2	14	16	—	6	1	8	5
15. Unclassified	1	—	—	—	—	1	—	—	—	—
Total	**70**	**81**	**149**	**172**	**321**	**100**	**100**	**100**	**100**	**100**

TABLE XIV

PRINCIPAL REASONS FOR RETURN CLASSIFIED ACCORDING TO AGE AND BOROUGH
(Chapter VI)

Reasons for return	*Numbers*						*Percentages*					
	Children less than 12 years old			*Children more than 12 years old*			*Children less than 12 years old*			*Children more than 12 years old*		
	Tottenham	*Islington*	*Both Boro's*	*Tottenham*	*Islington*	*Both Boro's*	*Tottenham*	*Islington*	*Both Boro's*	*Tottenham*	*Islington*	*Both Boro's*
I. FAMILY RELATIONSHIPS	**11**	**23**	**34**	**12**	**10**	**22**	**33**	**40**	**37**	**34**	**42**	**37**
1. Parents anxious or lonely .	4	15	19	4	2	6	12	26	21	11	8	10
2. Child homesick or eager to return	4	4	8	7	7	14	12	7	9	20	29	24
3. Parents' visits disturbing .	—	1	1	—	—	—	—	2	1	—	—	—
4. Returned because of brother or sister	3	3	6	1	1	2	9	5	6	3	4	3
II. ECONOMIC	**5**	**11**	**16**	**4**	**5**	**9**	**14**	**20**	**18**	**12**	**21**	**15**
5. Billeting cost (actual or prospective)	5	11	16	2	1	3	14	20	18	6	4	5
6. Child's wages or help needed	—	—	—	2	4	6	—	—	—	6	16	10

III. RECEPTION CONDITIONS	**14**	**13**	**27**	**13**	**5**	**18**	**41**	**23**	**30**	**37**	**21**	**31**
7. Billet unsatisfactory . .	10	6	16	8	5	13	29	11	18	23	21	22
8. Change of billet (actual or prospective) . . .	4	7	11	5	—	5	12	12	12	14	—	9
IV. THE CHILD	**4**	**6**	**10**	**6**	**3**	**9**	**12**	**10**	**11**	**17**	**12**	**15**
9. Illness or accident . .	4	4	8	4	1	5	12	7	9	11	4	9
10. Nervous or difficult . .	—	2	2	2	—	2	—	3	2	6	—	3
11. Homesick (see 2) . .	....	....	....	....	....	....	....	....	....	....	....	....
12. Companions (misses or quarrels) . . .	—	—	—	—	2	2	—	—	—	—	8	3
V. OTHER REASONS	—	**4**	**4**	—	**1**	**1**	—	**7**	**4**	—	**4**	**2**
13. Returned for holidays .	—	4	4	—	1	1	—	7	4	—	4	2
Total	**34**	**57**	**91**	**35**	**24**	**59**	**100**	**100**	**100**	**100**	**100**	**100**

APPENDIX IV

FOSTER HOME INQUIRY

(*Strictly confidential. No names will be divulged.*)

N.B.—Instructions were given to tick one of the alternative answers here quoted in brackets.

1. Occupation of householder.
2. Estimated age of foster mother. (Under 40, 40–60, over 60.)
3. Foster child: name, sex, age.
4. Sleeping conditions of child. (Not known, own room, shared room, own bed, shared bed.)
5. London address of child.
6. Change of billet. (Not known, none, 1, 2, 3, 4. Number if over 4.)
7. Foster parent: name, Mrs., Miss, Mr.
8. Cambridge address.
9. What do the foster parents feel about the billeting money?
10. Have there been any difficulties about the child's clothes?
11. Have the child's own parents supplied any clothes since his arrival?
12. What does the foster mother feel about the extra work?
13. Have the foster parents asked to be relieved of *all* billeted children?
14. If so, for what reasons?
15. How does the child fit into the family? (Well, fairly, badly.)
16. Is the child happy? (Not known, very, fairly, no.)
17. Parents' visits. (Comments of foster parents about parents' visits to child, if any.)
18. Health: General. (Not known, good, fair, poor.)
    (Skin trouble, hair nits, body lice, not known.)
    Infectious illness. (Not known, no, yes.)
19. Is the child praised for any specially good qualities?
20. Have there been any special difficulties? (The list below includes all sorts of complaints which have been made from time to time about different children.) (Visitors are asked to indicate any problems this child may or may not have shown.) (Cries often, sleepless, drowsy or lethargic, nightmares, special fears, shy, homesick, food fads, greedy, bad table manners, bad language, sex talk, sex behaviour, steals, cruel, destructive, disobeys, lies, fights, loses temper, truants or wanders, noisy, excitable. Soils

himself often, sometimes, not known. Wets himself, often, sometimes, not known.)

21. Any further comments.

SCHOOL INQUIRY

(Strictly confidential. No names will be divulged.)

N.B.—Instructions given to tick one of alternative answers here quoted in brackets.

1. The child: names, sex, date of birth, age.
2. London home address.
3. Foster home address.
4. London Education Authority.
5. London school.
6. Cambridge school.
7. Are there any brothers or sisters of the child in the same billet?
8. Number of children in family. (1, 2, 3, 4. Number if over 4.)
9. Are there any other evacuated children in the same billet?
10. Ordinal position of this child. (Eldest, second, third, fourth; position if younger than fourth.)
11. Are there any Cambridge children in the billet?
12. Number of family now in Cambridge. (None, 1, 2, 3, 4. Number if over 4.)
13. Have there been any difficulties about the child's clothes?
14. Number of billets. (1, 2, 3, 4. Number if over 4.)
15. Details of difficulties about the child's clothes.
16. Reasons for changes of billet (if any).
17. Occupation of father.
18. Teacher's comparisons of homes (economic circumstances). The Cambridge home is (less well-to-do, about the same, more well-to-do).
19. Does the child seem happy?
20. Child's attitude to foster home, if known. (The child is not to be questioned.) (Is dissatisfied, tolerates, likes.)
21. Comments on parents' visits and letters.
22. Visits of parents to child. (None, less than monthly, monthly, more often than monthly.)
23. Letters of parents to child. (None, less than weekly, weekly, more often than weekly.)
24. Visits home. (None, number if any.)
25. Letters of child to parents. (None, less than weekly, weekly, more than weekly.)
26. State any difficulties which have been noted in Cambridge. (Only difficulties *observed* by the teacher.) (Cries often, special fears, shy, homesick, bad language, sex talk, sex behaviour, steals, bullies, destructive, disobeys, lies, fights, loses temper,

truants or wanders, noisy, excitable, soils himself often, soils himself sometimes, wets himself often, wets himself sometimes, lazy, fidgets, nervous movements.)

27. Child's relations with other children. (In London, if known, on arrival in Cambridge, at the present time.) (Friendly, quarrelsome, plays with others generally, plays with others seldom.)
28. Have there been any outstanding changes in the child since his arrival in Cambridge? (Happiness, behaviour, interests.) (Give details.)
29. Attitude in classroom. (On arrival in Cambridge, at the present time.) (Alert, ordinarily attentive, lazy or lethargic.)
30. General health. (On arrival in Cambridge, at the present time.) (Good, fair, poor.)
31. Infectious illness. (Since arrival in Cambridge.) (Specify.)
32. Cleanliness. (In London, if known, on arrival in Cambridge, at the present time.) (Skin trouble, hair nits, body lice.)
33. State any good qualities which have been noted in Cambridge.
34. Further comments.
35. Period of evacuation. (Start, last attendance, duration.)

RETURNED CHILDREN INQUIRY

(*Strictly confidential. No names will be divulged.*)

N.B.—Instructions given to tick one of alternative answers here quoted in brackets.

1. Home address.
2. Name, sex, date of birth, and age of child.
3. Education Authority.
4. London school.
5. Date of evacuation.
6. Date of return to London.
7. Reported number of billets in Cambridge. (1, 2, 3, 4. Number if over 4.)
8. Reasons given for changes, if any. (Please specify for each home.)
9. Did the parents visit the child in Cambridge? (Yes, no. Number of visits, if any.)
10. Reasons given by parents for child's return to London.
11. Reasons inferred by visitor. (Please state evidence.)
12. What do the parents feel about their payments, if any?
13. Has the child settled down well since his return home? (Please state informant.)
14. Child's attitude to war dangers. (Please state informant.)
15. Do the parents consider that there has been any change in the

child due to evacuation? (Health, happiness, behaviour, interests, attitude to parents, attitude to brothers and sisters.)

16. What do the parents feel about sending the child away again?
17. What do the parents feel about the general plan of evacuating children?
18. If they are in favour of evacuation, have they any suggestions as to how it should be carried out?
19. Has the child shown any particular difficulties? (Please enter (*a*) if before evacuation, and (*b*) if after evacuation.) (Cries often, sleepless, drowsy or lethargic, nightmares, special fears, shy, food fads, greedy, bad table manners, bad language, sex talk, sex behaviour, steals, cruel, destructive, disobeys, lies, fights, loses temper, wanders, noisy, excitable, fidgets, nervous movements, soils himself by day or by night, often or sometimes, wets himself by day or by night, often or sometimes.)
20. Is the child attending school?
21. Is he attending Club or Play Centre?
    Any further comments about the child?
22. Members of the family living at home. (Please give details of relationship to child.)
23. Parents, step-parents, or foster parents.
24. Brothers or step-brothers and sisters.
25. Usual occupation of father.
26. Present occupation of father.
27. Ordinal position of child in family.
28. Usual occupation of mother.
29. Present occupation of mother.
30. Estimated age of mother. (Under 40, 40–60, over 60.)
31. Economic standard of home. (Comfortable, moderate, marginal, dependent.)
32. Standard of housekeeping (care of physical needs). (Good, fair, poor.)
33. Does the child's Health Card record any visits to Cleansing Station?
34. Comments on family relationships.
35. Comments on parents' attitude towards child.

INQUIRY INTO WHAT THE TEACHERS SAY

(*Strictly confidential. No names will be divulged.*)

N.B.—Instructions given to tick one of alternative answers here quoted in brackets.

1. Type of school. (Secondary, Technical, Central, Senior, Junior, Infants.) (Boys, girls, mixed.)

2. Status and experience of teacher. (Head, assistant, man, woman, married, single.) (0–10 years' experience, 10–30, over 30 years.)
3. What changes have you noted in the following?
    YOUR health. (Not so good, about the same, better.) Comments.
    Patience (......)
    Attitude to work (......)
    Relations with colleagues (......)
    Relations with children (......)
    Financial position (......)
4. Have you met any difficulties in connexion with the following?
    YOUR expenses. (No, yes, details.)
    Removal from home (......)
    Own children (.......)
    Billet (......)
    Uncertain plans (......)
    Illness (......)
5. What changes have you noted in the following?
    CHILDREN'S health. (Not so good, about the same, better.) Comments.
    Personal appearance (......)
    Discipline (......)
    Attitude to school (......)
    Relations with teacher (......)
    Relations with fellows (......)
    Concentration (......)
    Self-reliance (......)
    Progress in work (......)
6. Have you met any difficulties in connexion with the following?
    CHILDREN'S billets. (No, yes, details.)
    Supply of clothing (......)
    Washing and mending (......)
    Relief of poverty (......)
    Illness (......)
    Homesickness (......)
    Meals (......)
    Travel to school (......)
    Out-of-school activities (......)
7. What changes have you noted in the following?
    School conditions.
    Building. (Not so good, about the same, better. Comments.)
    Laboratory accommodation (......)
    Handicraft rooms (......)
    Staff rooms (......)
    Number of rooms (......)

Size of classes (......)
Library facilities (......)
Facilities for recreation (......)

8. Have you met any difficulties in connexion with the following?
School conditions.
Changes of staff. (No, yes, details.)
Variations in roll (......)
Sharing of school (......)
Crowded conditions (......)
Stock (......)
Size of classes (......)
Holidays (......)
Facilities for recreations (......)

9. Comment on the effect of evacuation on the following. Please suggest reasons for change where possible.
YOUR
Spare time.
Family life.
CHILDREN
Social relationships.
General development and outlook.
Changes in speech.
SCHOOL CONDITIONS
School routine.
Extraneous duties.
Responsibilities.

10. (*a*) Comment on the present evacuation scheme.
(*b*) Give suggestions for future evacuation.

Note. The following details concerning name, address, and school may be given if desired, but they are not essential.
Name.
Address.
School.
Date.

BIBLIOGRAPHY

Alcock, A. T.: 'War Strain in Children', *British Medical Journal.* 1941. 4177, p. 124.

Association of Architects, Surveyors and Technical Assistants. Evacuation Committee: *Evacuation in Practice. A Study of a Rural Reception Area.* 1939. No. 123. Duplic., pp. 28.

— *Evacuation—The Under Fives.* 1940. No. 127. Duplic., pp. 34. The A.A.S.T.A., 57, New End, London, N.W.3, in collaboration with the A.A. School Rural Planning Group.

Body, Alfred H.: *Children in Flight. Some Pictures of Evacuation.* Foreword, Earl De La Warr. London. University of London Press, 1940, pp. 95.

British Association of Residential Settlements, 1, Museum Street. London. 1940. (Private Communication.)

Brothwood, W. C. V.: 'Experience of Evacuation in a County Reception Area', *Public Health.* 1940. 6. LIII, pp. 125–9.

Burt, Cyril: 'The Incidence of Neurotic Symptoms among Evacuated School Children', *British Journal of Educational Psychology.* 1940. X. I, pp. 8–15.

Cosens, M. E.: 'Evacuation. A Social Revolution', *Social Work.* 1940. I. 3, pp. 165–82.

Crosthwaite, Agnes A.: 'French Evacuation', *Social Work.* 1940. I. 5, pp. 298–301.

Davidson, May A., and Slade, I. M.: 'Results of a Survey of Senior School Evacuees', *British Journal of Educational Psychology.* 1940. X. III, pp. 179–95.

Education, Journal of: '"Education Problems of Evacuation", by one who has dealt with them', *Journal of Education.* 1939. 71. 844, pp. 699–701.

Education, Journal of: '"Evacuation from the Reception End", by one who was there', *Journal of Education.* 1939. 71. 843, pp. 653–4.

Evans, Capt. Frederick: 'Evacuation and its Problems', *Quarterly Review.* 1940. 543, pp. 50–64.

Gill, Samuel E.: 'Nocturnal Enuresis. Experiences with Evacuated Children', *British Medical Journal.* 1940.

Glover, Dr. J. Alison: 'Epidemological Aspects of Evacuation', *British Medical Journal.* 1940. 4136, pp. 629–31.

Henriques, J. Q.: 'Evacuation and Welfare', *Social Work.* 1940. I. 4, pp. 235–41.

Henshaw, Edna M.: 'Some Psychological Difficulties of Evacuation', *Mental Health.* 1940. I. 1, pp. 5–10.

Isaacs, Susan: 'Cambridge Evacuation Survey', *The Fortnightly*. 1940. June, pp. 619–30.

League of Nations. Health Organization: 'Medico-Social Questions Arising out of the Movements of Civil Populations'. Report of the Emergency Sub-Committee of the Health Committee. Geneva. 1940. Ch. 1448 (1), pp. 7.

— — 'Medical and Health Questions Connected with Evacuations'. Chronicle of the Health Organization. 1940. II. I, pp. 1 and 2.

Leslie, Isabel M.: 'Some Problems of a Hostel in a Reception Area', *Social Work*. 1940. I. 5, pp. 307–12.

Lissen, Leslie R.: 'Some Problems in a Reception Area', *Journal of Education*. 1939. 71. 845, pp. 742–4.

Mass Observation: *War Begins at Home*. London. Chatto & Windus. 1940. Chap. XII, pp. 425.

National Federation of Women's Institutes, 39, Eccleston Street, London, S.W.1. (Private Communication.) 1940.

New Education Fellowship: Rickman, J.; Isaacs, S.; Bowlby, J.; Winnicott, D. W.; Thomas, L.; Yates, S. L.; Milner, M.; Alcock, T. Foreword, Earl De La Warr. *Children in War-Time*. 1940. London, New Education Fellowship. Hull, A. Brown & Sons, Ltd., pp. 79.

Owen, A. D. K.: 'The Great Evacuation', *Political Quarterly*. 1940. XI. 1, pp. 30–44.

Padley, Richard, and Cole, Margaret: *Evacuation Survey. A Report to the Fabian Society*. London. Routledge & Sons, Ltd. 1940. pp. 296.

Paul, Leslie: 'How the Evacuation Went. Problems in the Reception Areas', *The Schoolmaster and Women Teachers' Chronicle*. 1939. CXXXVI. 1579, p. 330.

Plaut, P. I.: 'Refugee Children in England', *Mental Health*. London. 1940. I, pp. 37–41.

Ring, F. A.: 'Some Reflections on Evacuation', *Journal of Education*. 1939. 71. 845, pp. 747–8.

Robson, W. A.: 'Evacuation, Town Planning and the War', *Political Quarterly*. 1940. XI. 1, pp. 45–58.

Secondary Schoolmaster: 'Evacuation as I See It', *Journal of Education*. 1939. 71. 845, pp. 745–6.

Shakespeare, Geoffrey, M.P. (Committee under chairmanship of): *Report on Conditions in Reception Areas*. 1941. London, H.M. Stationery Office, pp. 18.

Strachey, Mrs. St. Loe, O.B.E., J.P. Introduction by Amabel Williams Ellis: *Borrowed Children. Evacuation Problems and their Remedies*. London. John Murray. 1940, pp. 134.

Straker, A., and Thouless, R. H.: 'Preliminary Results of Cambridge Survey of Evacuated Children', *British Journal of Educational Psychology*. 1940. 10, pp. 97–113.

Times Educational Supplement: 'Cambridge Survey of Evacuees'. 1940. (January 27th), p. 27; (February 3rd), p. 42.

University of Liverpool, Department of Social Science: *Preliminary Report on the Problems of Evacuation.* University Press of Liverpool. London. Hodder & Stoughton. 1939, pp. 32.

— — *Our War-Time Guests—Opportunity or Menace? A Psychological Approach to Evacuation.* University Press of Liverpool. London. Hodder & Stoughton. 1940, pp. 43.

Vernon, M. D.: 'A Study of Some Effects of Evacuation on Adolescent Girls', *British Journal of Educational Psychology.* 1940. 10, pp. 114–34.

Wagner, Gertrude: 'Evacuation', *Social Welfare.* 1940. IV. 6, pp. 98–107.

GOVERNMENT PUBLICATIONS

Board of Education. Circulars 1461, 1467, 1469, 1474, 1535. His Majesty's Stationery Office, Kingsway, W.C.2.

Ministry of Health. Revised list and index of documents in course of preparation. H.M.S.O.

INDEX

PRINTED BY
JARROLD AND SONS LTD.
NORWICH